"*The Second Curve* shines like a beacon through the 'future' fog, illuminating new ideas and stimulating strategic thinking. Through the use of other-industry analogs and parables, Ian Morrison provides *déjà vu* tension to jolt first-curve managers into second-curve thinking."
—Jerry Karabelas, President
SmithKline Beecham, NA

"How vivid and economical! Ian Morrison describes a law that governs everything that is developing and evolving—the continual renewal of the first and second curves. If change is the constant, the variable is the period of the cycles. For business, industry, and even nations, knowing where you stand on the curves and managing your position on the curves could well be the key to survival and prosperity."
—Zhouying Jin
Professor, Center for Technology
Innovation and Strategy Studies
Institute for Quanti-Economics
and Techno-Economics Research
Chinese Academy of Social Studies

THE
SECOND
CURVE

Managing the Velocity of Change

IAN MORRISON

BALLANTINE BOOKS

New York

http://www.randomhouse.com

LIBRARY OF CONGRESS CATALOGING-IN-PUBLICATION DATA
Morrison, J. Ian, 1952–
The second curve : managing the velocity of change / Ian Morrison. — 1st ed.
p.   cm.
Includes index.
ISBN 0-345-40541-2
1. Organizational change—Management.   I. Title.
HD58.8.M655   1996
658.4'06—dc20   96-14754

Text design by Fritz Metsch

Manufactured in the United States of America
First Edition: May 1996
10 9 8 7 6 5 4 3 2 1

Acknowledgments

THE SECOND CURVE came from ten years of research and consulting on long-term structural change and how it affects the overall business environment, companies, and individuals. Over that time I have been fortunate to be associated with the Institute for the Future (IFTF)—for the first five years as a research director, and for the last five years as president. IFTF is a unique organization, a think tank structured as a nonprofit organization and dedicated to helping organizations, both public and private, think systematically about the long run. I am deeply grateful for the opportunity to work with IFTF, its board, its clients, its affiliates, and its staff.

Like any book, *The Second Curve* is the product of many people, and would not have happened without each and every one of them. Mari-Pat Boughner, head of business development at IFTF, managed me as well as the overall project, and deserves enormous credit for pulling the team together, encouraging us to meet deadlines, and providing the essential liaison between IFTF, our agent, and our publishers. She managed to achieve all of this with an assertive good humor.

My deepest thanks go to my literary agent, Rafe Sagalyn, who encouraged me to turn the "second curve" idea into a book, and who put me together with the incredible folks at Ballantine with whom it has been my pleasure to work. Special thanks to Leona Nevler, Senior Vice President and Editorial Director at Ballantine, who has been immensely supportive of the project and uncannily accurate in her editorial comments and recommendations; Linda Grey, President and Publisher; Clare Ferraro, Senior Vice President and Publisher; senior editor Susan Randol for her meticulous reviews of the material; Steve Black, Senior Vice President and Director of Sales; Gilbert Perlman, Executive Vice President; Liz Williams, Vice President; and Kim Hovey, Publicity Director, for their energy, enthusiasm, and support for the book; and to Alberto Vitale, CEO of Ballantine parent Random House, who has so enthusiastically embraced the second curve throughout his organization.

Bo Caldwell was the perfect collaborator. She took my rough words and often incoherent sentence structures and turned them into flowing prose. Chris Budd diligently checked and rechecked the facts and figures partially stored in my brain, and conducted significant research in support of the many examples in the book. Lotus deserves praise for the Notes technology that allowed the manuscript to be produced in four months, from August to December 1995, with individuals in four different locations and on three different operating systems working on the same material. Much of this book was written on planes and in hotel rooms and was in my colleagues' hands the same day for review. Thanks to Stephanie Schachter at the Institute, we all rapidly became Lotus Notes literate. The miracle of online searches verified data on a turnaround basis and contributed to making a challenging deadline realizable.

My colleagues at the Institute for the Future, past and present, have been instrumental in pushing me to develop my thinking about the second curve. In particular, Roy Amara, my predecessor at IFTF, whose mentoring and whose Amara's Law—"There is a tendency to overestimate the impact of phenomena in the short run and underestimate it in the long run"—had a profound impact on me. My colleague Paul Saffo, whose Thirty-Year Zen of Change theory, which explains the lag from introduction to successes of new technology, gave me critical components of second-curve thinking. Gregory Schmid, Director of the Institute's Corporate Associates Program in Strategic Planning, gave generously of his time, his materials, and his intellectual support to this project. He helped me frame the outline of the book, and provided many great examples. In addition, I drew substantially on the work of Greg and his team (including Nancy Ozawa and Robert Mittman), who prepared the report "Changing Distribution Patterns: Who Owns the Customer?" in the retailing and distribution chapter. Greg also coproduced, with IFTF's Outlook Team (Bob Johansen and Andrea Saveri, with Ruth Kaplan, Tomi Nagai-Rothe, Nancy Ozawa, Paul Saffo, David Sibbet, and Rob Swigart), "21st Century Organizations: Reconciling Control and Empowerment," which heavily influenced the analysis of organizational implications of the second curve. Special thanks are also due to Willie Pietersen, Chairman of IFTF's Board of Trustees, for his significant contributions on the subject of the future of brands. Much of the original thinking on brands came from a chapter we wrote together for the "Changing Distribution Patterns" report.

Mark Vogel, a veteran of twenty years at the forefront of change in the banking industry, educated me with facts and challenged me with ideas about the future of financial services. His help was invaluable in shaping the analysis of the financial services market. Bob Johansen and Jeff Charles, who direct the Outlook Program at IFTF, have taught me about the world of emerging technology; their patient teaching is reflected in these pages. My colleagues in the Institute's two health care programs, Health Care Outlook and Health Care Information Infrastructure, are well ahead of the curve in their thinking. My thanks to Robert Mittman, Sandra Tripp, Matthew Holt, Ellen Morrison, David Hansen, and Tom Moloney, as well as our Health Care Outlook partners: Bob Blendon at Harvard School of Public Health, Department of Health Policy and Management; and Bob Leitman and Humphrey Taylor at Louis Harris & Associates. Their breadth and depth of knowledge on health care issues is staggering, and our work together has helped enlighten me about the second curve and the pace of change. Institute Director Mary O'Hara-Devereaux leads IFTF's public sector initiatives with Rod Falcon, assessing the delivery of health care services to vulnerable populations. No second-curve thinking would be complete without factoring in the needs of the vulnerable in our society.

Mary O'Hara-Devereaux and IFTF affiliate Peter Yim have played a key role in opening my eyes to the realities of the markets emerging geographically, particularly in China, and have been responsible for the Institute's new collaborative relationships with research organizations in that country. My thanks to Professor Zhouying Jin of the Center for Technology Innovation and Strategy Studies, Institute for Quanti-Economics and Techno-Economics Research at the Chinese Academy of Social Studies, for her guidance and friendship. Bill Fuller, President of the Asia Foundation and a member of IFTF's Board of Trustees, was extremely helpful in raising my awareness and understanding of emerging markets in Asia.

The final manuscript was helped enormously by inputs from several thoughtful readers. Brian Kelly was especially helpful with his incisive review.

My executive assistant, Charlotte Gould, has kept me organized throughout an incredibly busy period. Never once did I board the wrong plane, arrive at the wrong meeting, or attempt to check into a hotel that wasn't expecting me. She did a great deal to make this process possible.

My fellow directors at Interim Services—Al Sorensen, Cinda Hallman, Harold Toppel, Jerry Grossman, Bill Evans, Michael Victory, and CEO Ray Marcy and his colleagues—have taught me an immense amount about the challenges and joys of leading and managing a publicly traded company. I am very grateful.

Books, in large measure, are reflections based on the accumulation of intellectual experiences and perceptions gained from mentors, friends, and family. I would like to thank David and Walter Hardwick, Bob Evans, Morris Barer, Bob Murdoch, Colin Campbell, Mike Palmer, Fred Cadham, David Paradine, Peter Kelly, John Salmon, Bruce Juhola, Brad Miller, Jane and Craig Williams, Peggy O'Kane, Richard Smith, and Larry Leisure, who have helped me understand the second curve (even though they may not realize it) by sharing their time and their stories over the years.

To family and friends in Scotland, Canada, and California: Your encouragement, friendship, and support are greatly appreciated.

Nora, David, Caitlin, and Bullet the retriever put up with a lot: too many plane rides and nights away. But they make everything worthwhile. Thank you.

To Pat Stern, who wasn't with us to see an idea turned into a book: You are missed.

Finally, to the clients of the Institute, many of whose stories appear on these pages, who are living the day-to-day dilemmas described in this book: My thanks for the privilege of working with you, and for making me aware of the challenge and opportunity of the Second Curve.

Ian Morrison
Menlo Park
January 1996

To Nora, David, Caitlin, and Bullet
with love

Contents

Introduction

YOU'VE DONE EVERYTHING RIGHT in business. You've searched for excellence and found it. You've stuck to your knitting and focused on what works. You've reengineered your business processes and developed the discipline of a market leader. But, even with all of that, you're worried—and with good reason. If you're not at least a little bit paranoid about your future, you're going to be blindsided by the second curve.

Here's what I mean by that. Say a company—maybe your company—is going along quite nicely, doing what it's always done, on a course of business that represents the vast majority of its revenues and profits. Call that its first curve. But everyone has a sneaking suspicion that in the long run, that curve is going to play out and be replaced by a new business—a second curve, if you will.

If you're lucky, there may be signs, but maybe all you have to go on is that feeling in your gut. Or maybe revenue growth is flattening out, even declining slightly. Maybe new players are showing up, guys with a new technology and a slightly different way of doing things, and they're making inroads into what you thought were secure markets. Maybe new geographic markets are springing up like gopher holes, and there are just too many to deal with. What do you do? You could stay where you are playing that first curve, maybe put a little bit more into R&D for the next generation of products or cut costs in your internal processes. Not bad ideas, and there's nothing *wrong* with them; there's just not enough *right* with them. And, by not at least acknowledging those second curves, you might miss that Big Opportunity and end up kicking yourself for the next ten years. But maybe you're feeling lucky, or smart, or (on a good day) both. You could go for it, abandon ship and jump to that second curve. Gutsy but also risky. You might jump too soon.

Welcome to the world according to two curves. It's a world in which the present is hard, but the future is doubly difficult—and the only certainty is change. Managing in this world is a lot like playing three-dimensional chess where you've got to see both near and far at the same time as you prepare to move up, down, across, and sideways.

To start with, you must understand the sources of the second curve, a phenomenon that is fueled by massive forces of change over which you have no control: new technology, new consumers, and new markets. As such, the second curve will fundamentally change the threats and opportunities you face. To survive, not to mention succeed, you have to learn to anticipate these changes. We live in a world where new technology means that everything has to happen better, faster, cheaper. Where new consumers demand anything, anytime, anyplace. Where growth in massive emerging economies like China, India, and Brazil will create new markets and new competitors. You have to be able to put these changes in context—and, in addition to understanding where the second curve comes from, you have to understand the pace of change and how the changes will play out in various sectors of the economy. We look at three areas: retail and distribution, where the second curve has already come in a big way; health care, which is in the midst of a supposed second-curve transformation; and financial services, where a massive second curve is building.

The second curve isn't limited to large organizations; individuals are affected too, and are forced to face second-curve realities in their own careers. You'll have to confront second-curve career choices. Do you hang on to the perceived stability of a dying first curve? Do you jump to the second? We'll help you judge the pace of change and provide some clues about when and where to jump, because even what was once a second-curve Camelot can falter. You're thirty-something. You work for Apple in 1985. You have the world by the tail. The place becomes first-curve in its thinking—all about margins, not about magic. The crazies leave, the magic goes, and eventually so do the margins. So ask yourself this: Are you working for an Apple of 1985? Or a Kmart of 1980, or an IBM of 1970? A Sears of 1960?

Staying put may be a mistake, but jumping too soon to a premature second curve can also get you in trouble. You have to balance the risks and rewards with the pace of change. Do you go with Steve Jobs to Next Computer when he leaves Apple? What about when he goes on to Pixar? Next stumbles despite Ross Perot's help. Pixar makes Jobs a billionaire (albeit briefly) all over again. Be ready to jump, but don't live in the future before it happens.

This book is based on my ten years of experience at the Institute for the Future (IFTF) working with large organizations, both public and private, as they think about their long-term prospects. IFTF is a nonprofit research and consulting group founded in 1968 and dedicated to a systematic evaluation of social, technological, and business trends and their consequences for organizations and citizens. This book draws on the lessons learned from working with corporations, from those as large as Fortune 100s to nonprofit organizations, as they confront the fundamental structural changes of the second curve. What has continued to strike me over the years is the consistent applicability of the second-curve model to organizations, regardless of their size or profit orientation, and to individuals, regardless of life stage or career path.

All business books (this one included) are basically a rewriting of common sense. This was written to help you develop a healthy sense of paranoia about what's around the corner—fog lights for the road ahead. By knowing where the second curve has come from and what it means for you and your business, you'll get a jump start on the future. You can formulate strategies—both personal and professional—that will help you deal with change, whether you're a CEO or among the ranks of the recently reengineered. Because the biggest mistake—the fatal mistake—is to do nothing.

The Two-Curve Challenge

A DECADE AGO two relatively new retailers—Kmart and Wal-Mart—were fighting for supremacy in the market, each appealing to the new consumer's search for value. Kmart was the country's largest retailer and had a good track record in building new stores that presented choice and value to customers. But they took a wrong turn by wanting to move up with their customers to specialty stores. They purchased a number of specialty retail stores, covering everything from books to shoes. In contrast, Wal-Mart focused all of their investment on what they saw as the critical element of the second curve—consumer choice and private label value in purchasing basic goods. They put all of their investment in computer controlled inventory and distribution systems and continued to build new stores. In January 1996, *Fortune* wrote the obituary for Kmart. They weren't dead yet, but the business press was writing them off. Wal-Mart had well over double the revenues of Kmart, with sixteen times the market capitalization. Kmart was being dismissed. What happened? Wal-Mart responded well to the second curve and Kmart didn't.

Sony and Disney are another example of two companies that have both read the second curve signs, yet one is making it and one is scrambling. Why? They're certainly both expanding. Sony made a major move into media delivery, buying Columbia Pictures in 1989, as well as part of Traema, a French music producer. It also entered into joint ventures with Interactive Network, Blockbuster, and Time Warner to create radio programming, and it has additional joint ventures with Viacom, MTV, TCI, HBO, IMAX, Netscape Internet Access Group, Children's Television Workshop, and Jim Henson Productions. In early 1996, its U.S. entertainment investments through Sony Pictures Entertainment are in jeopardy. Now look at Disney, a company that's expanding on its strengths in entertainment, making a fluid move to a second curve with joint ventures with Ziff-Davis Publishing Co., Ameritech, BellSouth, and Southwestern Bell to develop markets and deliver video products. And it has joint ventures with Luxembourg Géoise de Télédiffusion in Belgium and Newscorp B Sky B in the U.K. and investments in Times Square hotel and theater refurbishments; in addition, California baseball and hockey franchises, Florida Wild Animal Theme Parks, and advertising production with Coca-Cola leverage new markets and new technologies. What's the difference? Sony is an electronics company buying its way into a new world, a second curve it neither understands nor is culturally comfortable managing—it made the leap but the gap was too large—while Disney continues to bring new consumers what it knows best: the magic of entertainment.

Or look at Air France versus British Airways. The United Kingdom and France are similar-sized economies that had a similar approach to nationalized airlines until the 1980s. The similarities end there. British Airways has embraced today's sophisticated consumer and emerging global market, and become "the world's favorite," growing both revenues and net income handsomely over the last decade. Air France, on the other hand, turned instead to its domestic market, focusing on Air Inter, its domestic regional subsidiary, and has experienced a decelerating rate of growth and mounting losses. Growth is on the second curve of bringing the world to the urbane international traveler, and British Airways is doing the job.

Or you can go a little further back in time. In the 1950s, U.S. railroad executives knew that their world was about to be turned upside down. Trucks on the coming interstates would grab critical pieces of their freight business, while the arrival of commercial aircraft like the 707 would soak up their most elite passenger business. They faced the classic two-curve problem: their current industry was on a stable, even lucrative, curve, but around the bend was change that would transform the business fundamentally, completely, and irrevocably.

Management wasn't stupid. They responded to the external changes by redefining their industry. They were in the *transportation* business, not the railroad business, they said, and they looked for new opportunities, from renting rights of way for communications lines to moving freight in new ways, such as piggyback truck trailers and slurry pipelines. They sold off their downtown space to office developers; they diversified with the cash. Many failed ultimately, but not out of ignorance. They correctly perceived the shape of the future intellectually; they just never made the shift emotionally. They loved trains too much.

These are not isolated incidents. As we head toward the next century, *every* business is threatened with becoming a railroad of the twenty-first century, and companies in *every* industry will have to learn to manage on two curves. A second curve is emerging—one based on changes in technology, consumer behavior, and geography. It will require new skills, new strategies, and new ways of thinking.

Ask Pitney Bowes, a company that, so far, is facing these dilemmas successfully. In 1993, Pitney Bowes had its best year ever. Sales were $3.5 billion, up nearly 40 percent in five years, and net income was $353 million, the highest for thirty years. The company had just introduced its successful Paragon mail processor, a state-of-the-art wonder that could move 240 pieces a minute.

You would have thought life was good. Pitney Bowes's core business—supporting paper-based mail—was more successful than ever. And yet management was worried: the infrastructure for electronic communications and information technologies, especially to the home, was expanding exponentially. Business-to-home mail represented 70 percent of the mail stream, and a good portion of Pitney Bowes's business; if any part of that traditional mail stream was replaced by information technologies—if, say, a good number of account holders started receiving their bank statements online; or if consumers started sending payments electronically; or if businesses that relied on direct mail decided it was more cost-effective to install a home page on the World Wide Web—depending on the rate and extent to which any of these occurred, a significant proportion of Pitney Bowes's core business could be seriously eroded. The second curve was approaching.

Defining Our Curves

A COMPANY'S FIRST CURVE IS its traditional business base representing the majority of its current revenues—in Pitney Bowes's case, supporting the paper-based mail stream. You might be doing fine on that curve, maybe even very well, and maybe even for a long time. But sooner or later things begin to change—you sense that your first curve isn't going to do it forever—and you know you have to respond. You might invest more heavily in R&D; Pitney Bowes did, investing $325 million in developing Paragon and other technologies from 1990 to 1992. A good move: the investment has paid off handsomely. But it was still an investment in the first curve, in what the company had always done well, and these days it simply won't be enough.

That's the second-curve dilemma. To continue to grow and thrive, Pitney Bowes has to start thinking about getting on that second curve. Almost every successful first-curve business was a second-curve business in its day. Pitney Bowes revolutionized the collection of postal revenues with the invention of the postage meter in the 1970s. IBM has been on the second curve twice, first as a tabulating machine company, then as a second-curve office equipment player that came to first-curve dominance in the 1960s and 1970s. Eventually, every business has to face the second curve because it's caused by external changes over which a company has no control, and what this means is that the first-curve investment is no longer enough, and the company must face very real—and very complicated—strategic dilemmas. Do you make the jump to the second curve—a second business—at all? If so, do you jump now and risk losing your best customers—and your solid first curve? If you jump too soon you may be walking away from all the profit and (worse yet) putting yourself in head-to-head competition with yourself or your best customers. If you stay on the old curve too long, you may never get a chance to play on the second curve. But when do you jump, and how? Can you play both curves? Are these second curve guys for real?

A potentially daunting scenario, but one, nevertheless, that every business, in every industry, will face. There are things you can do— strategies to follow, ways to handle the coming changes. But before looking at those, it's helpful to understand how we got where we are. Often the *why* of change is as important as the *what*. The key challenge of the second curve is to recognize the components of change.

Sources of the Second Curve:
What's Driving the Change?

SO WHERE DOES the second curve come from? In studies of companies undergoing this kind of market transformation, you can see three forces driving the second curve: new technologies, new consumers, and new geographical market frontiers—forces that are changing our world, singly and in combination, faster than ever.

THE NEW TECHNOLOGY IS FASTER, BETTER,
AND CHEAPER

Understanding the effects of new technologies—especially information technologies—is critical for managing on two curves. You could argue that without the vast and rapid proliferation of information technologies in the last twenty years, there would be no second curve. It is, in fact, the ability of new technologies to fundamentally transform a given industry that creates the discontinuities that define most second curves. For example, powerful new electronic tools make highly tailored customer service possible for companies such as Federal Express, AT&T, and United Airlines.

It takes thirty years for technologies to become overnight successes. Forecasting the next big technology application is a lot like picking who will make it to the Olympics in 2016 by sorting through baby pictures. But despite the difficulties inherent in a long time curve, you can learn a few things about the diffusion of technology and try to spot the moments when something really big starts happening.

THE NEW CONSUMER WANTS ANYTHING,
ANYTIME, ANYPLACE

Smarter, richer, choosier, more demanding: today's consumers have high expectations in quality, service, design—and they want low cost. Their expectations are transforming the marketplace dramatically, creating a second curve for the companies that serve them. The new consumer is a powerful enough force to change the types of products and services coming to market, and to transform the way products and services are sold. And there are more of them every year.

The volatility of contemporary consumers—their willingness to change—is at the heart of the second curve. There wouldn't even be such a pronounced second curve if customers hadn't shown such a willingness to jump from one type of product and service to any other without warning. You can't begin to understand how or when to move from one curve to another without understanding the new consumer.

They're better educated. They're more affluent—the larger number of households with large annual incomes means there are more consumers who have some discretion over purchases, which in turn means they can be more demanding and more volatile in their purchases. They're used to sophisticated information. And they're more skeptical—a much harder sell, if you will. Consumers, more than ever, are willing to shift loyalties and experiment with the new and different.

The demands of these new consumers—and vendors' responses to those demands—have had huge effects. Companies have gone through a distribution revolution to win over and retain the loyalty of the new consumer. Time to market is down while choice is up; take a look at the choices you have at the supermarket for a single item now as compared to ten years ago, whether it's snack foods, prepared meals, or the ever-expanding array in the freezer aisle. The number of ways of reaching the customer is radically different; think of everything from factory outlets and warehouse stores to direct mail catalogs and TV shopping. And the value of a brand name has changed dramatically. In the past, brand names denoted value by promising a standard of quality. Now that standard of quality is conferred by the retailer himself, who can carry a wide variety of brands (some of his own making), all of which have an image of quality but some of which can be discounted because they don't need to be advertised individually.

So the dilemma of selling to the new consumer goes something like this: Do you try to do the best you can with what you have, or do you scrap the whole system for something newer and better?

THE NEW MARKET FRONTIER COMES FROM THE GROWTH IN EMERGING MARKETS

The emerging markets of Asia, Eastern Europe, and Latin America are singly and in combination creating second curves for companies the world over. They will be key markets—and key competitors. For example, China: it will be a larger economy than the United States sometime early in the next century—the only question is when, not if. All the emerging markets have extremely high growth potential for consumer products, capital goods, infrastructure, high technology, and services.

But knowing there's a big new second curve in the long run doesn't guarantee the right response at the right time. Sorting out the sequence and the relative level of commitment to make to each of the emerging markets and subregions of the countries involved is a hugely complex task. Clearly Asia and Latin America will grow, but at different rates in different areas.

Which is not to say that American primacy in world markets will fade anytime soon. The United States will continue to be a large and growing economy and the most influential on the planet, in large part because of its cultural exports. American popular culture has become a key component of the U.S. economic base: Coke, Marlboro, Madonna, Levi Strauss, American movies, and *Married . . . with Children* reruns are everywhere. Sixty percent of *Jurassic Park*'s revenues were earned outside the United States. And another U.S. export—the Internet—is a window on the future of the global market, an electronically mediated bazaar that allows ideas and cash to zap around the world, enabling virtual deals to be done on a global basis.

Part of shifting to the second curve is redefining what a market is. For many years, the "market"—to American companies—meant the United States. Gradually, between 1970 and 1990, came the realization that the true market for American firms at least crossed the North Atlantic and included the countries of Western Europe. Now we are suddenly confronted with a new concept of "market"—one that includes many of the emerging countries of the world.

Where We Are Now

THE BOTTOM-LINE REALITY of the second curve is, of course, change. This includes transformation on many levels: society, the marketplace, even the individual. And most certainly on a business level. Corporations are experiencing transformation within—on an internal organization level—as well as without—throughout each industry as a whole.

In the rapidly changing global marketplace, many businesses are finding that their traditional organizations are more of an obstacle than an advantage in leveraging opportunities. Traditionally, organizations have been structured on models governed by mechanistic, linear metaphors, such as the military-style organizations of the early twentieth century. Reengineering is the ultimate mechanistic metaphor. These models worked well in regionally isolated markets with little competition, but now that markets are global, dynamic, and connected in a complex ecology of economic relationships, the old models are no longer effective—a classic second-curve problem. To compete in this world, companies must develop new organizational models. The metaphors for these models are more organic than mechanistic, more a set of dynamic processes than a static org chart. For example, traditional hierarchical organizations—the army and some large corporations—are moving to a "fishnet organization"—a network of constantly changing, ad hoc hierarchies linked and managed by information technology, an organization that gives them greater flexibility to meet the demands of the merging, fast-paced global market. As we move into the twenty-first century, these new forms of organization will increasingly present two-curve dilemmas for companies and their employees.

The world's major industries are being hugely affected by the second curve. New technology, new consumers, and new geography are creating change that isn't the limited, albeit dramatic, sort a company might experience because of a strategic error or a market shift. This is massive and fundamental change—a redefinition of terms—for an entire industry or market, resulting from the confluence of powerful driving forces. In particular, retail and distribution, health care, and financial services are dramatically affected by the second curve.

Retail and distribution. The second-curve dilemma faced by retail and distribution is the elimination of the middleman. As a result of the new consumer, the electronic infrastructure, more intense competition, and new distribution channels, retailers are scrambling. And they are coming up with some interesting responses, from Wal-Mart's virtual integration (embedding the retailer's systems electronically in the vendor's inventory and supply system) to Spiegel's all-out direct marketing, where mail-order and catalog sales are taken to the limit.

Health care. In health care, talk of two curves abounds. The traditional fee-for-service world is being replaced by managed care; the
inpatient environment is changing over to the ambulatory environment; and pharmaceutical R&D firms are moving from traditional
mechanisms for finding drugs (screening obscure, naturally occurring compounds for therapeutic effects) to a biotechnology-based
mechanism whereby large molecules are designed to have a specific
therapeutic effect. But even with all these changes, the real health
care second curve, where all Americans can be covered in a cost-
effective way, has not yet been clearly articulated.

Financial services. You see the confluence of new brands, new
channels, new consumers, and new technologies (everything from
the Internet to the smart card) transforming the global financial services industries, particularly the retail segment. Traditional financial
services companies are trying to avoid disintermediation—that is,
watching their deposits go elsewhere—by the second curve, which
will devastate the unsuspecting of Wall Street, Hartford, London,
Hong Kong, and Zurich.

Embracing Change: The Key to Success in the Second Curve World

AS USUAL, Yogi Berra put it well: "Prediction is very hard, especially when it's about the future." It is, of course, not only difficult
but simply impossible to predict the future, if by predicting you
mean reaching out into the future to pluck fully realized events like
so much ripe fruit.

Which is not to say that we can't think systematically about the
future, that we can't make sense of the trends, developing issues, and
emerging technologies, and in so doing become more informed
about what is likely to happen. When we are constantly looking
ahead and reviewing the longer-term driving forces that create
change in the business environment, the world becomes less random. Patterns emerge, new threats are foreseen and avoided, new
opportunities are identified and exploited. By taking the best available thinking and information, you can create forecasts that help
businesses and individuals make informed long-term strategic decisions. And that is probably the reason you're reading this book.

So what kind of forecasts can you make about the second curve? Given that you can't predict the pace of change for either of the two curves, and given that you're dealing with a multitude of false starts on the second curve, can you develop a strategy?

A resounding *yes*: there's a lot we don't know, but there's also a lot that we do. The second curve is about facing the challenge of change. You're doing well, running fast—but take a good look over your shoulder and see who's gaining on you. You'll be surprised.

Global beverage giants like Coke and Pepsi got hit hard by the private-label colas.

Health insurance giants like Traveler's and Metropolitan got side-swiped by managed care organizations like Oxford Health Plans, United HealthCare, and U.S. Healthcare, who outperformed them with a different paradigm.

Japanese semiconductor manufacturers who themselves had been the second curve in the early 1980s were overwhelmed by new second-curve semiconductor technology from Intel, Advanced Micro Devices, and the brains of Silicon Valley in the late 1980s and 1990s. By focusing on advanced microprocessors, the U.S. semiconductor industry engineered a second-curve comeback. But this isn't an easy change. You don't become second-curve overnight. You might not be up to it—as a company or an individual. That's why managing on two curves is the exciting and enjoyable challenge of the emerging global business scene, where technology, political change that opens new geographic markets, and sophisticated new consumers are creating new curves by the thousands.

Managing on two curves is extremely difficult and few pull it off, and if it sounds as if there's a lot of uncertainty in all this—well, there is. And there's only one thing to do with that uncertainty: learn to live with it. In the final analysis, managing on two curves is a juggling act. You can get comfortable with it if you develop an awareness of change and the tools to deal with it. That's the skill: to use change to provide the creative tension that keeps you and your company moving forward.

The World According to Two Curves

THE SECOND CURVE has effects that are far-reaching and far-felt, affecting us as individuals, changing the marketplace, reorganizing corporations, and even transforming major industries. There are fundamental transformations under way as we move from the first to the second curve, tensions that are summarized in the table below. Understanding how different the curves are is an important first step in being able to deal with them. Recognizing that the second curve has very different characteristics from the first is the best way to begin to manage on two curves.

FROM FIRST CURVE TO SECOND CURVE

First Curve	Second Curve
MARKET	
Capital	Knowledge
Producer	Consumer
Atlantic	Pacific
Japan	China
International Trade	Electronic Commerce
Computers	Internet
Money	People
ORGANIZATION	
Mechanistic	Organic
Engineering	Ecology
Corporations	Individuals and Networks
Horizontal and Vertical Integration	Virtual Integration
Business Processes	Culture
THE INDIVIDUAL	
Hard Work	Hypereffectiveness
Security	Uncertainty
Current Career	Future Career
Faith	Hope
Loyalty	Courage

The Second-Curve Marketplace

THE FORCES of technology, consumers, and geography have created second-curve markets, which are hypercompetitive. Competition
comes not only from first-curve players, but from new second-curve
actors. It's an odd mixture: you have a huge clash of the titans, and at
the same time you have a bunch of piranhas nipping at your heels. A
bad metaphor, but it makes the point of the strangeness of the competitive environment.

These new markets are also dynamic and uncertain, driven by technology in the hands of users with rapidly changing consumer preferences. Political wild cards compound the uncertainty. The second

curve is like that, and succeeding in markets in the future will require bold actions.

Increasingly, these markets will be interdependent. Taking linear thinking—simply dividing the world into bite-size chunks—then overlaying command-and-control militaristic-type hierarchies on a complex rich global second-curve soup makes little sense. What's required is systemic thinking on the part of corporations and of individuals who can weave together the interdependent elements of this marketplace, rather than just carving out particular areas and claiming them as territory. More and more, your territory will be part of somebody else's territory, and everyone—think of the wildebeest, lions, and zebras in the Serengeti—is going to have to get along.

There are several key trends that characterize the shift from first curve to second curve in the marketplace:

From Capital to Knowledge

When the transformation is being made from capital to knowledge, it is important to put this in a geographic context. On one hand, there is a substantial amount of capital amassing in developing countries. In 1995, for the first time, foreign exchange reserves of developing countries exceeded those of developed countries. The other key shift that will occur in the future is the location of the technological and business knowledge capital of the planet.

Professor Zhang-Liang Chen is the vice president of Peking University, the elite university of China. When I met with him, we were talking about the activities of his students in the biochemistry department. The best and the brightest of a gene pool of 1.2 billion people end up making it to Peking University, and biochemistry is one of the strongest departments there. Consequently, virtually all of the graduates of the biochemistry department of Peking University would be capable of entering Ph.D. programs in biochemistry in the major universities in North America and Europe, and many do so. Currently, 95 percent of the graduates from those Ph.D. programs who had their original training at Peking University stay in the U.S. or in Europe. They don't return to China. And this is a pattern we've seen with other emerging countries. To put the pattern in context, you have to understand that over 50 percent of the Ph.D.'s granted in engineering and science in the United States are to foreign nationals, and disproportionately to Asians. In the past people who came to the United States for advanced training in science, mathematics, and engineering remained in the country and became part of the knowledge base and the human capital base of the United States, fueling the information economy. But the numbers are shifting markedly: for example, the share of Ph.D. recipients from Taiwan remaining in the United States after graduation fell from 53 percent in 1980 to 32 percent in 1991. In that same period, the share of Korean graduates remaining in the United States fell from 41 percent to 23 percent.

I asked Professor Chen whether he believed his graduates would continue to study and remain abroad. "Right now it's appropriate because we have no jobs for them," he said. I said, "That won't be true in the future." And he said, "Absolutely not. We will follow a similar pattern where that resource will stay within China."

The implication here is clear, and a similar story can be imagined when you think about the vast intellectual resources of the Indian subcontinent and what appears to be a strong cultural affinity, both in the Indian subcontinent and in Asia generally, for science and mathematics, which is underscored by superior SAT results for Asians in mathematics in the United States. The implication is that as we move to a knowledge economy that is increasingly footless, global, and a second curve that can be anywhere, the anywhere isn't necessarily going to be Silicon Valley or Boston or Seattle. It may increasingly be Shanghai or Beijing or Bangalore because the sheer weight of numbers and the potential excellence in raw research will be shifted to those nations.

Now this doesn't mean that we all leave Silicon Valley, because to turn pure academic research into new wealth, new jobs, and new understanding requires a very complex infrastructure beyond simply having a bunch of smart Ph.D. people. In Menlo Park, where the Institute for the Future is based, within a mile of our office on Sand Hill Road is a very significant percentage of the venture capital money in the country. We are surrounded by specialized lawyers, consultants, venture capitalists—each of whom plays a role in a complex ecology that makes Silicon Valley the success it is. A good description of this phenomenon, which geographers call agglomeration economies, is in *Regional Advantage: Culture and Competition in Silicon Valley and Route 128*, AnnaLee Saxenian's book on Silicon Valley, a thoughtful analysis of the success of Silicon Valley as a network of intellectual resources.

Nevertheless, the shift toward knowledge means that the knowledge base can move. Perhaps the single biggest attraction that will maintain Silicon Valley's preeminence in the Information Age is the fact that not only does it have San Francisco, Stanford, and Berkeley and the existing infrastructures of Sand Hill Road and Silicon Valley, but it also has a Mediterranean climate, which most human beings prefer. And so we're not moving—because the weather is nice.

From Producer to Consumer

The critical distinction between the first and second curves is that the first curve is focused much more on making products or services. It's a production-oriented phenomenon, whereas the second curve nearly always has a sort of passionate and deep understanding of consumer needs. The best way to describe the transformations of the second curve is to say that owning consumers is going to be much more critically important than owning the factors of production.

From the Atlantic to the Pacific

If the first curve's geographic axis is the North Atlantic, the second curve clearly is a Pacific curve. The growth anticipated in China and India, added to the continued importance of Japan and the dynamism of the Asian Four Tigers and the western Americas, makes the Pacific the nexus of the second curve. Although Japan is an aging, maturing economy, it clearly has a significant investor role throughout Asia and will continue to be a major world force. But the rise of the Asia-Pacific region will be relentless over the next twenty years and will mean a significant shift in orientation from the first axis of New York and London to an axis much more oriented toward California and the Pacific Rim. Within this larger shift there are some extremely interesting flows of key actors between such places as Vancouver and Hong Kong. The ascendancy of particular cities in this global stew is an interesting one to observe.

One hundred of the Global Fortune 500 companies are headquartered in Tokyo and thirty-two are based on Osaka. The revenue generated by companies based in Tokyo accounts for nearly 24 percent of the Global Fortune 500 total revenue. Osaka-based companies account for a further 10 percent. The U.S. has 151 of the Global Fortune 500, compared to second-place Japan with 149. But Japan accounts for 37 percent of the revenues, compared to 29 percent for the U.S., while profits of the U.S. companies were five times greater than the Japanese companies'.

From Japan to China

Within this shift to the Pacific region, Japan was clearly seen as the first curve of Asia and it has begun to fall on hard times, in a relative sense, for three fundamental reasons.

First, as a society, Japan is the most rapidly aging society in the world. Among the OECD nations it has gone from being among the youngest in terms of percentage of population over sixty-five to a situation where by 2010 it will have one of the oldest populations of all advanced nations. This puts enormous stress on the dependency ratio (that is, the proportion of nonworking to working individuals). It will stretch the pension, social security, and health care systems, which have been enormous reservoirs of capital for Japan in the past. The lack of immigration and of natural increase in population have meant that Japan has had to look elsewhere in Asia and in North America for its labor force. And increasingly it will be a nation that will deploy capital and knowledge to other parts of the globe and have checks sent home to provide for the needs and expenses of an aging population.

The second reason for some concern about Japan's ability to become a second-curve actor in and of itself is that the Japanese form of capitalism involves unbelievably interconnected investment protocols which limit both speed and flexibility. Japan's great strength is in preserving and taking the long view. Japan's weakness is perhaps an inability to respond. The Internet phenomenon is not peopled by Japanese companies for two reasons: the fact that software development is not a Japanese strength, and the fact that using the Internet in Japan is very expensive. But the dark side and the threatening side for this interconnection is what some analysts call the house of cards of capital relationships, where banks are much more heavily leveraged through guarantees and interrelationships. The true scale of the Japanese leverage in such areas as real estate is understated. Some analysts argued that the U.S., for all its faults, appropriately bit the bullet on the savings and loan crisis, whereas Japan has not been as responsive in either recognizing or responding to the enormous debt overhang that it faces.

A third reason why Japan's transformation to the second curve may be less easy is that if the second curve is about volatility and uncertainty, there may be less cultural capacity in Japanese society to respond to that volatility and uncertainty.

From International Trade to Electronic Commerce

The first-curve world of the last twenty years has been about trade between advanced nations. The second curve involves a shift toward trade with emerging countries. But beyond that, it also involves a shift in location away from trade in physical space toward trade in digital space. Electronic commerce doesn't know the same boundaries that nations impose. And this will raise some very interesting and bizarre questions with regard to the production, consumption, and sale of goods and services. For example, it is quite conceivable that new software products will be developed over the Net in several different countries in a collaborative effort among a variety of different entities. Sorting out the relative tariffs and trades in these kinds of production processes will become increasingly difficult over time. It will be more and more difficult as we shift from products which are manufactured and have value added, created by the addition of labor in a specific place. It will be increasingly a situation where the value will be added through global teams working across virtual space, adding value to a product which is increasingly more software-embodied than physical technology–embodied. And what that means is that our whole sets of conventions of accounting for where goods and services and final value are created is going to be extremely difficult to document and sort out, blurring the national boundaries and indeed muddying the trade statistics even more than perhaps they are already. Easy money flow across global financial networks will further blur these boundaries.

From Computers to the Internet

If the first-curve market is one in which stand-alone computing was the information paradigm, the second curve is best embodied in the Internet. As I write, the *San Francisco Chronicle* has a story on Internet companies the day that Netscape stock reached 140. The euphoria is likened to the tulip mania of seventeenth-century Holland, where speculative fever sent the price of individual tulip bulbs higher than the price of a house. We may be seeing such a phenomenon with the Internet. There have to be real revenues and substantial revenues from these companies in the future, and investors are gambling that the metaphor that allowed Microsoft to reach such market dominance will be a similar success on the Internet. This may be a false assumption. It's easy to see how a 70 percent market share of browsing tools could lead to the kind of hegemony that Microsoft has seen in the Microsoft/Intel world, but this may not be the case in a world of interoperability facilitated by extremely powerful technologies that allow any kind of machine to talk to any other. As horsepower and the speed of innovation increase, the moment in the sun for any individual actor may get shorter and shorter—Netscape then Java, Sun Microsystems' newest Internet tool—and this in turn may lead us to question whether anyone can truly dominate, and whether a global standard for something as important as the Internet, which is rapidly becoming the medium for both culture and trade, can be controlled by one company.

The Internet is certainly going to be a key phenomenon for the next twenty years. The question is, whose software will dominate and what kinds of market structure will those tools be embedded in? Will it be a monopoly or will it be a much more competitive, dynamic, and interoperable set of tools and techniques? Second-curve theory says the latter.

From Money to People

The first curve is dependent on money. It is where capital is important, where profit is important, where margin is important, and it is the basis for current cash in hand. The second curve, in contrast, is more about people. It is incredibly dependent on the capacities of individual human beings rather than simply on financial dimensions. And this presents the fundamental dilemma. Simply having money doesn't mean you can build a second curve. You can't do it without people and the right kind of people. The second curve needs people who can change, who can accept new ways of doing things, who embrace the strange, the foreign, and the weird. But most of all, the second curve belongs to diverse organizations who mix talents, skills, and interests.

Second-curve success stories have had the right mix of people. In the chapters that follow, we will highlight some examples, but perhaps the best is Netscape's combination: the young software innovator (Marc Andreesen) with the successful entrepreneur visionary (Jim Clark of Silicon Graphics fame) and the experienced big-time operator of second-curve companies (Jim Barksdale of Federal Express and McCaw Cellular experience). This is the quintessential second-curve team.

Second-Curve Organizations

IN TERMS OF CORPORATE ORGANIZATION, what used to work often doesn't anymore, causing a move from control and coordination to creativity and freedom, and creating hybrid organizational forms. In Michael Rothschild's book on bionomics (*Bionomics: Economy as Ecosystem*), he talks about the shift to an economy in which the laws of biology and economics are combined. Paul Hawken, founder of Smith & Hawken, an environmentally sensitive—and profitable—chain of gardening stores, takes it a step further in *The Ecology of Commerce*, claiming that the earth is lost unless profit-seeking capitalists gravitate toward environmentally sensitive and ecologically stable opportunities where the notions of conservation and recycling are built into the manufacturing process itself.

The following are trends that characterize the shift from first- to second-curve organizations:

Mechanistic to Organic

The first curve likes hierarchy, military command and control, and organizational charts. The second curve is organic, chaotic, a little bit wild, and it resists static forms of organizational control. As a consequence, the metaphors and language of first-curve versus second-curve organizations are very different. The mechanical first-curve organization tends to use the language of the military: divisions, units, sections. These are all militaristic terms that are embedded in business and really are reflective of a first-curve mentality.

The second-curve organization is built up of networks and alliances. It focuses more on relationships and personal connections than on organizational charts, hard mechanistic job descriptions, and reporting relationships. Visitors to high technology companies on a roll—Netscape today or Apple in the mid-1980s—are hard-pressed to find anyone who even claims to be in charge. Companies like those are out of control and loving it. But even among the saner second-curve companies, there is a fluidity of relationships and roles that is very different from the traditional corporate hierarchies, where most of American business is still stuck.

Engineering Versus Ecology

"Reengineering" has been the buzzword of the last five years. It is the ultimate mechanistic metaphor and it is the ultimate first-curve play. Reengineering is an attempt to wring the most out of the first curve. It is Taylorism—the principles of scientific management developed by F. W. Taylor in the 1910s—applied to the utmost. It is essentially arguing that every last piece of inefficiency must be eliminated from the first curve in order to maintain profitability. This is a perfectly reasonable response to the kind of global pressures that we've described. But it's not the second curve. You cannot reengineer your way to greatness. You cannot reengineer your way into a second-curve transformation because the act of reengineering is likely to focus the company's money on the first curve and get rid of the crazy people trying to build something amazingly different on the second. Any good reengineer will probably destroy second-curve activities found in the organization because those activities don't fit with critical business processes.

The second curve is about ecological relationships rather than engineering ones, and it is likely that the consultants will find themselves creating a new, much more ecological form of intervention that they can go and sell because clearly reengineering has left a bad taste in the mouth of the reengineered. It feels as though a bunch of overpaid reengineers came in and gutted the soul of the company. In 1985, when I first came to the United States, I began to travel extensively, and would fly with executives from the blue-chip companies—IBM, Du Pont, Chevron. The executives were passionate zealots for their companies. They were like Moonies. No longer. Many corporations have downsized, rightsized, and reengineered to the point where the spirit has gone. Bob Johansen and Rob Swigart's latest IFTF research report, "In Good Company," focuses on the spiritual vacuum and lack of meaning felt by many of the reengineered organizations as companies stumble on the first curve.

Corporations Versus Individuals and Networks

It may be true that the corporation is a first-curve phenomenon and that second-curve organizations are much more likely to be individuals and networks and various combinations of individuals and networks that create value. That doesn't mean that all corporations as business entities will disappear. That seems unlikely because we have existing frameworks that function effectively and are increasingly being adopted around the globe, such as stock markets, limited companies, and the ability to raise money because of a particular corporate entity having both the legal and financial infrastructure to raise capital, keep standard sets of accounts, and declare profits or losses which can be judged independently by shareholders. Such apparatus is inherently valuable and indeed most of the second-curve companies have used the market to the hilt, to wit: the Netscapes, Silicon Graphics, Intuits of the world. Great wealth has been created on the second curve through the traditional stock market mechanisms. But increasingly, within the organization and within the corporation, the entities that are important are going to be much more closely tied to the individuals involved and to the networks. The same would be true in most emerging, second-curve companies created by venture capitalists. The idea is not enough. It's who's behind it, what the management team looks like, and what their Rolodexes look like.

Horizontal and Vertical Integration Versus Virtual Integration

The first curve is about horizontal and vertical integration. In the chapters that follow we will lay out how first and second curves are playing out in various industry segments. And a theme that occurs over and over again is that much of the scrambling action on the first curve is either horizontal or vertical integration in response to greater competitive pressures experienced both as the first curve consolidates and clamps down and as the second curve nips away at the heels of the first.

The business response in times of great uncertainty is often, *If you don't understand it, buy it.* Many attempts have been made by first-curve players who perceive the threat of a second curve and think that they can simply purchase it as a mechanism of corporate salvation. Some examples of this include Merck's purchase of Medco, which was perhaps the most extreme case of the first curve trying to learn quickly about managed care by owning what they perceived to be a leading proponent of the future. It is an expensive seminar to pay $6 billion to find out what's going on. Other examples include some of the aborted attempts in the mergers of cable companies and telcos that—because of the perceived value the other guy had—scrambled mightily to put themselves together to build the mother of all communications companies, only to have the deals undone or diluted by regulatory impediments, cultural incompatibility, and the speed of technological change.

Some vertical integration has taken place, but much more prevalent has been horizontal integration on the first curve. There are going to be fewer and fewer banks in the future, as the first curve consolidates in response to a highly uncertain second curve in financial services. The first-curve response in many industries is to try and organize for economies of scale. It's happening in telecommunications. It's happening in most fields.

Indeed, one variant on the second curve is actors who correctly perceive the potential in consolidation of what may be sleepy first-curve industries. The founder of Waste Management, H. Wayne Huizenga, built a billion-dollar company, then went on to found another, Blockbuster Entertainment. He's now starting a company called Republic that will be a holding company in trash management, billboards, and alarm systems—which doesn't sound particularly second-curve, but what he's essentially doing is consolidating horizontally in very fragmented industries where there are potential market share plays and economies of scale. He really understands the whole notion of rental businesses and how to make money in rental businesses, which is the common denominator in waste management and in video rental.

The second curve tends to be more about virtual integration rather than vertical or horizontal integration. Examples abound in the electronics business. Computer and communications companies rarely make all of the elements of the products they sell. They create the kind of virtual corporation that Bill Davidow (coauthor of *The Virtual Corporation*) and his colleagues described eloquently—where various pieces of the product are created by a web of subcontractors linked through contract relationships, partnerships, and alliances. A similar story can be told of some of the successful managed health care organizations discussed in chapter ten. Virtual integration is a hallmark of the second curve.

Business Processes Versus Culture

Much recent work at the Institute for the Future has focused on describing alternate visions of the twenty-first century organization and identifying six archetypes arrayed across the two curves, from the mechanistic to the more organic nonlinear, from a focus on business processes to a focus on culture.

The Hyperfocused Firm. The classic Silicon Valley start-up or the large company division bearing down on a focused object, bounded only by its core competencies. An example of this would be IBM's microelectronics division, which has recently begun to concentrate, in a hyperfocused way, on becoming a player again in chips and semiconductors.

The Cultural Juggernaut. The large organization that exerts long-lasting and wide-ranging control by means of shared values and norms. The Catholic Church, the Korean *chaebol*, the powerful interlocking ties of Chinese business families in South Asia, and the families of Monterrey, Mexico, are all examples of cultural juggernauts.

The Extended Enterprise. The vertically integrated enterprise intent on carving out fewer, deeper, and more meaningful relationships with its suppliers and distributors. Ultimately, the whole business system goes under the brand or imprimatur of the parent company. One example is MCI and News Corporation of America getting together in a joint venture where they'll form an extended enterprise in the publishing area. But the large automakers are the best examples. Volvo, for instance, is intent on trying to build a global extended enterprise with the Volvo values of engineering, quality, safety, and environmental sensitivity, and applying those values across the range of suppliers and distributors of Volvo products in their various divisions. The car companies are increasingly trying to build extended enterprises not only with suppliers, but with the various global pieces of their businesses, as is the case with the Ford Mondeo, a world car conceived for a world market.

The Shared-Risk Alliance. The attempt by corporations to build value through joint ventures and alliances, whereby competencies may be shared to mutual benefit. The relationships don't have to be permanent or exclusive; in fact, most often they're not. You can see examples in the outsourcing of R&D, which is increasingly happening among some of the larger corporations that don't want to bring all of it in-house, and in pharmaceuticals, where increasingly the large pharmaceutical companies recognize that they can't assure themselves of having a blockbuster drug come from their in-house R&D programs, no matter how big they are and how much they have invested in R&D. Many have made minority investments, and in some cases a majority investment, in smaller research-and-development–oriented biotechnology companies. This is a form of a shared-risk alliance.

The other place in which the shared-risk alliance is used increasingly is the managed health care business. Large health maintenance organizations (HMOs) such as Health Net, PacifiCare, FHP, U.S. Healthcare, and United HealthCare have built shared-risk alliances.

In most cases, these organizations don't actually own anything; they have contractual relationships with groups of providers, either medical groups or hospitals, who are prepared to take on some of the risks of managing care—to become, in effect, insurers in their own right. By sharing risk in developing networks, they add value to their customers, the employers, and the patients they serve. In the whole health care enterprise, they are the ones who seem to have been most successful in managing the two-curve transition over the last few years. They've made money and been rewarded for creating a second curve.

The Fishnet Organization. A web of constantly changing hierarchies linked and managed by information technology, with multiple centers of activity and responsibility that can change quickly to adapt to market conditions. The large global consulting firms are perhaps the quintessential fishnets. (The phrase comes out of *Upsizing the Individual in the Downsized Organization* by Robert Johansen and Rob Swigart, and *Globalwork: Bridging Distance, Culture, and Time* by Mary O'Hara-Devereaux and Robert Johansen.)

The nature of the fishnet is such that it tries to be responsive to a rapidly changing environment. Bob Johansen has characterized it as growing from the edges, with the center of the fishnet the dull part, and the edge the important part. It's only as strong as the nodes in the network and the links between them. In other words, it relies heavily on contacts and communication networks for its strength, resilience, and ability to perform the task. The large consulting companies like Andersen, McKinsey, Booz Allen & Hamilton, and Price Waterhouse are very much fishnet organizations. Among the tools necessary to support fishnets are advanced forms of groupware. Lotus Notes is often categorized as the first real groupware product, and it's no accident that fishnet organizations like Andersen, Price Waterhouse, and McKinsey are among the largest and earliest users of Lotus Notes technology.

Chaord. A neologism that combines chaos and order, coined by Dee Hawks, the founder of Visa. It speaks to the concept of the self-generating organization, which is the most organic, free-form enterprise, driven by spontaneous adaptation to market niches. These organizations are seemingly bereft of central control, growing in response to and almost in conjunction with the environments in which they are serving. The chaotic small enterprise (perhaps even the Institute for the Future) may be in this category; this kind of organization is fluid, flat, and—one hopes—responsive to a changing environmental context. On a larger scale, Virgin Group is really a chaord in some sense, in that its focus and ability to adjust to customer requirements are really quite organic, in terms of its ability to act.

Together these models represent steps on a continuum, from detailed central control to control at the edges; from mechanistic to organic; from predictable, directed situations to creative chaos. For the next decade and beyond, companies will most likely use all of these models to compete in the global marketplace. What the models really are, of course, is a diagnostic, a way to think about organizations of the future. There is not necessarily one prescriptive model, and you can't really see an organization being a pure form of any of them; most organizations will be hybrids. Because each model has specific strategic advantages, companies will probably try different models, and a single company may try different models at different times. Companies may even use a combination of these models at the same time—for example, the hyperfocused model for their marketing of one particular product, the fishnet for running their sales and service business, and chaord for their most advanced research departments. The models may vary across companies.

As we move into the twenty-first century, these new forms of organization will increasingly present a two-curve dilemma for their companies and their employees. Indeed, organizations are jumping from the first curve to the second curve as they move from the traditional command-and-control hierarchical structure to the more fluid dynamics of the decentralized organization, which empowers small groups to respond quickly and flexibly, whether it be a chaord, a fishnet, or a shared-risk alliance.

The Second Curve and the Individual

AMERICAN COMPANIES have gone through a startling transformation in their use of labor over the last decade. Just fifteen years ago, they were increasing their use of labor at tremendous rates, regarding labor as a seemingly endless source of cheap and talented input for growth. Today companies treat labor as a costly, inefficiently used input that offers wide opportunity for cost cutting in a more competitive environment. This rapid reversal in the role of labor is at the heart of a major reorientation of job roles, responsibilities, and the place of workers in twenty-first-century organizations.

Most industries and most second-curve companies have discovered that they can get along with fewer workers. Manufacturing firms learned this lesson early as foreign competition encroached on many of their markets in the 1960s and 1970s. Service-sector firms picked up the idea with the general slowdown in the economy in the late 1980s and early 1990s. While a few industries continue to hire new workers, most industries are now either cutting back on workers or holding the number of workers at current levels. This last group includes virtually all of the service industries that created the bulk of the new jobs in the previous three decades. The service sector is improving productivity by using fewer workers per unit of sales, but because the overall service sector is growing—new firms are being added, particularly in business services—overall service employment will continue to rise.

One way of dealing with the rising cost of workers is to cut what accounts for the most rapid rise. Benefits and costs of associated social payments have been rising much faster than the cost of wages. In response, employers now provide benefits to fewer workers. Over the last decade, the share of workers receiving health or pension plans has fallen dramatically. Employers have done this by cutting coverage where possible, by cutting the benefits offered, by hiring more part-time employees with few or no benefits, and by contracting work to small firms whose benefits are limited. Bank of America shifted all of its teller jobs from full-time to part-time to increase their own flexibility and to ease the cost of full-time benefits for a position that attracts many part-time workers.

Outsourcing has grown sharply in the last decade, not only as a means of avoiding benefit costs, but as a fundamentally different way of organizing. The temporary help industry—Manpower, Kelly, Interim, Olsten, and so forth—as an entire industry employs some 2 percent of the labor force. Coming out of the 1990–1992 recession, however, temporary help accounted for almost 20 percent of the net new jobs. Leaders in the industry, like Ray Marcy, CEO of Interim Services, believe that instead of providing temps in the future, Interim and others will be in the business of managing the entire human resource function for their clients. The early signs of this vision are there. Pitney Bowes has an almost billion-dollar business providing a service to large companies that outsources the logistics, equipment, and management of mail rooms. Pitney Bowes in turn has contracted with Interim to manage the staffing and recruitment dimensions of the business. In health insurance, insurers find that the billions of claims they receive are too much for them, and they outsource like crazy to Electronic Data Systems or First Data Corporation for MIS activity, to Chase Manhattan Bank for check processing, even to the Caribbean Data Systems group of American Airlines, where offshore clerks in the Caribbean do the data entry for your airline ticket and your medical claim. These webs of relationships are mediated by technology and enable organizations to focus on their key competencies and client relationships.

New technologies have also affected individuals in the workplace. Technology enables workers to do what they couldn't do on their own in the past, which isn't so much a revolution in technology as it is a mind shift for workers and managers, a breakthrough in learning how to integrate technology and the worker. Not only does the nature of the work itself change, the experiences of individual workers and teams change as well. The "anytime/anyplace" office that author Stan Davis predicted in 1987 (*Future Perfect: A Startling Vision of the Future We Should Be Managing Now*) is, in many companies, a reality today. And the new tools are enabling companies to change business processes on the basis of new kinds of assumptions about where work can be done, how much complexity individual workers can handle, and where within the organization decisions will be made. New tools facilitate new tasks, which then require new attributes. For example, thousands of field sales and service personnel in a variety of industries are already using portable computers or specialized information appliances to record transactions, access data, support decision-making activities in the field, and transmit the results of their work to corporate offices, factories, and distribution centers.

Selling was once a highly interpersonal role in which sales were made on the basis of personal relationships within a context of predefined procedures and price ranges. Today, however, field sales professionals can be their own financial analysts. With a personal computer, analytic software, and corporate economic models, they can explore alternative pricing, promotion, and delivery terms with their customers in real time. This capability allows the buyer and seller to negotiate mutually beneficial deals that are far more complex and far more accurate than was previously possible—and to do so far more quickly. The results of the deals can be communicated back to the corporate offices to influence production schedules, shipping dates, and sales monitoring systems.

The combination of these changes is affecting individuals in several major ways. The shifts in individuals' attitudes can be characterized in the following ways:

Hard Work Versus Hypereffectiveness

The hallmark of the first-curve employee is a hardworking, motivated, driven individual—the success model of putting in time, being productive, and getting good results through energy, time, and talent.

The second curve is about hypereffective employees. Leaders in the software industry estimate that there might be a fiftyfold difference in productivity between best and worst programmers. This is really a reflection of the fact that writing lines of code is not the end point at which one should judge software productivity. It is how quickly an individual or a team can create a functioning product that runs effectively and accurately with few errors. Perhaps the single best example of this is a former colleague at the Institute for the Future, Hubert Lipinski, who went on to cofound the company that became CC Mail, now a division of Lotus, an internal division of IBM. Hubert basically wrote in his head object-oriented programming before the term was invented and was capable of stringing together in his brain many lines of code into little objects that could be brought to bear on a particular set of subroutines in writing the original source code that would eventually become the CC Mail product. Hubert is an exceptional individual, but he is typical of many great software geniuses who have enormous capacity to store complex sets of relationships in their heads and seem to take great joy in being able to produce elegantly written code that functions sweetly.

With the development of CASE tools (computer-aided software engineering tools), such genius need not be required to write software code. Object-oriented programming, and all of the tools available and tools yet to be developed in the software world, promises that the productivity of software creation will improve radically over time. Nevertheless, it will still be true that certain individuals can master these tools in much more effective ways than others, and the variation in output, given that these tools are for the arrangement of symbols, is going to bestow maestro-like qualities on certain workers. Organizing around maestros is very different from organizing in a hierarchical framework. The concept of a fifteen-thousand-person symphony orchestra is not necessarily one that would be any better than a one-hundred-person symphony orchestra.

Security Versus Uncertainty

The nice thing about the first curve is that it feels fairly secure. It's where you get your money. It's what keeps you employed. It's where your office is. It's the place, the people, and the company you belong to. It's what you know. It's what you know you can do. It's what you feel capable of delivering on a daily basis. The second curve is uncertain. It is not clear that what you are doing is right. The second curve is a little bit scary because it's not about an obvious transformation, another set of business processes you ought to be doing. It is a very difficult shift. Why would anyone move? Why would anyone leave the security of the first curve for the second? This is at the core of the second-curve dilemma.

The reason is that the security of the first curve is a false security. It is a sense that just because it's working now doesn't mean it will work forever. And fundamentally, the psychology of the second curve is perhaps the most difficult dimension of management. As the baby boom generation ages, we are going to become more and more risk averse. We are no longer the pot smoking, freewheeling, don't-trust-anyone-over-thirty types that we once were. Americans are thickening in the middle, in both demographic and physical terms. The number of people in the forty-five-to-fifty-five-year-old age range will double in the U.S. between 1990 and 2010 as the baby boom moves through like a pig through an anaconda. That shifts the psychology of the nation from risk taking to risk avoiding, from the celebration of the new to the need to preserve, maintain, and prepare for the responsibilities of middle to later years. Many baby boomers are confronting a challenge of highly leveraged mortgage situations, fiercely competitive work situations, and the prospects of the triple whammy: kids' college education looming, parents in retirement homes with insufficient savings necessary to weather a long-term-care episode, *and* a bunch of reengineering consultants who are scheduled to visit their office a week from Monday.

This kind of anxiety compounds the difficulty that many middle-aged, middle-class workers have in dealing with the second curve. It's a hell of a lot easier to be hip about the second curve if you're a Generation X-er than it is if you're a middle-class baby boomer. The Net is your way of fighting back if you're a Generation X-er. It's different if you're a forty-five-year-old baby boomer working for a Fortune 500 company who may get vaporized by some Netscape-based loonies. And so for managers, the psychology of the second curve will be a very significant challenge over the next decade: how to inculcate among a worried, aging, and vulnerable middle-aged baby boom workforce the notion that their organizations have to change to meet these new challenges.

When I was in China in the summer of 1995, I thought a lot

about my children. They are nine and eleven. And I thought about the world they will be competing in, about their competing against Professor Chen's students of Peking University, about how they could possibly emulate the lifestyle and the kind of jobs and responsibilities that we have managed to reach in a world that was less global, less competitive. Then I came home and was reassured because they are curious, they are talented, and they are smart. They will find a way, I hope, maybe with a little help from their parents, to be able to compete in the twenty-first century. But clearly our kids and we ourselves are going to have to be very careful and very diligent about learning and looking for the second curve. In the meantime, it's a little daunting to think about how to make the right career choices in terms of a transformation from the first to the second curve.

Current Career Versus Future Career

The second curve is a little scary. If you see it coming at you, you know it can mean big changes, and no matter how many opportunities you can see in that emerging second curve, it's still alien and new, and it can be frightening. For managers and employees alike, the second curve is tough to deal with. As Random House CEO Alberto Vitale says, *Now everyone has two jobs.* You have to be working your second-curve career even though you're committed to the first.

For the manager, there are those gnawing feelings in the gut. *Is this a real second curve? Do we really have what it takes to pull it off? Am I the right leader for the second curve? What happens if we fail— to the company, and to me?* In short, the second curve tests leadership abilities, and it demands vision, persuasive powers, and courage. You have to be very cool and a little bit nuts.

For the employee, the second curve brings new pressures. *How can I do my reengineered job and still participate on the second curve? What is it that they want of me? Can I do it? Do I fit?* Employees need to be both challenged and reassured at the same time. The pressures are particularly intense for the middle-aged boomer with family obligations.

But these pressures—on managers or workers—shouldn't lead to despair. All of the growth—personal, professional, financial—will be on the second curve. With a little luck and a lot of common sense, you'll be a winner. And in that spirit, here are some tips for managing second-curve careers:

Build on what you have. It's nice to reinvent yourself, but build your new career on existing interests and competencies. Connect with the second curve through one or more of your current strengths.

Bring the two-curve model home. If you have a spouse, a partner, a significant other, you have an opportunity to work the second curve as a team. The home-based business. The second-curve start-up. The flaky new assignment.

Listen to Nike. Sometimes *Just Do It* is the best advice. Nobody knows exactly how the second curve will play out in your business. Look for the signs and signals described in this book, and then just do it.

Faith and Loyalty Versus Hope and Courage

The key attributes of a first-curve success are faith and loyalty. Faith that the company can deliver what it says in terms of products and services and loyalty to the organization. The second curve is about hope and is certainly about courage. The second curve is a pretty scary place because, as we have laid out, uncertainty abounds and the technology, the infrastructure, and the volatility of the markets stretch the capacities of individuals to believe in themselves and in the future.

Lessons Learned

WE CAN LEARN A FEW LESSONS about the world according to two curves:

DON'T MISTAKE THE SECOND CURVE FOR AN ORDERLY NEW WORLD

The second curve is the Wild West. It is the frontier. It is the change area. And that means you cannot rely on having the apparatus, the institutions, or the security of the first curve. The biggest mistake that one can make is to assume that the second-curve phenomenon is just like the first-curve only in a different place: just like New Jersey, only with good food.

HOW AND WHEN THESE SHIFTS OCCUR
IS EXTREMELY UNCERTAIN

The dirty little secret of futurism is that we cannot predict the future. We can think more systematically than most about what lies ahead, but because the future hasn't happened yet, we don't know what's going to happen and a lot of it depends on the choices and actions taken by key individuals. That's why, as an organization dedicated to helping people think about the longer term, the Institute for the Future works with decision-makers to help them *inform* their decisions, not necessarily to give them predictions of what will happen no matter what because the no-matter-whats just aren't firmly fixed.

But there are some no-matter-whats in terms of demography. We age one year at a time. We can make some fairly intelligent predictions about what the structure of demographics might look like over a five- or ten-year period. Prediction fails somewhat over a thirty-year period because you can miss certain fundamental shifts, such as the shift in fertility rates that occurred in the U.S. in 1968, when the combined effects of the Beatles and the pill radically altered the birthrate in America.

PEOPLE TEND TO OVERESTIMATE THE IMPACT
OF CHANGE IN THE SHORT RUN, AND TO
UNDERESTIMATE IT IN THE LONG RUN

We really do have this fundamental problem: We amplify change in certain dimensions and minimize it in others. The Internet is a prime example of that. One would believe that everybody in America was surfing the Net at night and not watching *Seinfeld* and not watching video rentals and not having meals with their family. The Net is certainly a phenomenon that's growing rapidly, but it hasn't consumed all of us yet. People read books. People only have so much time in their day, and time is becoming such an increasingly scarce resource that it will limit the transformations envisioned by the hype. In a world of competing claims from books, the Net, the movies, there will certainly be growth in the Net, but not eradication of the other channels. Simply because surfing the Net is a compelling thing to do doesn't mean that it will come to dominate my utility function in a way where I will do nothing else. Addiction is a model of marketing. It is a powerful one, but most of us despite our flaws manage to overcome our addictions and maintain a semblance of balance in our lives.

GROUND THE FUTURE IN INFORMATION
ABOUT THE PRESENT

Finally, in thinking about the second-curve world and the anxieties associated with it, it's crucial to understand what's going on in the here and now. There's a description of the future (attributed to "Goose" Gossage, former pitcher for the New York Yankees) that says *The future is a lot like the present, only longer.* There's some truth in that: if you take a look at the sweep of history, you can see there is tremendous compression of the future in the thinking of many individuals. They tend to believe that far out phenomena are actually much closer than they appear to be. As my colleague Paul Saffo of the Institute for the Future says, "You must never mistake a clear view for a short distance."

The New Technology:
Faster, Better, Cheaper

TECHNOLOGY PLAYS a huge role in creating a second curve, so much so that without it there probably wouldn't be one. But it's important to keep things in perspective and not get too carried away with the notion that technology causes change, or even that it determines the exact direction and pace of change. What technology is really about is enabling change and amplifying the direction that it takes. The direction of change isn't dictated by the technology; in many instances, it's dictated by choices—choices made by individuals, corporations, even governments. New technologies can drive the second curve in two ways. They create second curves in the industries that develop them, and they enable the changes that bring about second curves in the companies and industries that use them. An example of the first is the move from mainframes to PCs in the computer industry, of the second is the effect networked PCs are having on the way retailers organize or banks operate.

The second curve can come to all technologies, but the innovations in the areas of information and communications technology in particular are affecting just about every kind of business you can name, and they drive the second curve in a particular way.

Smoother Operating for Smooth Operators: The Power of Technology

IN TODAY'S TECHNOLOGY, power is the name of the game. What computers do these days wasn't even a twinkle in a techie's eye ten years ago, and the list of things you can do with a computer is growing at an astonishing rate. The advances are all the more impressive when you look at them in context.

One of the major changes in technology since World War II is the emergence of solid-state electronics and the microprocessor. Gordon Moore, one of the fathers of the semiconductor and computer industry, codified what is known as Moore's Law, a remarkable forecast of the capacities of information technology. It basically states that the number of transistors per chip doubles every eighteen months— which has meant an enormous increase in the horsepower available to drive information technology applications in all dimensions. Similarly, in other technologies developing in parallel (such as optical storage, relational databases, network controllers, and so on), there've been enormous leaps forward in the capacities, power, and performance of computers. Simply put, we're seeing smaller devices with more power at lower cost, and because of innovation in communications, these devices are more connected, more interoperable, and more mobile than ever.

It would be easy to get lost in all that power and dwell on its impressiveness strictly in and of itself the way you gaze at a work of art (because it is, in a way), but of course there's more to it than that. The point of all that power is what it can do, and the answer is a lot. It's made all kinds of never-would-have-believed-it things possible, things that hit very close to home for just about all of us. For example, when I was a student at Edinburgh University in the early '70s, dealing with the computer center—advanced as it was—was a complete pain. You would type a series of instructions on a card-punch machine, one card per line of code; then you'd submit that to a card reader in a batch-job mode. Submitting the job was a tedious process in itself: you took the cards and put them in a little basket, and came back a day or two later, because as a groveling undergraduate your status in the computing world was low. So you'd come back two days later to collect your output, only to find you'd made a typo in the first or second card of your fifty-card stack, leaving you in tears, or at the very least ready to go to the pub a little earlier than usual. Computers were very definitely "user-ugly" devices. They didn't seem to help with anything, and they made the process painful to boot.

Contrast the computing capacities in that environment (not to mention the environment itself) with the Macintosh sitting on my desk, a PowerBook Duo. When I walk into the office in the morning and plug it in (or, more often, when I dial in from a hotel room), not only do I access our e-mail and Lotus Notes servers and interact with my colleagues, but a click of a button away is the Internet and everybody on the planet you could want to waste time with. That's a fairly powerful shift in a relatively short period of time.

That dramatic increase in the sheer power of computers has made, and continues to make, new things possible. For example, it provides more ways to interact with the computer. We're no longer limited to keyboard and touch-screen; computers understand voice commands as well. And increased power has essentially brought large-scale data processing to the desk, the briefcase, and the palm in a way that was inconceivable twenty years ago. And not only is all that possible; it is available. It's what Mark Weiser of Xerox PARC calls "ubiquitous computing"—computers have become so cheap that they can be everywhere. Almost like paper and pen, there isn't much value attached to the computers themselves; in fact, we may be moving to a world where the devices can be essentially free, as cellular phones are today. A simple example is the Christmas card—or the Absolut Vodka ad with a vodka bottle—that sings, thanks to a chip and a small speaker device that's so cheap you can throw it away.

France's Minitel is another example. The French government thought that computers had become so cheap that they could use them to replace the telephone directory and provide an electronic platform for other services (as well as spawn a new French industry making the devices). The Minitel System was a forced-fit idea, and while it's made many French households computer literate, it has, to some extent, locked itself into a technology standard that is a little out of date.

The Minitel terminal is old-fashioned looking, the screen is fuzzy, the keyboard is small and hard to use, and many people find the screens slow and the menus hard to follow. But despite all that, after twelve years of operation, Minitel has become part of everyday life in France. And with good reason: the service we're talking about is extensive, and it includes 6.5 million terminals used by 14.4 million people, a little under a third of the adult population, almost equally represented by men and women, city and country dwellers, with the largest single age group of users being middle-aged adults. In 1994, turnover reached $1.2 billion (FFr 6.6 billion), compared with just $582 million for CompuServe, America's most popular commercial online service. While most of the services carried by the network have not been subsidized, the network itself has been. France Telecom has given away so many machines that the system is not expected to pay off its investment until 1996 at the earliest.

In its early days, Minitel's mainstays, despite the absence of sound and high-quality images, were games and sex (so-called *services bleus*), which introduced people to the system and taught them how to use it. Since 1991 that kind of use has fallen from 22 percent of the total (comprising banking, tourism, and local official information, and excluding directory inquiries) to 14 percent.

Today Minitel's most popular services are those that field inquiries; the system offers 24,600 services, provided by over 10,000 companies. Almost a fifth of the people with an account at Crédit Commercial de France, a medium-size French bank, use their Minitel for banking. And SNCF, the French railway, receives 24 million queries a year, most of them about timetables and routes. Such service providers earned royalties worth FFr 3.1 billion in 1994 on the call charges levied by France Telecom. In 1994 Minitel introduced a Minitel model capable of reading credit cards. They are also working on models that can send and receive data at faster rates.

Increasingly, computers are everywhere doing everything, changing the way we live and work. And the two areas of technology that affect us most are information and communications.

Everything You Always Wanted to Know: Information Technology

ALL THIS INNOVATION, and the possibilities it allows, can't help but affect the way we think about using information, everywhere from the business environment to the home.

Business first. In the old days (a few years ago), there was a big distinction between data that had to be online, and data that could be archived. The only data you kept online, in real time, was what was necessary for conducting the daily business, and you archived everything else. But, more and more, just about everything is available online. The USAA insurance company that serves former members of the United States military is one of the best examples of this. Fifteen years ago, the company committed to having essentially online data records, probably before the second curve of technology allowed it to happen. Their strategy is to automate all of their incoming activities as well as their older records, so that when you call USAA, the customer service rep can bring up all of your data records on the screen while you're on the phone, thanks to optical storage and sophisticated customer service computers. That's a pretty amazing feat, given the high volume of transactions and information involved in the insurance business.

Large corporations aren't the only ones making good use of the power of computers to make data available; individuals are doing it as well. I flew in an airplane once with an attorney who worked for a major law firm based in New Orleans. He'd decided he wanted to live in a place that was quiet and sane, so he moved to Boulder, Colorado, and established his practice there, but continued to maintain a very sophisticated global clientele in a specialized area of the law. He did this by making a commitment very early on (the mid-1980s) essentially to keep every piece of correspondence online. Everything—correspondence that he initiated, as well as correspondence that he received (thanks to scanners and storage technology)—would be stored online. The result? Impressive. When a client calls, this lawyer has available, at the touch of a button, all documentation relating to all previous contact with that client. And this extends not only to his clients, but to acquaintances. His system gives him an enormous range of opportunities that wouldn't be possible without the power of today's technology.

The power of information technology opens up new vistas for just about every business, large to small, to think about how they want to operate. The old limitation of "we can't do that, we're too small" just doesn't apply much anymore. The basic building blocks of a global business are PCs, not giant mainframes that cost millions of dollars. More and more, the technological power available to a typical small business provides all kinds of new opportunities: for new products, for new services, and, in the bigger picture, for new entrepreneurs to find whole new businesses.

Talk to Me, Baby: Communications Technology

SO NOW, thanks to the microprocessor, we've got these amazingly powerful computers. We've got PCs, and a decentralized environment. But meanwhile, back at the ranch, there's something going on with communications, something big. The inventions and innovations in communications technology have transformed those PCs from almost stale imitations of typewriters into exciting new business platforms. And more and more (as Paul Saffo has pointed out), what's important isn't the computer itself as a useful device, but what it's connected to.

The technologies underlying the development of communications horsepower are many and varied, and include developments like these:

- Communications laser, fiber optics, and large computer-switching systems, which together increase the speed and capacity of the telephone network;
- Data compression technologies, which make it possible to get more out of existing networks by using those infrastructures for otherwise high-bandwidth applications (such as graphic images, movie clips, and full-motion video), thereby not requiring the installation of major new infrastructures like fiber optics;
- So-called ATM (asynchronous transfer mode) technologies that can transform a simple twisted pair of telephone wires into a close approximation of a high-bandwidth fiber optic or coaxial cable network.

We're not there yet, but such advances in data compression and more efficient mechanisms for using computer communication networks point to the potential for enormous expansion in higher bandwidths of what formerly had been lower-bandwidth capacity without necessarily digging holes all over the planet—although for those parts of the world that have an opportunity to invest in infrastructure afresh, enormous bandwidth capacity is a good starting point. For example, the Chinese, with the help of Hongkong Telecom and some other vendors, are about to lay a major fiber optic access through the highly developed coastal cites of East China. This will dramatically increase that country's communications capacity. Similarly, the growth of cellular communications in developing countries is a sort of leapfrogging over the wired world to give low-bandwidth ubiquitous access to computers and to communications by using wireless technology that cuts out the need for enormous investments in fixed infrastructure, such as laying fiber optic cable. The question will obviously be this: As the demand for broadband service increases, can wireless technology sufficiently service the needs of a rapidly growing economy?

This is a fundamental dilemma for anyone trying to provide telecommunications, including China's leaders. On one hand is a very rapidly growing demand for basic telephony services; on the other, the potential future growth of broadband services. Given that wireless and broadband don't go together, it's going to be interesting to see how this dilemma is resolved.

What'll They Think of Next?
The Combo Platter

THE BOTTOM LINE is that the increased power of computers is making information extremely available. And thanks to today's communications technology, just about anybody can hook up with just about anybody else. When you combine the power of today's information technology with the capabilities of today's communications technology, it seems the sky's the limit. Take a look.

The Internet

The Internet is possibly the best manifestation of the intersection of computer and communications technology taken to their extremes. While the Net itself may not be the platform for all of the twenty-first century, it does give us the early inklings of what networks of the future may look like. It will clearly be a major force because of the momentum behind it, both in the popular culture and, increasingly, in the commercial culture. The Net is beginning to touch many more households worldwide as we move from a phenomenon that was once exclusively the domain of closet techies, to more of a mainstream cultural medium. It's certainly that in the United States. More and more, it will become so around the world as well, as Internet access becomes more affordable through the policy initiatives of countries like Japan, where access is currently fairly expensive—but probably not for long.

The Internet is also a precursor for new private networks. The private networks of the future are likely to combine the basic characteristics of the current Internet: a mix of media—voice, data, graphics, images, and movie clips—as well as the software applications themselves will be available over a globally facilitated network, making an amazing variety of information available. Indeed, the hottest emerging Internet application is what some call the "Intranet," where the Internet tools are used as an internal operating system, which allows interoperability across platforms and between the company's systems and the Internet itself. Two dimensions of the Internet that are worth improving are the security of transactions (although much work is being done on that issue) and, more important, editorial overlays, which will allow people to not only navigate, but to be confident that searches for information are thorough and reliable in terms of content. Despite all the surf hype, wandering through the Internet these days is a bit like roaming through an amazing electronic bazaar where you're certainly entertained, but you're just not sure what it is you're buying.

The Internet represents an important experiment of twenty-first-century life. Computer horsepower, communications horsepower, compelling applications, and usability are being combined in an electronic infrastructure that is being made available to the planet at large. And it's from the connection of these sophisticated tools with the population that new applications and ideas will emerge. The Internet is spawning an enormous variety of experiments, and while many of these will fail, the Internet is nevertheless unparalleled as a source of second-curve businesses, ideas, and insights.

Customer Service

When you bring information and communications technology together, the potential for improvements in customer service is huge. Look at AT&T's 1-800-COMPARE, a service aimed at small-business customers that want to compare the cost of their current phone carrier to a competitor—AT&T versus service provided by MCI or Sprint. The service runs on a Silicon Graphics workstation and uses a data mining application to search through the caller's phone records and construct a side-by-side comparative table using actual data of the caller's historical use of long distance. It then provides a spreadsheet on the spot that tells the caller whether or not changing long distance services would save money—and it's all done on line—in the old-fashioned sense, while the caller is on the phone. A rather remarkable use of information and technology: you wouldn't think of AT&T's basic phone records as being very valuable in terms of real-time direct marketing, but with today's data mining technology they are. A basic company resource becomes a marketing tool—it's like finding big nuggets in the tailings of a gold mine.

Remote Service

Remote services, like customer service technologies, are born of the combined power of communications and technology. Think of the AT&T ad where the surgeon gives a diagnosis remotely. Although telemedicine has been on the horizon for a long time and actually has yet to be used much (some would say we don't need robo-surgeons; we've already got too many real ones), there are situations that call for remote service technology. Where there was great physical discomfort, for example, or a lack of specialized skills, or difficulty in simply reaching someone who needed care, the situation might require a set of technologies that support remote service. The largest telemedicine project in the United States involves the Texas prisons, where over 2,500 prisoners were treated through telemedicine in 1995. Using an integrated computer supplied by AT&T Global Information Solutions, Radiance videoconferencing systems provided by Compression Labs Inc., and specially designed medical peripherals and cameras, the University of Texas Medical Branch (UTMB) at Galveston operates the only tertiary-care prison hospital in the state.

The need is not limited to the field of medicine, of course. As an example, think of an aircraft technician, in the wheel arch of a major jet, who discovers a problem and wants to look at the manual for a particular item; through CD-ROM technology or remote access to a broadcast database, specific information that would help in the repair could be—and is—available on a video display headset (a one- or two-inch TV monitor attached to the technician's helmet).

Direct Marketing

The combination of computer and communications technology has been one of the key factors behind the emergence of direct marketing in the United States and globally. Desktop publishing and the creation of customer-specific information by the direct marketing, magazine, and newspaper industries have allowed publishers and advertisers to target individual users with highly segmented information. The magazine ad or mail piece is customized for me, at either the household level, by way of the zip code, or, even more specifically, for me personally, as the result of some declared preferences which have been collected and stored and are available to the person sending me the publication or the direct mail piece. The increasing power of technology allows for these direct marketing tools not only to generate mindless lists, but to keep these lists accurate, and—potentially, in the future—to have these lists for kinds of bargaining between consumers and list users that we haven't even thought of. For example, it's not out of the question that you could enter a dialogue with these vendors to negotiate access to particular services over the Internet, interactive television programs, or print offerings which would be made available at varying discounted rates (including free) in return for information about your buying preferences.

Advances in technology will also be brought to bear on the existing mound of transactional information that's kept increasingly by banks and other credit card companies who not only know considerably more about you than your mother does, but who, like your mother, have some very particular ideas about how you should spend your money.

Personal Jeans

One of the most extreme examples of the use of new technology is Levi Strauss's Personal Pair jeans, jeans made specifically for you, based on your measurements and your having tried on generic sizes. The process works like this: at a Levi's store, your measurements are taken and, with your name, are punched into a computer, which then tells you which of some four hundred pairs of prototype jeans, based on Levi's 512s, are closest to your measurements. You try on a pair to figure out the exact measurements—the supposed perfect fit—then choose black, bleached, natural, stonewashed, or white. The system produces a stock code number for your personal jean pattern and sends your specifications to the Levi Strauss factory, where, with the help of computerized fabric-cutting equipment, the pieces are cut, tagged with bar codes (which are scanned into your customer file so that you can use that code in the future to order more jeans), washed, and sewn. Levi's promises that the jeans will be delivered (to you or to the store) in three weeks, and they claim that they consistently beat that deadline. The jeans cost about 12 percent over normal rack price.

The technology for all this, developed by Custom Clothing Technology Corp. of Newton, Massachusetts, uses Lotus Notes. In the U.S., Levi's offers Personal Jeans at their Original Levi's Stores, and at sixteen locations in Canada. The jeans are being tested in London and Belgium, and Levi's is considering Japan as a future market. They'd better fit, though—the new consumer won't pay a premium for a gimmick that doesn't work.

Small Goes Global

It's becoming easier for small organizations to act like big ones these days. Scale and sophistication are no longer the prerogatives of the Fortune 500; today you see small organizations doing what big ones do, including operating on a global basis, wooing consumers, building virtual linkages to other partners, and participating in the value chain. The Institute for the Future is a pretty good example. It's an organization of about thirty full-time employees, and recently it has been actively involved in research and consulting with businesses in China, Hong Kong, Japan, Singapore, Sweden, France, Britain, Germany, Peru, Canada, Mexico, and Italy, as well as all over the United States. The Institute is able to do this by using many of the tools of technology (fax, e-mail, Lotus Notes, and the Internet, for example); it could not have supported such a global consultancy twenty years ago.

Visual Computing

Silicon Graphics (profiled later in this chapter) is a leader in visual computing. What a lot of people know them for is providing slick special effects for Hollywood, but there's more here than meets the eye. More important is the core technology underlying those special effects, a sophisticated workstation geared to the rapid manipulation of complex images and the creation of spaces and virtual spaces where you can view information in interesting ways. It's likely that in the future, visual computing will be the cornerstone of business: more complex information will have to be managed, and leaders who need an overview of this information will have to get that overview from complex visual images. Accessing information will increasingly be like circling a sort of graphical mountain of information rather than gathering it from a simple two-dimensional model. The whole notion of displaying complex information in four dimensions—the three physical dimensions plus time to show sort of an animated dynamic—will provide a very rich set of tools for the twenty-first-century manager.

Second Curves: Coming Soon to a Theater Near You

THE POWER OF TECHNOLOGY is already creating second curves, and that trend isn't about to slow down; we'll see more and more second curves over the next decade. We haven't yet reached the edge of physics, and if anything Moore's Law understates future capacities, in terms of speed, power, and the ability to make new technologies available at lower cost to more people.

So the second-curve question here isn't *if*; it's *when*, and after that, *how fast*. The unknowns are the speed at which these curves will be created, and—most important from a practical perspective— how you can tell whether a new technology is true innovation or a phantom.

Spotting Impostors and Finding the Real McCoy

THERE IS A TENDENCY to overestimate the impact of phenomena in the short run and to underestimate the impact in the long run, per Roy Amara, my predecessor as president of the Institute for the Future. Nowhere could this be more true than with technology. For many of us, especially Americans, the desire to see the innovation of the week as a major life-transforming event is practically an inbred trait. It's what you might call premature extrapolation, and the best examples of it are in the writing and thinking of futurists over the last one hundred years, where the potential of technology is taken almost to absurdity—what you could call "personal helicopters by the year 2000." Much of the hype around the second curve is just that: hype. A lot of people have an interest in creating an unrealistic expectation on that second curve, and it presents very difficult problems for managers trying to think about the second curve of technology. How do you really know whether this is the beginning of something very important, versus a complete waste of time?

There are lots of cases of mistaken identity in the world of the second curve, for lots of different reasons. We'll try to categorize them here, to impose some order on this second-curve chaos.

The "Break-Through" Versus the "Me-Too"

OFTEN WHAT LOOK LIKE technology second curves at first
glance aren't fundamental breakthroughs at all; they're just incremental improvements on existing technologies. You see this a lot in
the pharmaceutical industry, where the distinction is often made
between "break-through" drugs and "me-too" drugs. The irony, of
course, is that no one sets out to design a me-too drug. The full in-
tention, given the ten-year time horizon required to develop a new
pharmaceutical product, is always to be first. But because of the
research difficulties and the exigencies of trying to make this happen, somebody ends up being second. Not that the nipping-at-your-
heels, coming-in-second guys don't have an effect and haven't made
money. Their incremental improvements contribute to the path of
innovation, and until recently me-too's were profitable. They just
aren't as dramatic as the breakthroughs.

Unhappily there is no guarantee—or even much of a suggestion—
that the real breakthroughs (technical or commercial) will be sig-
naled as such very far in advance. If you think about the great false
starts over the last few years, you see real question marks around
some of the early innovators like the Osborne Computers, Ataris,
and Hayes Modems who were hailed as ahead of their time, only to
be out of business a few years later. It isn't just the Smith Coronas
(the typewriter makers) of the world that disappear. Often it's early
second-curve pioneers who (a) can't keep up with the pace of innovation, for whatever reason; or (b) simply become too comfortable
too soon—they're just a little early, and end up, ironically enough, as
first-curve players in a second-curve world.

The Technical Sweetness Factor

ANOTHER REASON that something that looks like it's going to
become a second curve in technology doesn't is that technology
innovation often comes from people who aren't commercially oriented.
A lot of technological innovation is driven by what Robert Oppen-
heimer, in reference to the Manhattan Project, called "the technical
sweetness of it": the push for the innovation is not motivated by wealth
but by innovation purely for the sake of innovation. The technical
sweetness factor has played a huge role in Silicon Valley, where the pio-

neers and visionaries were zealots about technology before they became zealots about money—though it's also true that in recent years the length of time it takes for a techno-zealot to become a money-zealot has grown shorter. Enter Netscape, profiled later in this chapter.

The Never-Ending Search for
the Better Mousetrap

THE BELIEF that there ought to be a better mousetrap, even when the current mousetrap is working perfectly well, is the push behind a lot of second-curve impostors. When innovation is honored and admired and sought out, almost to the point where the innovation is valued ahead of the market, it becomes difficult to tell what's what.

A good example of this is Newsweek Interactive, which was so hot among advertisers that they were allocating space on the interactive CD-ROM product if the advertisers were prepared to take real space in *Newsweek*. Now think about this: While the demographics for CD-ROM-based versions of Newsweek Interactive are good, the service actually has lousy audience pickup. For the moment it's a boutique service and product, with very few people actually using it, and yet the attraction of the innovation—a cool way to receive *Newsweek*—had advertisers basically begging to be put on a medium that wasn't delivering any volume. It's ironic, all right, but it's also pretty illustrative of what the second curve comes to mean to people: when it comes to technology, there's tremendous pressure to become a second-curve player, whether you make any money at it or not. Jump first, figure out if it's lucrative later.

Turtle Stuck in a Half Shell: Permanently
Emerging Technology

WHEN YOU UNMASK second-curve impostors you also find a lot of permanently emerging technologies that just never get going. They never really take off, but they never go away either, even after several market failures. Their developers and marketers see huge markets

that never become real. Why? Very simple: there's no compelling
need for them. Despite the fact that the odd granny might want a
stilled slow-scan video image of her new grandson, most would prefer
a plane ticket to come visit. Or a nice clear picture in the mail. Video-
phones are a permanently emerging technology. Despite the fact that
the technology receives a lot of attention, it struggles continuously to
be a mainstream technology. It will most likely still be an emerging
big deal "ten years from now"—whenever "now" happens to be.

Second-Curve Snipe Hunting: The Search for the Killer Application

ALL THIS PHANTOM ACTIVITY does more than just confuse the
issue; it sparks a hunt, a search for the great white snipe, the killer
application. Somehow people begin to believe that somewhere out
there is the application, the application to end all applications, the
one that lots of people will pay lots of money to have. It only needs
to be discovered. The problem with this theory (we'll be generous
and call it that) is that it presupposes this latent demand for a particular form of technology. This just doesn't ring true; killer applications
are, in actuality, discovered by users and vendors together. They
don't just exist and need only to be found. Just the opposite is true:
they don't exist, and have to be created, and that's best done by
users messing around with neat stuff. Fortunately, second-curve
technology enterprises are catching on, and it's why a company like
Netscape succeeds. They essentially give away their product, rather
than trying to sell it in a new market. They build up users by pricing
it low (read "free"), then they learn with those users about how their
product can be used. *Et voilà*: a true second-curve technology.

Doesn't it seem rather arrogant to presume that there's a killer application out there like the "field of dreams" effect: *If you build it,
they will come*? And isn't sticking a given application (or product, or
service) under a consumer's nose until he or she finally declares,
"You've found the killer application!" a rather arrogant form of marketing? (The interactive video trials in various parts of the country
are examples of this.) What really needs to be done is to figure out
new ways to experiment with technologies and find compelling applications that effectively utilize those technologies.

Killer applications almost always emerge from—what else?—sex, drugs, and rock 'n' roll. Beepers, pagers, cellular phones, and 1-900 numbers were the domain of hookers and dealers long before they reached doctors and real estate agents. And if you look at who were the cutting-edge vendors and users of technologies for sending video images or still images on the Internet, chances are that some of the rapidly growing applications and the initial stages of those particular technologies were oriented toward illicit activities of a certain (baser) kind. In fact, in late December 1995, in response to a directive from the prosecutor's office in Germany, CompuServe temporarily restricted access to more than two hundred sex-related computer databases pending legislation in that country against indecent content.

Software piracy may be the killer application of the twenty-first century. Case in point: When I was in Hong Kong recently, the scuttlebutt in the local news was about the daily closings of illicit software stores there. These stores were raided periodically and would open again a day later. And the interesting thing about it was that this visit took place a month before the official release date of Windows 95—and the popular driver behind these illicit stores was to sell a CD-ROM drive which had Windows 95 and few other applications, all for $35 U.S. Pirates had gotten hold of early prerelease copies of Windows 95 and were gleefully manufacturing hundreds and thousands of copies of them for sale to an equally gleeful set of software consumers in Hong Kong—and everyone kind of thought it was okay.

The story illustrates a couple of interesting points: First, the degree to which there are cultural differences across the planet in terms of respect for intellectual property, notwithstanding legal and court systems to support those claims. And second, the fact that—predictably and sadly—the power of technology can be used for evil as well as for good. It's just as available to pirates and other bad actors as it is to the good guys.

Estimating the Speed of a Shooting Star

OKAY, you've ridden all the impostors out to the edge of town. Now what? Once you're sure (or as close as you can be, given the fact that we're talking about the future) that you've spotted a real McCoy second curve, you next need to try to understand how fast it's moving, to estimate the pace of change. How fast can things change? How fast will they change?

Everyone who thinks they've spotted a true second curve would, of course, like to believe that they're getting in on the ground floor of a technology about to take off on that classic and longed-for hockey stick curve, where growth rates and profits go through the roof. But often hockey sticks are lazier—meaning slower—in taking off than you think; indeed, Paul Saffo has codified his views of the diffusion of technology in a classic "Zen of Change" piece called "Paul Saffo and the Thirty-Year Rule" in *Design World*, Nov. 24, 1992, where he describes a thirty-year time constant which has held true for many types of technology over many centuries in terms of the diffusion of a technology into a meaningful business or cultural phenomenon. It takes thirty years to go from invention to full market acceptance. This slow adaptation seems to have held true from the invention of the printing press in the fifteenth century to the introduction of the telephone and automobile at the end of the nineteenth century, to radio, television, and fax machines in the twentieth.

The first issue to look at is that of scale. At what level do you define the technology—and, by extension, the trend? The notion of a thirty-year transition may be valid at a very high level of aggregation, in thinking about information technology and very broad societal and economic changes. But when you take it down to the level of an individual technology, thirty years is probably too long. There are plenty of examples of individual technologies that have swept through a market relatively quickly and still had dramatic effects: personal computers between 1981 and 1986; fax machines in the mid- to late 1980s; cellular phones in the early 1990s.

There is also an important distinction to make between deeper underlying technologies—such as electron beam photolithography for making microchips—that have huge long-term effects, and consumer or business implementations of those technologies. Look at the fundamental tension between, on one hand, this thirty-year argument and Moore's Law, the idea that the capacity of a semiconductor chip will double every year and a half. This law has held true since 1960, and is likely to continue to do so until at least the year 2000—an interesting two-curve situation in and of itself.

Ev Rogers, the father of diffusion theory, makes the case that the old thirty-year paradigm has become less applicable, arguing that

from the end of World War II to about 1985, there was not a sufficiently large installed base of technology in people's home and work
lives—the technology simply wasn't there for people to use. But
these days we're becoming acculturated to technology, first at work,
then at home, as a result of the dramatic rise in the penetration of
information technology during the last decade. And the fact that the
world we live in is increasingly technology-driven has resulted in a
dramatic shift in the awareness and use of technology. We know how
to use technology, and we expect to use it; it's always there, from the
microchip that tells us we left the lights on in the car, to the ATM
(automated teller machine) card we use to get cash to satisfy a
2 A.M. attack of the munchies. Rogers concludes that the curves are
going to be much shorter in the future.

All of which underscores the need to define the technology variable being diffused. Rogers did work on the diffusion of the personal
computer and eventually concluded that was the wrong variable.
What he actually should have been measuring was the diffusion of
the microprocessor, because the personal computer was in fact a
packaging of the microprocessor for a particular application.

Definitions and measurement become incredibly important and
incredibly difficult on the second curve. What is the unit of analysis
for the second curve? This difficulty applies to technology especially,
but it's true of all second-curve phenomena. In fact, the second
curve can be so fuzzy that it becomes a series of multiple curves, a
blend of false starts, weird early signals, and true pioneers. But there
are times and conditions when we as a society are prepared to jump
to the next curve: when the case is so compelling, when the pains
and problems of the old order become too much, when the infrastructure to support change reaches a critical mass.

Breakthroughs That Aren't

THE ALREADY DIFFICULT TASKS presented by a second curve
that comes from technology—spotting impostors and measuring the
speed of the real McCoys—are made even more difficult when you
put money into the equation. The first curve is dull but profitable;
the second curve is sexy but illusory. Bankers and businessmen gravitate toward the first curve, while techies gravitate toward the second.

The conflict between the two curves is basically old-world technology versus emerging technology, installed base versus innovation. The future margins are clearly going to come from the second curve, but the problem is they're not there at the start; they're not real margins. There's not much real revenue coming out of Netscape, for example; there simply isn't real profit in General Magic. An interesting armchair dilemma, but it gets pretty real, with pretty real consequences, if you're running a large business, and trying to stay in business while you're at it. How can you possibly justify investing on the second curve? Because the money comes from the installed base, the innovator has to persuade consumers (and investors) of superior value in order to be able to drive a wedge and create some kind of growth. For example:

IBM Versus Apple

Put yourself in IBM's position in the late 1970s and early 1980s when Steve Jobs and Steve Wozniak were building Apple Computer. While Apple was struggling to produce a product that would be salable beyond the hobbyist market, IBM was making a ton of money from its existing mainframe business. It would have been incredibly difficult for senior IBM executives not only to countenance the demise of that source of revenue, but also to imagine that the Apple II technology could ever mature to a point where they would be a serious threat in the global business environment, and, more to the point, to the power of Big Blue—its reliability and performance in mainframe computers. You can certainly sympathize with IBM top management, given the dilemma. It's the tyranny of the installed base.

Ironically, twenty years later the tables have turned. With the announcement of Windows 95, the IBM PC platform—with the Microsoft/Intel axis and installed base—has basically caught up with where the Mac operating system was ten years ago. So in some senses Microsoft and Intel, which were clearly among the second-curve players in the early 1980s, have themselves become first-curve players. The question now is, will they maintain that first curve or will they be threatened by a second curve? They're one of the big first curves as we enter the twenty-first century. And the future of Apple is one of the big second-curve questions: Will Steve Jobs and friends come back to rescue Apple, or will Apple go the way of Atari or Hayes Modems—pioneers who couldn't hang in there?

The RBOCs

Virtually all of the Regional Bell Operating Companies (RBOCs) at one time or another have had to examine the relative future growth of plain old telephone service (POTS)—their first curve— versus new media, whether that means fax, data, video conferencing, online services, or something else—the second curve. The Institute for the Future, in working with these companies, consistently generated scenarios and forecasts that showed that the speed with which new media would grow would be a lot slower than the eager Regional Bell Operating Companies had hoped, and that generally speaking, telephony (basic voice telephony) would still account for a vast majority of the revenues for longer than they might think. That forecast has proved accurate, despite the explosion in the use of cellular phones and fax. In 1994, the total revenue for the seven Baby Bells (Ameritech, Bell Atlantic, Bell-South, NYNEX, Pacific Telesis, SBC Communications, and U S West) was $88,218 million, 85 percent of which came from basic local service, including related features such as call waiting. The remaining 15 percent came from new services, comprising cellular, paging, computer, and other services.

A Look at a Few of the Players

THE INSTALLED BASE VERSUS INNOVATION CONFLICT is probably best illustrated by the dilemmas faced by some of the key players in technology-based business.

Pitney Bowes

THERE IS AN INHERENT CONFLICT between the first curve (installed base) and the second curve of new technology. Once you see the conflict, the challenge is establishing communication between the two groups to really help sort out what's real, what's illusory, and what's feasible in the longer run. Leadership is obviously important here; someone has to be able to balance the cool heads, who make measured responses based on experience, with the crazy people of the second curve, who just want to play with new stuff.

A few years ago, Pitney Bowes chairman George Harvey characterized the dilemma his company was facing. On one hand, he knew there was potential for a second curve to emerge in terms of technology substitution for the mail. He could see evidence in their business and they had made provisions for it in terms of the business-to-business segment of communications—investments in copiers, fax machines, dictaphone and voice messaging systems. He recognized that traditional business-to-business mail for large users in the United States, which Pitney Bowes had supported through both mail meters and production mail capacities, would not continue to be the most rapidly growing business segment. The new growth would come in services in the small business sector and the global market and from new definitions of mail. Similarly, on the business-to-home side, there were concerns within the organization about potential substitution of business-to-home mail. Information generated by both financial services (statements, bills, credit cards, etc.) and direct marketing could potentially shift over to electronic media once an infrastructure had been established in the household. But, as Harvey correctly ascertained, premature abandonment of first-curve businesses made no sense either strategically or financially in the short run. The uncertainty of the second curve was inherent, but it was also real, and Harvey brought a great deal of experience to his decision. He'd been in this movie before; he'd seen others' premature attempts at bringing about the paperless office—but the paperless office never came to pass. One of the best things that ever happened to paper was the computer, enabling an explosion in many dimensions: desktop publishing, directories, and the use of paper as interface.

Most organizations that succeed in playing two curves have a combination of cool heads and enthusiastic experimenters. In Pitney Bowes's case, much of the thinking about the second curve came from the futures group, which was chaired by cool-headed George Harvey, but which included some of the young up-and-coming middle-to-senior managers, who viewed the company as their company for the twenty-first century and wanted to point out and help grow second-curve businesses inside Pitney Bowes.

Silicon Graphics Inc.

SGI SMELLS of the second curve. Founded by people at Stanford and Hewlett-Packard, it has focused on high-end graphic workstations, and the company's method of operation is to try to build faster and better computers. SGI is an example of a rapidly growing company in terms of products, head count, and the way they're perceived in Silicon Valley—as a leading company in embodying the second curve. In particular, SGI likes to start late and still be ahead of the market, a concept that's both a method of operation and, to some extent, a metaphor for their business process. The only way to do that well, of course—without being able to predict the future—is to get your business processes down so fast that you can catch up and get ahead of people. One way SGI does this is by keeping head count low through subcontracting processes that the company has determined are not strategic. The smaller head count lets SGI move quickly and change direction easily, when necessary.

SGI was founded in 1982 by Jim Clark, who left his position as a professor at Stanford in 1981 to develop and market 3-D computer graphics technology. That year SGI introduced the first 3-D terminal, and two years later the company followed with the first 3-D workstation, priced at $75,000. In 1986, SGI—already the leading producer of high-end 3-D workstations for the technical and scientific market—went public, and was faced with some major decisions regarding its future. The company could remain a high-end player, or take the technology into the low end; they decided to try both. With the $50,000-to-$100,000 systems, SGI stays close to high-end players and keeps track of how their changing needs will affect the computers SGI produces. The company's most creative R&D people see what leading-edge customers (Industrial Light & Magic, NASA, Boeing, Disney, Merck, and the military, for example) might want in the future, and they come away with new product ideas. And R&D isn't the only part of the company that has contact with customers; engineers are evaluated in part by the amount of time they spend with customers.

Jim Clark left SGI in 1994 to start Netscape, and that same year SGI and AT&T agreed to codevelop an interactive communication system. The following year saw the dream team: SGI and Dreamworks SKG cocreated a $50 million digital animation studio able to support five hundred animators. SGI also worked with Rocket Science Games to develop authoring tools (tools that allow you to write software much more quickly) for the next generation of computer games. SGI is famous for the special effects in *Forrest Gump* (which included scenes depicting Tom Hanks meeting, among others, John F. Kennedy and John Lennon) and *Jurassic Park* (where those hide-behind-your-seats dinosaurs were in fact generated by computers). The same machines are being used in automobile design and airplane wing design, where they cut down on the time from development process—design to prototype to finished plane—significantly. In these applications, SGI computers handle huge amounts of data and detailed 3-D images that can be moved and viewed from any angle, then changed; for example, designers can look at airflow without setting foot in the wind tunnel. And SGI machines have a substantial presence in the medical world. Researchers use SGI machines to study cell surfaces and immune response; doctors use them to pinpoint the locations of tumors in victims of once-inoperable brain cancer; and future surgeons use them to practice surgery. Today SGI is trying to move from an exclusively workstation environment into other server applications like Internet Server and "data mining"—where you can go back and do neat things with essentially old systems, such as AT&T's 1-800-COMPARE service, mentioned earlier.

CEO Ed McCracken believes that the only source of competitive advantage in the high tech market is staying on the cutting edge of innovation. I followed him as a speaker a few years ago and he basically said that he wasn't smart enough to predict the future, he didn't believe in strategic planning, and that what he was trying to do in his company was to get his decision-making processes and his business processes so fast that he could afford to start late and still be ahead of the market. Thanks, Ed, a great introduction to a futurist.

McCracken is an unusual CEO. For starters, he comes from a Midwestern farming family, is an electrical engineer by training, teaches meditation classes for stressed execs, and doesn't allow managers to plan products more than two years in advance, his reasoning being that in the world of high tech, nobody is smart enough to plan long term. Instead he believes in compressing product development cycles, making them as short as possible—twelve to eighteen months—citing as an example the Indy workstation, a high-end, powerful graphics workstation, which, according to McCracken, wouldn't have included a new digital camera if the design on the machine had started just three months earlier. McCracken has led SGI during a period in which the company has made some interesting partnerships. Time Warner's Interactive TV, which provides movies on demand, educational resources, interactive video games, and home shopping, uses SGI video servers and set-top boxes that are built around SGI chips. Nintendo and SGI are jointly designing a video machine. And the company has worked with Disney to develop the Aladdin ride at Epcot.

SGI gives customer needs high priority. The company responds quickly to company requests and consistently and aggressively tries to solve even complicated problems. McCracken is a strong believer in R&D—a hallmark of second-curve commitment—and the company (along with Intel) spends more money than most companies on R&D. In 1994, SGI spent 12 percent of its revenue—$177.2 million—on R&D. SGI's top management is asked to make sure that the corporate organizational structure encourages the brightest technologists to stay close to customers, who are segmented by their needs and the technology that will meet those needs. Management assigns a project team to each customer segment; together they design the answer to the customer's needs.

SGI's fame spreads beyond the high tech world of Silicon Valley. When President Clinton and Vice President Gore announced their technology policy, SGI was the only corporate visit. McCracken, a lifelong Republican, became a Clinton supporter because of Clinton's technology policies. In January of 1994, President Clinton founded the National Information Infrastructure Advisory Council (NIIAC) to aid in the development of the National Information Infrastructure—which influences communications policy and makes recommendations to Congress in the areas of service, privacy, and security privacy—guided by Department of Commerce Secretary Ron Brown and the Interagency Infrastructure Task Force. The NIIAC, composed of thirty-seven members from the telecommunications, cable, and broadcasting industries, is cochaired by McCracken and National Public Radio President and CEO Delano Lewis.

In September of 1995, it was announced that President Clinton would present McCracken with the National Medal of Technology, given annually by the President and the highest honor in the United States for technical achievement—a kind of Oscar for the second curve—for McCracken's work in affordable 3-D visual computing and supercomputing technologies, and for his technical leadership skills in making SGI into an advanced global technological company.

Netscape

THE STORY OF NETSCAPE is the story of a young visionary in the bowels of the University of Illinois computer science department who invented an Internet World Wide Web–surfing search tool and within the space of four years went from being an obscure hero of the Internet community to one of the founders of an initial public offering that came out at a $2.6 billion market capitalization. All that despite the fact that his product was originally simply given away, and that its net income until months after its IPO offering was negative. The technical visionaries, pure as they are, can somehow be converted to capitalism in fairly short order.

Netscape, founded in early 1994, is the producer of Navigator, the most widely used software browser for the World Wide Web. Navigator's incredible and almost instant popularity is due to its novelty—it was the first tool available to help novice users point and click their way through the Net. (Its popularity was also, at the start, due to pricing: for a while they were *giving* it away.) Netscape's numbers are impressive and unique. By the end of 1995, Netscape had a market capitalization approaching $4 billion, with sales for the first half of 1995 at $16.6 million—but no profits. The company's debut in the stock market was stunning, with the stock originally offered at $28, opening at $71, and reaching an astonishing high of $130 by late November of 1995.

It started at the University of Illinois in 1992, where Marc Andreessen, then a twenty-one-year-old student, was one of a small group of programmers who created Mosaic, a prototype of Navigator. Mosaic was practically an overnight success: it was the first browser program that made surfing the World Wide Web easy, *and it was free to download*—the University of Illinois was giving it away. Eighteen months later, the number of Internet users was at 20 million, almost triple what it had been, and the number of World Wide Web sites had grown more than a hundredfold. Andreessen graduated and got a job with a small Silicon Valley company called Enterprise Integration Technologies, which developed security products for the Internet. A month into his job, Andreessen received e-mail from SGI founder Jim Clark, who had gotten interested in the Internet—specifically in developing tools and interfaces that would make the Internet a friendlier and easier place to surf. In April 1994, using $4 million of Clark's own money, Clark and Andreessen founded Mosaic Communications, which they renamed Netscape Communica-

tions Corporation in November 1994, to sidestep legal troubles with
the University of Illinois. Clark hired most of Andreessen's University of Illinois buddies to develop a new version of Mosaic, which included built-in security, was faster, and could handle sophisticated
graphics. In December 1994, Netscape released Navigator, with what
just about all of us would call success: seven months later, Navigator
accounted for two-thirds of the nine million browsers used on the
World Wide Web. In January 1995, Jim Barksdale joined Netscape
as their CEO. Could be a natural: Barksdale was previously the CEO
of McCaw Cellular, and before that he was COO at Federal Express,
when it went from $1 billion to $7.7 billion in revenues. Barksdale
had managed the second curve before.

Netscape is a company that spotted the Internet as a great opportunity for business early on. Of course, Netscape isn't the only one;
other companies are seeing the same light, but Netscape knows its
competition: roughly half of Netscape's three-hundred-plus employees work in research and development. Netscape has to fulfill its
promise of the second curve. Can it generate the earnings to match
the price? The key will be in turning high market share of a free good
into money. An early example of how the Netscape hegemony could
be turned into profit is its selling the rights to be the first Netscape
search engine screen to replace Yahoo—the search engine of choice
for most Net freaks.

Lessons Learned

THE ISSUES HERE are varied and complex, and there is much to
understand, but the experience of others has yielded some valuable
lessons. Here is a sort of cheat sheet of the basics.

POWERFUL TECHNOLOGIES WILL SPAWN
NEW CURVES

In particular, the Internet is a global primordial soup of change. New
second-curve ideas will emerge from the Internet at a very rapid
pace. Computer and communication capacities, cost effectiveness,
and usability will increase over the next decade, and regardless of

what happens with the economy, the tools of information technology will be greatly expanded and will open up new opportunities.
This means that corporations have to adjust to a world where new
products and services will be a reality even though we cannot conceive of exactly what those products and services will be; we have to
prepare for a world where they will exist. In other words, using current products and services as a benchmark is inadequate. We need
to stop benchmarking against each other and start benchmarking
against this uncertain but powerful future. Otherwise, we're all going
to be left behind.

TECHNOLOGY FORECASTING IS
INCREDIBLY DIFFICULT

This is not a lesson as much as it is a reminder, something to reassure you, in a perverse way. The profound irony here is that we know
there will be more powerful technologies; we know that they will
make an enormous difference and present enormous opportunities;
but it is almost impossible to forecast precisely their form, their
shape, and their function. Even though at the Institute of the Future
we make a living looking out ten years, we find it hard to push the
envelope that far on the technology front. A major effort is under
way at the Institute to push the horizon of the information technology world by projecting the technical capacities we see coming
from the labs of our vendor clients onto the shifts in business anticipated by our leading user clients. By putting cutting-edge users and
vendors in the same room, new trends and application ideas can
emerge as described below. But it is incredibly difficult given the
likely shifts and turns that may occur because of fundamental shifts
in technology and huge uncertainty about how new technologies will
play in the hands of users. Many systems, subsystems, tools, and
technologies are being created simultaneously. The possible combinations of these new capabilities are mind-boggling. The direction is
clear, and it's clear that the pace will be rapid, but the consequences
are still somewhat murky.

Evolving Technology

As information technologies continue to evolve, and today's innovations become tomorrow's everyday tools, business processes will in-

evitably change. A successful organization will be the one that can harness these new tools to be proactive about change—to create new options and possibilities. In the next decade, we can expect the following broad trends to continue:

The tools will become smaller and more powerful. Microchips will be faster, more powerful, and less expensive; multiple processing capabilities will be common; memory storage devices will be more reliable and less expensive; and batteries will be more powerful and lighter, and will last longer. As a result, devices like portable computers and personal communicators will become smaller, more powerful, and easier to use. At the institutional level, corporate information systems will continue to migrate from mainframe computers to desktop platforms. Massive parallel processing (essentially powerful microprocessors operating in tandem) will allow an even greater amount of information to be processed more quickly and efficiently.

The cost of processing will decrease. The cost of processing is already much lower on desktop machines than on mainframes; and distributed systems (so-called client-server computing) provide significant advantages in flexibility. This trend will continue as microchip manufacturers make breakthroughs like Intel's Pentium and the Apple-IBM-Motorola consortium's PowerPC.

Nontechnical people will interact with computers more easily. Desktop video, powerful graphical displays, voice recognition and synthesis, and pen-based input will make computers more natural to use and more ubiquitous.

Information technology will invade the home. The home environment will change as much in the next ten years as the office has in the past ten. Television will become digital and interactive, with a panoply of information services for consumers (customized programming, video on demand, home banking, information services, interactive games). Telephones, cable television, and computers will converge to create a multipurpose, multimedia information and entertainment capability. One consequence of this development will be an acceleration of telework, as the home office becomes a completely functional extension of the corporate office. Overwork at home has become one of the killer applications of the late 1990s.

Connectivity will define the power of technology. The real story has been the growth in connectivity among computers. In the early 1980s most personal computers were just that: *personal* computers. In 1985, just 1 percent of the personal computers then in use in the labor force were connected to a local area network. But by the year

2000 almost one-third of the desktop workstations will be connected to a local network, and a growing number will also have access to external networks, databases, and e-mail. There is even talk of TANs (tiny area networks) to connect multiple computers within the home. In addition, virtually all laptop personal computers now have built-in communications capabilities. And there is a whole category of simpler devices and software products whose sole purpose is to provide access: cellular phones, pagers, fax machines, personal communicators, videoconferencing, voice mail, and e-mail. In fact, groupware—information tools that help groups work together—may be the most rapidly growing segment of the information technology industry.

The Paradigm Shift

Realistically, just because these technologies are available doesn't mean they will be used, or are even desirable. But remember the takeoff point for information technologies in the late 1980s. New technologies usually take longer than expected to achieve marketplace acceptance, but when they do take off, their growth rate and impact on work processes often exceed expectations. Tomorrow's information toolkit includes the following:

Data superhighway. Using fiber optic cable with high bandwidths, the national data superhighway will be able to transmit more data than ever before, including video data. Along with the new wireless communications, this will provide access to anyone in the world at any time. Businesses will expand dramatically their use of wide-area networks for such purposes as electronic data interchange, funds transfers, and real-time market research because the high bandwidth will enable them to send more data and higher-quality images.

Information agents. Information is useless unless it's meaningful. Information "agents" will screen the fire hose of data, going off to search hundreds of databases to select information needed for the task at hand. These kinds of searching and screening protocols will enable businesses to effectively use the massive amounts of information soon to be available.

Computers with full voice and handwriting recognition. Voice and handwriting recognition will combine to make human-computer interaction more natural and more widespread. These systems will enable computerphobes and, with the addition of language translators, workers who don't speak the host language to use computers easily, creating a new kind of work community.

Integrated multimedia. With enhanced video compression technologies, full-motion video on the desktop integrated with the telephone network will be capable of providing full videoconferencing capacity anywhere, anytime—if, as, and when the market wants it. Electronic mail systems will incorporate video clips, voice annotations, and complex graphic displays. Businesses will be able to make real-time presentations anywhere in the world.

Virtual reality. By means of simulated exercises, virtual reality will allow mission-critical training of those professionals whose work is life-threatening, including military and commercial pilots, police officers, firefighters, doctors, and nurses. Look for virtual reality to help move training out of the classroom and into the field by supporting just-in-time, experience-based learning.

Groupware. Groupware is a set of computer tools that helps groups work together more effectively. These tools can enhance communications (screen sharing, teleconferencing, and group writing), support group processes (workflow software), and provide a group memory bank (filing/retrieving and filtering/refining). These tools are especially helpful for crosscultural teamwork, making global team collaboration a reality, and for creating customized tools for groups in any firm.

Information appliances. These low-cost, portable devices will provide the ultimate in mobile connectivity, bringing the traditional tools of the office into the field. With built-in wireless, users can send and receive faxes and e-mail, receive the latest changes in the stock market, access company databases, and track press releases in their fields of interest. These appliances will change the shape of knowledge work by extending the scope of anywhere/anytime business practices.

Local area networks (LANs). LANs are changing the personal computer into the interpersonal computer, defining information tools not by what they are but by what they connect to. LANs can access corporate databases from any location within the corporation, for example, making the information available to anyone who needs it. This may alter the power structure of traditional corporate hierarchies.

Our fascination with the power and capabilities of the individual tools often overshadows the broader importance of these developments. In the most basic sense, we are at the edge of another revolution in the nature of information technology and its impact on organizations. Technology that first replaced individuals and later empowered them is now creating communities by linking people with each other and with the information they need. This paradigm shift in technology is leading to very different ways of thinking about work and working relationships.

FAILURE IS ENDEMIC TO THE SECOND CURVE

Most of us like to believe that the second curve is about predictable emergence of new technology. Unfortunately, most of the second-curve technologies turn out to be worthless junk, or, if you're lucky, they become important sacrifice flies on the way to a better technology future. It is pretty hard to think about technologies without thinking about risks. Indeed, in a recent major study on the future of America's research-intensive industries, we commissioned a paper from Stanford University's leading economists who have thought about technological change, and they (in an elegant review of the literature) conclude that there will be a systematic underinvestment by society in new technology because of the inherent risks and uncertainties and the difficulty of really capturing privately the benefits of technology innovation. In large measure, people who play on the second curve are in it for the technical sweetness—not the money—and most, if not all, will be doomed to failure. The question is this: As a society, will we continue to support the second-curve technology actors? At one level we appear to be putting great faith in them by buying their stock, even though the risks are high, but at another level, we are failing to make the investment in basic R&D at the government and corporate level that fueled all this stuff in the first place.

TECHNOLOGY'S SHEER POWER WILL AMPLIFY THE POIGNANCY OF THE TWO-CURVE DILEMMA

H&R Block (the parent of CompuServe) and its competitors like America Online are beginning to quake in their boots at the prospect of one of two competitors eliminating them entirely. Either the Microsoft network becomes so powerful because of its access through Windows 95 that it comes to dominate the online service business, or Microsoft, America Online, CompuServe, and Delphi all become irrelevancies to the phenomenon that is the Internet, which requires no per-member, per-month intermediary between you and the wild electronic frontier. The answer may be somewhere in the middle, where users have become comfortable with the online services as gateways to the Internet and as gateways to the wired world. They may continue their brand loyalty to online services, provided these services are priced competitively and the services are compelling.

The other part of this poignancy is the converse of the point made earlier about Mark Andreessen and the time-lapse between technical genius and grubby commercialism getting shorter. Leading-edge second-curve companies are going to have shorter moments in the sun. As the power of technology amplifies, and as the connectivity of a global wired world increases, these moments in the sun shorten for second-curve pioneers. And the speed with which new curves have to be built becomes even greater.

BUILDING SUSTAINABLE TECHNOLOGY COMPANIES MAY GET MORE DIFFICULT IN THE FUTURE

In the U.S., we are seeing research and development—particularly basic research—under threat because the Soviet Union is no longer cooperating as an enemy; thus we as a society have a less compelling reason to invest in basic science, now that the cold war is over. On the other hand, innovation, whether it be in the computer business, the pharmaceutical business, or the semiconductor business, is increasingly predicated on software, not hardware. This is worrisome in that there seems to be a global disrespect for intellectual property, which may have deep-seated cultural roots and may be difficult to overcome. That lack of respect coupled with a lack of support for basic R&D may undermine some of the innovation and some of the capacities of the research-intensive industries of the future. Technology clearly has contributed enormously to the increase in the global standard of living in the last twenty-five years and it will continue to do so in the future. But some of today's attitudes may impede this engine of growth and slow the penetration of innovation and in turn slow the productivity engine that leads to higher global standards of living.

The New Consumer:
Anything, Anytime, Anyplace

CONSUMERS ARE NOT what they used to be. Sophisticated, affluent, college-educated, they have expectations that say they can have
any product, anytime, anyplace—and they expect to get it at low
cost. The number of new consumers grows every year, and their presence is transforming the marketplace dramatically. They're more discriminating than their predecessors, and they're no longer sold by a
label alone, or by a low price.

What does all this mean for the businesses trying to sell to them?
As a start, it's difficult just to get this consumer's attention, let alone
make a sale, and even if you do get it, he or she may or may not believe
you. Many of those with disposable incomes are from two-income
households, where they're trying to be supermom, or, less commonly,
superdad. Today's consumers are overtired and overworked, and, as if
that weren't enough, they're a little jaded, making the easy sale a thing
of the past. These days the only true leisure class is the unemployed.

Consumers *are not* what they used to be, and neither is the market. Time to market is down, choice is up, the authority of brand names is no sure thing—all of which leaves a lot of markets up for grabs. New consumers demand change, and second-curve companies had better listen up.

New and Improved: Today's Consumer

THE BASIC SOURCE of the new consumer is the rise of the baby boom, which, in the United States, accounts for a third of the population. Baby boomers have managed to dominate every institution they've come in contact with, from kindergarten, elementary school, and college to the workplace. (And come the year 2020, they will dominate nursing homes.) They're well-informed, plugged in, and online, and they're motivated to make good decisions. And along with all that has come a profound skepticism of perceived authority. Consumers, more than ever, are willing to shift loyalties and experiment with the new and different.

In short, they're different from consumers of the past in five major ways:

They're better educated.
They're discriminating.
They're better informed.
They're more individualistic.
What they value has changed.

The Education of the Consumer Class

MOST STRIKING ABOUT THE BABY BOOMERS—and by extension today's consumers—is their education. Over half of this group made it to college, and half of that half graduated. As a result, they have a higher level of education than any previous group of consumers. But that's not all: the groups following them also have extremely high levels of education. In the U.S., among the consumers who disappear from consumption patterns at the end of life, typically less than 10 percent have college educations. But the new consumers who replace that group have a different background: 60 percent of them have had some college experience, and some 25 to 30 percent have college degrees. So as time goes on, the education level of the consuming public will continue to increase, thanks to the replacement of old consumers with new consumers. And this isn't exclusively in the United States; it's a phenomenon you see worldwide.

That rise in college education has created customers who are not only capable of making choices, but eager to do so, and unafraid of challenging vendor authority, something people just didn't do in the past; a brand name could sell a product, as could a low price. Today's equation isn't nearly so simple; consumers have minds of their own.

A Question of Taste

WITH EDUCATION comes discrimination in terms of taste. The level of quality and sophistication that people want—across the board, including product design and appearance and service—is extremely high. The increased number of households with large annual incomes means that there are more consumers who have some discretion over purchases, which means that they can be more demanding and more volatile in their purchases. More and more, consumers are making the rules.

Start Me Up: Infomated Consumers

TECHNOLOGY HAS PLAYED A KEY ROLE in the emergence of the new consumer by giving people the tools to learn what their options are and to then choose efficiently. And it's allowed manufacturers and distributors to respond much more quickly to consumer desires. The combination of new consumers and new technology allows enormous change, giving vendors new ways to reach consumers, and giving consumers new ways to reach, control, and manage vendors.

And it's not only a privileged few we're talking about. Over half of the workers in the United States have access to a computer, from an interconnected PC at the desk of a professional to the handheld inventory control device in the hands of the inventory clerk, to the point-of-sale terminal at the checkout counter. Three quarters of all new jobs created during the last decade have such devices. People not only deal with the gathering and analysis of information, but see how the workplace is transformed by that information every day.

The availability of technology isn't limited to the workplace. Thirty-seven percent of today's households have a computer, and approximately 40 percent of those households are connected by modem to the outside world, a proportion that will only increase as more personal computers are shipped with internal modem and fax connections. The online world is still a relatively small proportion of American households; approximately 4 percent of today's households have online access in general, and the number of American households plugged in to the Internet is somewhere between 4 and 7 percent, although active users are probably a subset of less than 1 percent (albeit those numbers are growing rapidly). How big the Internet can become is uncertain. One possibility is that it may be the laboratory for twenty-first-century commerce, communication, and entertainment, in that it brings together the increasing power of computers, the increasing capacities of communication, and the increasing array of options that a planet engaged with these machines can offer. And it has the kind of freewheeling wildness that leads to enormous financial growth.

While technology in and of itself doesn't necessarily change consumption patterns, it does give consumers access to tools they can use in making purchasing decisions. As more households become infused with information technology, consumers will have new choices available. In particular, there's a segment of what the Institute for the Future calls "infomated" households, households that have at least five out of the following eight technologies: VCRs, CDs, laser discs, fax machines, answering machines, voice mail services, computers, and cellular phones. In 1993, when this measure was first developed, approximately 11 percent of households in a national sample conducted by Louis Harris were found to be infomated by this definition. By early 1995 that number had increased to over 20 percent, and it is growing rapidly. And this segment isn't a bunch of technology freaks; on the contrary, it represents people from a variety of walks of life who tend to be college-educated, affluent baby boomers who are using technology to enhance their lives in very everyday ways, including the ways in which they interact as consumers.

H&R Block is a company that has done well in managing change. Henry Bloch built an enormous business on a very simple premise for the mid- to low-end consumer market: preparing tax returns for ordinary working people. Henry and Richard Bloch started the company, then called United Business, in 1946, and included free tax preparation as part of their service. In 1955, when the IRS stopped offering individual tax preparation service, the Bloch brothers reorganized, focusing their business on what was a sideline—preparing taxes—and reincorporated as H&R Block. Business went well; in 1962, 75,000 shares were sold in a public offering.

Sixteen years later, the company began to expand in terms of direction. In 1978, they acquired Personnel Pool of America, a temporary services company, and in 1980, CompuServe, as well as 80 percent of Hyatt Legal Services, a chain of law offices (which they subsequently sold, in 1987). In 1985 they bought Path Management, a seminar business (also sold, in 1990). In 1991, Personnel Pool of America bought Interim Services. In 1992 Henry Bloch's son Tom succeeded him as president. In 1994, the company jettisoned the temporary services unit in an IPO in order to focus on electronic and computer services.

The company's tremendous success over the years has been largely due to incredible discipline on the part of Henry Bloch and his colleagues, and to a sense of frugality and good business practices. When I first met Henry Bloch, his son Tom was CEO of the firm, and I was being considered as a board member of Interim Services, still a subsidiary. I went to Kansas City on the way back from a trip to the East Coast, and when I got to Block's headquarters, I was surprised at the office space, which was relatively modest for a Fortune 200 company. I walked into the office building and the receptionist said, "Oh you must be Ian," and asked me to sit down in the foyer of the building. No more than a couple of minutes later, Henry Bloch walked out and said, "Ian, it's nice to meet you." It's not often that you're greeted in the foyer directly by the CEO of a major company. (A side note: interestingly, Ed McCracken of Silicon Graphics has a similar style, which is very different from the typical corporate encampment in which CEOs are cloistered behind the door with a dragon lady and a great deal of difficulty between you and them.) It's a testimony to Henry Bloch's character and personality that it was important for him to represent that kind of image—only it's not an image. It's who he is.

Part of the Bloch second-curve story is a technology story, because clearly they could see that in the long run, the preparation of taxes, while a useful service, could increasingly become part of the electronic infrastructure, either on a stand-alone PC or online. They recognized that their cash cow was not necessarily the best use of funds and that there might be better ways in which they could make investments. So they bought CompuServe, and they bought Interim. The reason for Block's interest in the temporary services business was that, since tax preparation was an enormous annual event with significant numbers of temporary employees brought in and trained by Bloch, they felt they had two relevant core competencies: management of the temporary work force, and of franchise businesses (which is what the Block system really works off of). Interim Services (then called Personnel Pool of America) represented a mid-size temporary service, with ambitions to grow. In 1990, new CEO Ray Marcy joined, and shortly thereafter they made an aggressive purchase of Interim Services, and some other acquisitions. They adopted the Interim name and have continued to grow the business. In 1994 Interim was spun off as a separate organization as an IPO on NASDAQ. The cash that Block generated from that deal was used partly to purchase MECA software (which subsequently was sold).

Block understands the second curve and knows how to get in early—and get out at a profit. Temporary help is one example. But the current key second-curve player in the Block linup is CompuServe: an asset that represents an increasing share of Block's market value. The Block style has been to give a lot of autonomy, including independent boards of directors, to its subsidiaries, although the final authority always rested with the parent Block company, and indeed with the Bloch family itself. Tom Bloch is a very smart, engaging, decent man whom most people would describe as too decent to be a CEO. In August of 1995, Tom decided to step down as a leader of the company, and he handed over the company reins to an outside CEO. Shortly thereafter Richard H. Brown, the vice chairman of Ameritech, was named president and CEO, a step that in essence consummates the transition of H&R Block from the first curve to the second. Today they have a strong play online, serving the new infomated consumer, and with a legacy on the first curve of a cash cow built on a low-tech business serving hardworking Americans.

The Customized Customer

INCREASINGLY, individual consumers are just that: individuals, beyond the point of being easily characterized in the mass, or even in major segments. More and more, today's consumer has a unique set

of preferences, unlike anyone else's. Consumers may have shared
interests, and can perhaps be classified in a limited way, but their interests tend to be so specific, and so varied, that they can't be characterized in the general ways of the recent past.

This presents quite a challenge for the mass marketers on the first
curve. Increasingly the second curve will be about helping individuals fulfill their unique combination of needs and wants, instead of
finding as many people as you can who can fit certain criteria.

Matters of the Heart

UNDERNEATH THESE FOUR CHARACTERISTICS lies a fifth,
closely linked to each of them, in some cases the reason for the
change: simply put, consumers' values have changed, and you see the
difference in their attitudes and expectations. Environmentalism, for
example, is having a huge impact on the buying public, and, for reasons that are only too obvious, will most likely continue to be a core
value well into the twenty-first century. In particular, the continued
growth of Asian economies (discussed in chapter six) is likely to make
the environment even more of a concern and to raise even more trou-
bling questions of the sustainability of economic growth, or even the
sustainability of the planet given anticipated levels of economic
growth in major developing countries. A substantial group of consumers holds environmentalism very near and dear to their hearts; it's
often more than an intellectual decision, moving toward a matter of
the heart, almost like a religious preference, so much so that consumers can be swayed by a company's concern—or lack thereof—for
the environment, in terms of its marketing and production practices.

The change in the perceived importance of brand names is another example of change in values. Today's consumers are no longer
easily seduced by brand names that don't consistently deliver quality
at a fair price. Yet at the same time, consumers have demonstrated
an ability, and even a willingness, to support entirely new brands and
be amazingly loyal to them. The rise of companies like Starbucks, Intuit, Nike, and Reebok are testimony to the ability of the baby boom
generation to create and embrace brands they identify with, and to
back brands they perceive as providing value. Brand loyalty may be
down in the classic sense, but it's alive and well in the context of
changing values.

They Come Bearing Change:
The Consumer's Effect on the Market

CONSUMERS ARE, more and more, calling the shots. To survive, vendors have to listen and respond. The emergence of the new consumer has created five key characteristics of the second-curve market:

> *Time to market is down.*
> *Choice is up.*
> *Distribution channels have changed and fragmented.*
> *The value proposition has changed.*
> *Who owns the customer is blurred.*

You Want It *When?*

WHEREVER YOU LOOK, the speed with which economies operate is increasing. Consumers demand high response, and these days vendors are competing for speed. And that time-based competition, a very real factor in today's market, has had a huge impact on the market in a couple of ways.

First, time to market: today's consumers demand responsiveness, in terms of both service and product quality. For vendors and providers this means that whatever product or service they're offering must be delivered in a timely fashion—very timely. Vendors are under tremendous pressure to decrease the time between manufacturing and product availability—to get the product on the shelves—and they're succeeding: products are moving to market much more quickly than they did five to ten years ago. The average time between initial product design and that product's appearance on the shelf is down by one half in a broad range of product areas, from Sony's consumer electronics, to Toyota's cars, to AT&T's laptops. The innovations in point-of-sale transaction processing and information have helped to speed things up. Stores and retail outlets could not have been as responsive to customer needs as they have been without knowing exactly what the customer was buying (and not buying) and at what price, at any given time. Point-of-sale terminals have taken the place of clerks and distributors making educated guesses once a week and have dramatically reduced the time to market of products the consumers want.

And second, product availability: once a product's out there, consumers expect to be able to buy that product anytime, and anyplace. Some companies, such as Levi Strauss (discussed in chapter four), are endeavoring to retool and rework their entire business process so that they can turn around a customized product in record time. And provider and vendor responses to consumers' desire to have access to goods and services whenever and wherever they want are all around us, and all around the globe. Look at ATMs, the twenty-four-hour Safeway, and—probably the most amazing manifestation—the ubiquitous vending machine in Tokyo. You see attached to practically every building in that city some form of vending machine; get your money out and you can buy just about anything: Scotch, pantyhose, juice drinks, iced coffee, cigarettes, sandwiches, and all kinds of other foods and snacks. The range and quantity are incredible, and the innovation is a testimony to Japanese ingenuity. What's even more remarkable is the lack of vandalism. The fact that these seemingly vulnerable boxes of goodies remain unharmed bears witness to the stability of Japanese culture and the strength of Japan's social system.

What's really going on behind the time issue is the attempt to find new ways to serve consumers faster, better, and cheaper, and often this is done by harnessing the power of second-curve technology. For example, by investing in logical sequence scanner technology, computer integrated manufacturing, and sophisticated logistic systems, a vendor can deliver a customized product within a week; thus product life cycles are becoming shorter, and the ability to bring out a new product becomes a function of both creativity and speed. And as time to market continues to go down, the pace of competition will only go up.

Peppercorn Ranch–Flavored Cheese Bits

NOT ONLY ARE PRODUCTS on the shelves more quickly; there are more and more products to choose from. Choice is up, and you see it both in the products you can chose from, and in the methods of payment available. In fact, choice isn't just up, it's the name of the game. The number of new products introduced is up dramatically over the last five years, and the number of different products actually on the shelves of the average store has doubled over the last ten—if in doubt, just visit any supermarket in the United States. When I first came to North America in the mid-1970s, I used to visit Palm Springs in the wintertime to get away from the rain in Vancouver. And there, in the Vons Grocery Store, I was always struck by the sight of the cracker aisle. The fact that they even *had* a cracker aisle—that there could be *that many crackers!*—blew me away. But it wasn't only the quantity. It was also the incredible variety, the fact that there could be so many combinations, and that somebody was actually *buying* peppercorn ranch–flavored cheese bits, or whatever. It was mind-boggling.

But that cracker aisle is also a good example of the simple proliferation of product ideas, which really comes from the intersection of new technology and the new consumer. If you can develop and test products quickly, and if you can track the preferences of consumers through sophisticated scanner technology, then you can really push the limits of pluralism. And if you believe in an individualized lifestyle where instead of mass segments we have individual segments, the logical extension of that is what's been called one-to-one marketing, where individuals rather than segments are served. It is clear that this kind of marketing is a major driver of the growth in choice.

In short, people are trying to figure out ways to add value through innovation, whether you're talking about crackers or tortilla chips or silicon chips or computers. And we're trying, through differentiation, to find new ways of not being commodities, and if that means new products, so be it.

Choice is up not only in terms of products, but in terms of payment. It's increasingly possible to pay with cash, credit card, ATM direct debit card, or, soon, with virtual money in the form of money cards, smart cards, and virtual digital cash on the Internet. These methods of payment are creating opportunities for new forms of transactions to take place both physically and virtually. The sight of a fast-food vendor accepting a credit card is a little scary, but it wasn't *that* long ago that we felt the same way about groceries, and increasingly, people are using cards to pay for just about everything. They're using credit cards as tools for managing their money by using the float for thirty days, and they're using ATM cards (where the float doesn't apply) simply for their convenience—you don't need your checkbook anymore. So for a lot of us, purchasing with cards, of one kind or another, has become a way of life. We use cards everywhere, from fast-food places to gas stations, where, thanks to point-of-sale systems embedded in the pumps, you don't ever have to deal with a gas station attendant again. We're talking about a mercifully powerful technology.

The Armchair Shopper

ALL THAT CHOICE isn't limited to products and payment; we're seeing more choices in purchasing channels, in where and how we shop, as well as in how we pay. The combination of sophisticated consumers and new technology has had a huge effect on channels of distribution, and today the ways in which vendors reach customers are radically different—and far more varied—from what they were in the not-so-distant past. Thanks to credit cards, point-of-sale systems, and ATM networks, transaction processing is a global breeze, creating a whole new second curve of distribution channels. The combination of electronic commerce, empowered and enlightened consumers, a focus on service and speed, and exciting new technologies and entrepreneurial flair is creating radically different ways of distributing products and services.

You don't have to look far to get an idea of the variety: malls, discount centers, superstores, factory outlets, warehouse stores, direct mail catalogs, direct mail coupons, TV shopping, interactive kiosks, pay-point outlets, and PC malls all with extended (or even twenty-four-hours-a-day, seven-days-a-week) openings are just a few. The following are some of the major new channels.

New Mail-Order Channels

Mail order is a key channel, particularly in the U.S. but increasingly in Europe and Japan, where the mail-order segment is growing rapidly. Some argue that this may be saturating the market in the U.S., and that mail-order marketing may peak. But even if volume peaks, mail order will probably become even more valuable because of refinements and innovations in mail-order systems—as the underlying tools like preference engines (computers that help market analysts identify the preferences of individual consumers) become more sophisticated, as addressing and mailing systems become more clean and secure, and as the information targeting becomes more precise.

The Rise of the Internet as a Mechanism for Exchange

Some of the most exciting potential for the future in terms of retail channels is going to emerge from the Internet. Being able to access information globally, systematically, and serendipitously is quite a seductive combination of technologies. It's true that at the moment the

Internet is more fun than it is practical: fulfilling your desires (whether they be in the area of retail or amour or somewhere in between) can be messy, to say the least, because of the lack of reliable checks and balances you'd expect in a conventional retail or service exchange— simple things like knowing what products are available, and whether the store is open, and whether or not a transaction can be conducted securely. (Do you really want to share your credit card number with a hundred thousand other people?) But these barriers notwithstanding, the Internet is a very interesting experiment in commerce that will play out over the next decade. It may not be the backbone of electronic commerce of the future, but it could very well be the metaphor.

The Grocery Business

Some of the more interesting changes in channels have come in the most traditional retail segment, the grocery business. Safeway has pioneered the Peapod service, which is really the return of home delivery—only mediated by electronics. Peapod users keep what is essentially a spreadsheet of routine grocery requirements, then access Safeway's database of product prices and availability, and place their orders for delivery. Users say that the more prudent purchasing that results from doing online price comparisons, rather than impulse buying on sight, compensates for the fees, which can include combinations of starter, monthly, order, and delivery charges. Even so, the service has yet to gain widespread appeal. There's still something fundamentally human about wandering the aisle in search of the cracker of your choice, particularly if you are originally from Britain. Supermarkets are perhaps one of the more delightful dimensions of American culture, and it will take a long time before I give up the right to visit grocery stores.

Direct Marketing

Over 40 percent of the mail that households receive is direct marketing. Households with high incomes are the prime target for virtually all mail from businesses, and in many cases they receive from 50 to 100 percent more mail than lower-income households. While older households with members from fifty to sixty-four years of age get more nonprofit solicitations, magazines, and personal letters, younger baby boom households (with members from thirty to forty-nine years of age) receive more business solicitations, catalogs, and financial statements. This kind of targeted business mailing will most likely follow these boomer households as they age and grow wealthier.

With the growing number of well-educated, high-income households, advertisers have continued to target these markets. The response to traditional advertising has been high, especially among infomated households, which tend to be almost 50 percent more likely to respond to advertisements than the average U.S. household. And even though many surveyed households say that they wish they received less advertising mail, in practice a large portion of households find such mail useful and interesting—they actually read twice as much of the mail as they tell interviewers they do, as discovered in a household diary study conducted by the U.S. Postal Service. In traditional surveys that ask households if they would like to receive fewer advertisements, participants usually give a strong *yes*—mostly because that seems like the right answer. But the diary surveys show that people read much more than they admit in face-to-face interviews.

You *Wouldn't* Really Rather Have a Buick? The Change in Brand Names

THE KEY SHIFT occurring in the retail sector is a redefinition of value. In the past, value was sort of frowned upon as low-end. But today's sophisticated consumers are increasingly concerned about price and quality and service. They want the best brands at the lowest prices and they want to be treated well as part of the process. Wal-Mart is perhaps the cutting edge in understanding, supporting, and delivering on this difficult three-way promise. The company has been very focused about keeping costs down while providing outstanding value, both through their own private-label brands (which are discussed below) and through national brand leader–partners such as Procter & Gamble, and their efforts in these areas are totally integrated in their entire production, inventory, and logistic systems, all aimed at fulfilling consumers' needs.

Wal-Mart reached the consumer in a new way: large discount stores with a range of high-quality but reasonably priced products at out-of-town sites with plenty of parking. Their investment went into building new stores and improving the efficiency of getting product to customer. As the customer came to rely on the value of the products they had on the floor, they were able to keep prices down and variety up. Wal-Mart's share of total retail sales kept rising as that of the competition—specifically Sears Roebuck, JCPenney, and Kmart, companies that relied on older locations, or tried to spread out into areas that were more isolated, or didn't adapt the quality and variety of their offerings as quickly—leveled off or fell.

An upshot of this redefinition is decrease in the power of brand names. In the past, brand names denoted value by promising customers a certain standard of quality, but today a brand name doesn't sell a product like it used to. Consumers' concerns with price and quality and service outweigh the panache of a brand name, so that name simply isn't enough anymore. Now the standard of quality is often denoted by the retailer, who can carry a wide variety of brands (some of the retailer's own making), all of which carry an image of quality, but some of which are at discounted prices because they don't need to be individually advertised.

Divided Loyalties and Private Label

IN A WORLD in which channels are changing and fragmenting, where consumers are sophisticated, where the market is ripe with both choice and hype in terms of speed, the concept of customer loyalty gets blurred. In a more stable environment—one where brand loyalty was predictable, where innovation was rare, and where the manufacturer held sway over the consumer's tastes and preferences through mass media—the concept of brand loyalty was central to the success of the many great consumer products companies. Such brand loyalty indeed was carried as a metaphor over to other goods and services; some of the great brands have been not just in soaps and colas, but in financial services, like Chase, Wells Fargo, and Bank of America. Others have been automotive brands like Volvo, Mercedes, and BMW, and there have even been great brands in consulting—McKinsey & Co. and Bain & Co., for example.

A brand is not simply a product with a manufacturer's label on it. As much figurative as it is literal, a traditional brand is a product or service that the consumer perceives to have distinctive benefits beyond price and functional performance. A brand is a symbol that becomes part of the cultural imagination. It calls up a way of life, a unique set of associations, lifestyle attributes, and status. The brand may have social acceptability (Gillette razors, Pampers diapers, Coke, or Pepsi), it may be fashionable (Absolut vodka, Swatch watches), or it may be a badge of a lifestyle (BMW, Eddie Bauer, or Reebok). But no matter what, it must have a consistency and quality that continually forges a bond of trust between the manufacturer and the consumer.

A brand can sometimes command premium prices compared to its competitors, but it doesn't have to. Usually, the profitability of great brands is in the volume and economies of scale of mass appeal, not just in price per unit. And because the manufacturer controlled the traditional branded product, the manufacturer realized the profit.

Enter private label, the so-called generic knockoff, but really not that at all. Generic is one thing, nothing more than a no-label, no-brand, lower-quality item. Private label uses the power of the retail and distribution chain and its control over the channel to replicate the same kind of brand capacity that the manufacturer once had. The retailer makes the same investment in advertising, research, product quality, positioning, and packaging, so that the consumer perceives a product of equivalent if not superior quality and gains access to it at a very competitive price. The obvious attraction of private label for retailers is that because they're the ones making the investments and controlling the product selection decision, their margins on store brands are much higher than on manufacturers' brands. Retailers are able to do this—to sell products under their own labels—because of their clout. They own the customer, and they own the store, so they can display their private label products where they want, and they receive deep discounts from the source suppliers, who are often the brand manufacturers themselves. Retailers have control over the distribution channel as well.

Private label involves the management of a store-owned brand in the same way that a manufacturer creates and fosters a very specific and high-quality image for its best products. Safeway Select chocolate chip cookies are made with more butter and better chocolate than the leading manufacturers' brands, and they're promoted to the customer in a quality sense where freshness, taste, and appeal rival if not exceed customer expectations of leading brands. And Wal-Mart sells more Sams cola, its private-label value offering, than it does Coke.

The rise of private-label goods in American supermarkets has quickly followed the revolution that has taken place in Britain and Canada, the sources of the classic examples and forerunners of private label. Private label in Britain has been hugely successful: over 50 percent of retail grocery sales in the United Kingdom are private-label.

Aggressive private labelers have their own vendors, wine buyers, and sophisticated brand quality enforcement in areas such as wines and spirits, foods of all types, and goods which have previously had a lot of manufacturer brand loyalty. Marks & Spencer has pioneered private label for years. Their store is stocked only with the St. Michael brand, which has an excellent quality reputation in the segments they serve. Tesco in the U.K. has also followed very much the private label model. In Canada, Loblaw, the largest Canadian grocery chain, has been a pioneer in the use of private label. In fact, Loblaw's partnership with several retailers in the U.S. (including Safeway) helped to develop sophisticated private-label products. Loblaw is North America's most successful private-label retailer. Loblaw's No Name generic tier and President's Choice private-label tier have made enormous inroads on supermarket shelves across North America. Loblaw produces the number-one-selling cookie in Canada: President's Choice Decadent Chocolate Chip. It outsells Nabisco's Chips Ahoy! despite the fact that the Loblaw product is available in only 23 percent of the country's stores compared to 98 percent for Chips Ahoy!. The key to the cookie's success is not only that it costs less but that it tastes better: only 24 percent of a Chips Ahoy! cookie consists of chips, and the cookie is made with vegetable oil, whereas 40 percent of a President's Choice cookie consists of chips, and it is made with real butter.

According to *The New York Times* (February 6, 1994), Loblaw is invading the United States. By February 1994, its President's Choice retail brand was in more than 1,200 stores in the U.S., including chains like D'Agostino's in New York, Jewel in Chicago, and Lucky in California. Loblaw boosted its market penetration with its 1992 deal to help Wal-Mart, the world's largest retailer, generate what are now some six hundred private brands.

Some retailers don't just private-label their products; they private-label their processes as well. Wal-Mart has been on the cutting edge in both areas, automating its distribution centers, which cut shipping costs and time, and implementing a computerized inventory system that speeds up checkout and reordering. The second curve of retailing is one in which the retailer's brand is given equal if not greater weight, but also one in which the retailer has developed deep electronic and business partnerships with its vendors to ensure that they are capable of delivering the correct quantities of a product on time. Both sides support the product appropriately by completely embedding their inventory control systems and manufacturing systems between vendor and supplier. These complete integrations speak to the extended enterprise of the future, where more and more organizations will have established business integrations with vendors and distributors.

Private label is really about a fundamental shift in the value proposition, a revolution in which the power in the retail game is being driven down the distribution chain closer to the customer. Increasingly, this transformation of value and the shift toward private labels will create second-curve opportunities. We're likely to see similar manifestations of the private-label phenomenon in other areas of goods and services. We've already seen it to a large degree in health care, where managed health care plans are effectively private-labeling the services of some set of physicians and hospitals (leading brand), trying to "brand" those doctors and hospitals even though they have no exclusive relationships with them. And you see it in banking, where affinity cards create private labels for financial products where the core financial institution is a no-name bank in the bowels of the South.

Do brands have a future? Increasingly, marketing gurus are asking themselves this question, arguing that the emergence of private-label brands is compelling evidence that traditional brands are in trouble. This logic is false. The growth of private-label brands does not necessarily mean the demise of brands; private labels can themselves be real brands. Private-label products have moved from being parasites to becoming brands in their own right.

Once retailers caught on to this central truth, they moved into the brand business on their own, taking on the manufacturers at their own game. They purchased consumer goods from their suppliers, put a private label on them, and undercut the manufacturers' brands on price. But let's get clear. A knock-off competitor that mimics a market-leading brand is not a brand, it's a parasite competing with the brand on price. Like all parasites, it has no life of its own. If manufacturers were to match these private-label parasites on price, the private label would not survive. In most of the early cases, the private label had not made the investment in research or support to create the quality and consistency of the product and the trust with the consumer. It was taking a free ride on the margin created by someone else.

But increasingly brands are being built by retailers. The retail or private-label brand has developed the quality, consistency, and relationship with the consumer that are the hallmarks of traditional brands. These retail brands grew rapidly in Europe and Canada in the 1980s, and successes learned there are being imported into the United States. They likely will have a profound effect on the global consumer product business in the decade ahead. The premier retail analysts in the United States anticipate that the unit share of private labels will grow from 18 percent in 1993 to 33 percent by 2000 and will peak at 45 to 50 percent by 2004; in other words, unit share of private labels will more than double. We're seeing these other signs of the growth of private labels as well:

The strength of private label in Britain. Private-label brands account for 36 percent of sales in the grocery market in the United Kingdom, compared to approximately 15 percent across Western Europe as a whole and 14 percent in the United States. Private-label sales in Europe are growing at 11 percent per year while manufacturers' brands as a whole are growing at 6.5 percent.

The decline of brand loyalty in the United States. The Roper Organization has been tracking the steady decline in U.S. consumer preferences for well-known (that is, manufacturers') brands over a long period from 75 percent preference in 1975 down to 60 percent in 1993. Similarly, Gallup has found a consistent growth in the number of those who agree that store brands (private label) usually perform as well as nationally advertised brands, from 33 percent of those polled in 1981 to 67 percent in 1990.

The response of Black Friday. On Friday, April 2, 1993, Philip Morris slashed 40 cents off the price of a pack of Marlboro cigarettes in response to the consistently lower prices of private-label brands. The shock wave reverberated across the consumer products landscape, with most of the damage occurring on Wall Street. In one day—"Black Friday"—the top twenty-five brand manufacturers had lost almost $50 billion in market value. In response to private-label threats and everyday low prices by retail giants like Wal-Mart, other top companies have had to follow Philip Morris's example.

Six key forces are driving the change from manufacturers' to retail brands:

Manufacturers overindulged in pricing. Throughout the 1980s, manufacturers increased their brand prices at a rate well above the CPI. According to *Fortune* magazine, Ed Artzt, then CEO of consumer products giant Procter & Gamble, stated in 1992: "We learned by surprise that the premium [on manufacturers' brands versus retail brands] had grown too wide, to about 35 percent. At this point, manufacturers' brands start to lose market share to the retail brands."

Retail companies consolidated. England used to be a nation of shopkeepers, but now it is a nation of super retailers. In the United Kingdom, starting in the 1970s, and led by giants like Tesco and Sainsbury, grocery retailing has consolidated significantly. This trend is being followed in the United States, where everyday low-cost centers such as Target, Price/Costco, and Wal-Mart are taking ever larger shares of the traditional grocery retailing business. For example, Wal-Mart has the highest sales per square foot in retailing. Its 1993 sales were $73 billion, or about the same as Procter & Gamble, Coca-Cola, and RJR Nabisco combined. Such consolidation in the retail channel shifts the locus of power to the retailer. When this is coupled with the increasing gap in the margin between manufacturers' brands and private-label brands, it creates the necessary but not sufficient conditions for powerful retail brands.

The retail channel got it. Brands used to be the exclusive domain of manufacturers, who would do everything including research, product development, advertising, in-store promotions, and positioning. In the United Kingdom, however, large retailers such as Marks & Spencer, Tesco, and Sainsbury invested millions in positioning their whole retail outlet and the wide range of private-label products as a brand. Marks & Spencer became synonymous with high value in such varied consumer segments as underwear, potato chips, and knitwear. Sainsbury, focusing on grocery, wine, and liquor retailing, has been so successful in building the Sainsbury brand—and the product quality to merit it—that it can competitively market a Sainsbury cognac against Martell and Courvoisier. Giant retailers like Sainsbury or Marks & Spencer can spread their brand-building costs in research and advertising across an enormous product line, with huge economies of scale. As long as they don't let inferior quality in some segments tarnish the retail label, they can command brand recognition on what may seem like generic private-label offerings. To support the brand name, they are passionate about quality control in all their products. In the case of Tesco and Sainsbury, the retail channel understood what it took to create and maintain real brands.

The role of mass media is changing. The United Kingdom is rarely seen as the innovator in something as American as retailing. Why did private labels occur there so early? According to private-label guru David Nichol, president of Loblaw, part of the explanation may lie in the underdevelopment of the mass media in Europe. Unlike their counterparts in the United States, commercial radio did not exist in Europe, and commercial television was a relatively small part of viewers' lives. Americans grew up with product endorsements embedded in program content, first on radio, then on television. As a result, argues Nichol, American consumers knew 80 percent of the brands they were going to buy before they entered the supermarket. Not so in the United Kingdom, where consumers were stuck with the BBC and low-key, infrequent commercials on the single commercial channel. As a result, the manufacturers never built up as much brand power with the consumer. As media choices proliferate in the United States and as mass media wane as a vehicle for brand indoctrination, opportunities to capture the consumer through alternative channels (including private label, targeted couponing, and new media) seem likely to continue to erode the traditional manufacturer's-brand paradigm.

New technology changed the distribution chain. Information technology has also had an effect on the distribution chain. The growth in scanners, point-of-sale transaction processing, and database management systems has shifted the power of the market research engine from the manufacturers to the retailers further down the distribution chain. Store managers, not executives in New York, now have the information at their fingertips and can make real-time adjustments in pricing, positioning, and promotion.

The value era dawns. We have entered a new value era. This is a structural, not a cyclical change, and we had better get used to it. No matter what, any successful brand has to meet the new value equation that the increasingly sophisticated and educated consumer demands worldwide. Generic drugs, for example, are the choice of a smart generation. College-educated, affluent consumers are much more likely to ask for generics than consumers with less education. Similarly, value buyers are not poor. On the contrary, they will shop Target and Nordstrom, Price/Costco and Saks Fifth Avenue, the discounter and the specialty boutique, always in search of value. In a 1993 survey, Louis Harris & Associates found that the perception of value in private-label products compared to traditional brands increases with household income. The second curve belongs to private label.

Second-Curve Players in Search of the New Consumer

COMPANIES HAVE RESPONDED in a variety of ways to the demands and challenges of the new consumers. Herewith a few examples.

Direct Marketing Par Excellence: Spiegel

SPIEGEL IS A COMPANY that has perfected catalog marketing to the home. They run a portfolio of specialty catalog companies that includes a wide range, from their own clothing to Eddie Bauer, and they maintain address lists that reflect recent purchase patterns and responses to all kinds of direct mail. They have been able to combine four elements into a single business: computer-generated, up-to-date mailing lists of potential clients; a range of specialty producers of good-quality products; an extremely efficient distribution system that is able to get a customer order to the home in two or three days; and a solid reputation for product quality and customer service, including a policy of taking back anything that the customer isn't satisfied with at Spiegel's cost, no questions asked. Spiegel has managed simultaneously to create a market niche of their own and to establish an industry standard.

Joseph Spiegel founded the company in Chicago in 1865, shortly after his release from a Confederate prison. The company started by selling home furnishings. The Great Chicago Fire of 1871 destroyed the store, but Spiegel was not slowed down for long—he had kept much of his inventory in his backyard—and he was soon up and running again. Business grew, in part due to the railroad boom and the growing immigration rate, and in 1905 Spiegel began his mail-order business—a response partly to his son Arthur's suggestion (Arthur soon took over), but also as a response to the competition of two local mail-order companies, Montgomery Ward and Sears.

Spiegel began selling women's clothes in 1912, and soon the catalog business became the center of the business, to the point where Spiegel sold its retail operations during the Depression. The company's approach to catalog sales was new and very successful, with a number of firsts: the first mail-order company whose catalogs included photographs, and the first to put out a Christmas catalog. But its big first was credit, a move that played a large part in Spiegel's success. And while with World War II came restrictions on credit that steered Spiegel back into retail, that didn't last long, and the company was strictly mail order again by 1953.

Beneficial Corporation bought Spiegel in 1965, and by the mid-1970s mail order had grown and prospered, providing Spiegel with tough competition from the Sears, Montgomery Ward, Aldens, and JCPenney catalogs. Spiegel tried something new: its competitors all looked alike, so Spiegel went upscale and went after the upper middle class by offering labels: Ralph Lauren, Calvin Klein, Liz Claiborne. Otto Versand, a European catalog company, bought Spiegel in 1982, and sales tripled over the next four years. The company went public in 1987.

Then came the acquisitions. Spiegel bought Eddie Bauer in 1988, and First Consumer National Bank, which became the basis for Spiegel's credit card operations, in 1990. In 1993 Spiegel acquired New Hampton, now Newport News, whose catalogs are aimed at the lower middle market. Home shopping was next. In 1994 Spiegel and Time Warner announced a joint venture to create a new shopping channel, Catalog 1, aimed at more affluent consumers than the existing shopping channels. (That venture was cut back in 1994 after less than encouraging test marketing results: Spiegel discontinued television production of Catalog 1 and reduced programming from twenty-four hours a day to two hours on Saturday.) Spiegel also tested distribution using CD-ROMs and America Online.

Since 1994, Spiegel has gone global, starting with three Eddie Bauer stores in Tokyo and catalog sales in Japan and Germany. And they're big users of new technology. Spiegel's database of customer buying habits has basically replaced demographics as a basis for marketing and merchandising decisions. The company simply uses data kept on their customers' purchases to watch trends, spot emerging markets, and develop buyer profiles. Spiegel updates that database daily; information is kept right down to the SKU (the stock keeping unit—a stock number used for inventory and pricing) and customer level, and the company can use that data for spotting the latest trends and including those changes in new designs and the catalog itself. Spiegel can also summarize that data in the form of geographic customer profiles, which help in mailings that are targeted for particular locations. By analyzing customer profiles and buying information, Spiegel can tailor its catalog offerings in terms of frequency, timing, and the types of catalogs mailed to customers, a method at least as good as—company execs think better than—demographics. Eddie Bauer uses the same type of data in deciding where to open new stores—which is, of course, wherever there are concentrations of their catalog customers.

Despite a decline of overall sales in the catalog industry from $31.1 billion in 1992 to $29.3 billion in 1993, Spiegel built a significant second curve with mail order. Now Spiegel is carefully experimenting with new second-curve alternatives such as online services and broadcast media—and facing the second curve all over again.

Safeway: What Customers Want, They Get

A DECADE AGO Safeway was considered noncompetitive and stagnant; today they're a very strong competitor, one of the world's
largest food retailers, with 1,062 stores, most of which are in the
Western and mid-Atlantic regions of the United States and Canada.
Safeway also owns 35 percent of the Vons Companies, the largest
supermarket chain in Southern California, and 49 percent of Casa
Ley, S.A. de C.V., which operates food-variety and wholesale stores in
western Mexico. The manufacturing and processing facilities process
milk, bread, ice cream, cheese, soft drinks, fruit and vegetables, and
pet food. The Canadian company has a wholesale operation that dis-
tributes national and private-label products to independent grocery
stores and institutional customers.

Safeway's general method of operation has three distinct characteristics. They operate larger stores in the interest of efficiency; they offer a
wide variety of food and general merchandise; and they run in-house
specialty departments like pharmacies and deli/bakeries, which are historically high margin contributors. Store management is to a large degree decentralized by making store managers more autonomous in the
hope of allowing individual stores to respond to local market needs.
Safeway also tries to match merchandising strategy to customers' changing lifestyles, demographics, and product preferences; for example,
Value Pack products—economy-size packages that you'd expect to see
only at membership club stores—and low-fat single-serving meals.

Private label is big at Safeway, which with partners like Cott and
other manufacturers works to produce products under the Safeway
Select label. Most of the products sold by Safeway under different
private labels have been changed to the Safeway Select with new packaging, print ads, and in-store promotions to notify customers; as a result, the number of Safeway's private labels has gone from over a
hundred to about twelve, two of which are Lucerne and the Safeway
Select premium brand. In recent years Safeway introduced a line of
about 350 new private-label Safeway Select products; the plan is to do
more of the same.

The specialty departments and services that Safeway has brought in
recently are widely varied, and include video rentals, photo processing,
and in-store ATMs and bank branches. In some of the mid-Atlantic
stores, Safeway has even placed automated concert ticket kiosks, which
include video display screens and touch screens that let you select seats
using a seating chart. And they offer Peapod, described earlier.

In short, groceries may be a first-curve business, but Safeway is re-defining itself as a one-stop shop for the daily household, grocery, and food needs of the new consumer.

Lessons Learned

TODAY'S CONSUMERS come bearing change, all right. The market they're influencing is characterized by faster response to their needs, more choices for them, and new and multiple channels with a different value proposition where you earn customer loyalty daily by providing not only quality and price, but service with a smile to boot. The second curve is leading every segment of the market, not only traditional grocery retailing, but financial services, telecommunications, entertainment, health care, and on and on, and responsiveness to consumers will be critical to the success of any second-curve actor.

But they can also teach you some things, if you're alert, in particular the following key lessons.

BE ACTIVE, NOT PASSIVE

Most first-curve businesses treat consumers as not much more than fodder for their product; behind closed doors, they often talk about consumers in just those terms—a big mistake. Second-curve companies, on the other hand, generally embrace the consumer, are driven by—and even passionate about—his or her needs, wants, and aspirations. This characteristic is critical in recognizing second-curve companies as well as second-curve consumers: they're active, not passive; they don't sit back and take it. They're out there looking for value and they'll act aggressively to make sure they get it.

ADDRESS THE PARADOX CREATED BY
TODAY'S CONSUMERS

The second curve created by today's consumers has companies between a rock and a hard place. Marketing and selling are increasingly complicated processes: vendors are trying to sell their products (or services) by reaching out to consumers—even courting them—through a wide range of channels. At the same time, consumers are demanding that the products be made available faster, and that those products be both higher in quality and lower in cost. So as the complexity of the process increases, the cost of the product has to decrease, and that's a difficult balancing act to pull off. Technology offers some help, but it doesn't solve the problem. Organizations will have to be more and more creative in developing ways to overcome this paradox—for example, by turning the customer into a data entry clerk as Charles Schwab is doing with their StreetSmart software.

GIVE YOUR PEOPLE THE SIGNAL TO SERVE

It's a cliché that people respond to incentives, but it's true when it comes to customer service. You have to back up the exhortation to serve the customer with the training, empowerment, and incentives to do what it takes. It's not just Nordstrom and Wal-Mart doing this; it is Intuit in personal financial software, PacifiCare in health care, and Federal Express in shipping.

THERE IS NO SAFE HARBOR

It's often tempting for first-curve players to sit back and say, "This can't touch us." But the combination of new consumers and new technologies will, most likely, ferret out first-curve sleepy hollows wherever they may be. It's happened to hardware stores with the advent of Home Depot, it's happened to coffee shops with the advent of Starbucks. It's happened to banks, and to airlines and health care companies. Don't assume you're immune to the second-curve consumer or the second-curve technology simply because you're playing successfully on the first curve.

The New Frontier:
Growth in Emerging Markets

THE MARKETPLACE OF TODAY is a far cry from the market-place of the past, even the recent past. The political and economic changes of the last decade have transformed and expanded markets, turning them from local markets to global markets, and turning consumers from local to global as well. Together these shifts—the rise of new global consumers and of new global competitors—have changed the terms of trade in the new global marketplace.

The second curve belongs to emerging markets, but that isn't as simple as it sounds. The transition to those markets is difficult because the first curve holds much of the revenue, most of the capital, and a disproportionate share of the consumption—but the second curve has all the potential for growth, just as it does where new technology and new consumers are concerned.

The Global Consumer Explosion

THE GLOBAL CONSUMER EXPLOSION is the result of extremely large countries like China, India, Indonesia, Brazil, and Russia emerging from decades of poverty for reasons as varied as changes in market or political philosophies (or, in the case of South Africa, a somewhat smaller country, joining the global economy after apartheid). We know that the emergence of new large and vibrant economies will radically alter the global consumer landscape; what's uncertain is the trajectory of these growth markets, and the specific location of the growth within the countries and regions.

Emerging Markets

ANY REVIEW OF GROWTH in economies around the world indicates that sometime in the next century the markets of Asia will come to dominate the global scene. China, in particular, will dominate, and will grow into the largest economy in the world some time in the twenty-first century, barring major dislocations such as the cultural revolution of the 1960s. India too will grow as an economy, partly because of its huge population, and partly because of the liberalization of its policies and the capitalization on decades of investment in education, at least for the highly educated middle class, which in and of itself is the size of some large countries. And Indonesia, an overlooked giant with over 200 million people, is emerging rapidly as a world force and will be a significant factor in the Asian scene in the long run. The rise of the Four Tigers—South Korea, Singapore, Taiwan, and Hong Kong—is well documented. But beyond that there are really many new tigers within these emerging giants: Shanghai, the Pearl River Delta, and others will be city or state economies in and of themselves, with very rapid growth potential. We'll look closely at each of these Asian emerging markets in this chapter.

Latin America—Brazil in particular—is also becoming a major player. Latin American countries have gone through times when it was fashionable to focus on them as potential markets, but now the sheer scale and the embracing of market mechanisms clearly heralds a potential for significant growth.

The situation in Eastern Europe and the former Soviet Union is much more difficult: less difficult toward the Western European border, more difficult as one thinks about the future of Russia.

And there are cities and countries that are less impressive in their total population and total economic statistics, but that will nevertheless be absolute lightning rods for future development, in the way that Hong Kong and Singapore have been in the last thirty years. Vietnam, Thailand, and Malaysia are all experiencing rapid growth and will continue to be important anchors in the Asian economy of the future and the source of new global middle-class consumers.

If you look at any of these markets, the logical approach is to think about a progression, a path of development where markets move from emerging developing country status through a wave of industrialization to the maturity of an advanced economy. Japan today is a benchmark, and South Korea is where Japan was twenty years ago. Hong Kong is where Japan was twenty-five years ago, and so forth. Using that line of thinking as a model for emerging markets is correct in part: industrialization is clearly part of the development strategy of India and China and the other giants we've mentioned. But it would be false to assume that the extrapolation will be that pure and simple, for the following three reasons.

First, simply applying nineteenth-century industrial capitalism to the other 5 billion people in the world is a frightening prospect for the global environment. Pollution levels march side by side with urbanization and industrialization (at least through the industrialization phase; an information economy may be more environmentally friendly). But it's important to note the experience of London in the 1950s, when a ton of coal burned in a domestic grate was two hundred times more polluting than a ton of coal burned in a well-controlled industrial plant with appropriate scrubber technology. The prospect of rampant industrialization in the developing countries is frightening from an environmental point of view because of the drain on natural resources (such as the deforestation of the Amazonian Rain Forest) and the pollution and global warming effects of cities, factories, and transportation. This is of particular concern in China, with its 1.2 billion in rapidly industrializing population and its massive coal reserves.

Second, there is the potential for leapfrogging: certain countries may simply jump over stages. The skipped stage could have to do with their application of technology, or with their missing out on certain dimensions of the development cycle. For example, it's inconceivable that the cities of Asia will follow California's route, where everyone has an automobile as a personal means of transportation. Cities already clogged by traffic—Shanghai, Beijing, and Bangkok, for example—could never absorb 20 or 30 million car-using residents. So it's likely that they'll find new mass transit solutions, new solutions for the development of densely urban areas. The sheer scale of these cities is astonishing, and quite unlike that of the developed nations of Europe and North America. We marvel at New York and London, and yet the prospect of megacities in Asia—*cities with 25 to 35 million people*—is very real.

The third reason has to do with the contrast in the recent success of China versus Russia as an emerging economic power. Bill Overholt, the author of *The Rise of China: How Economic Reform Is Creating a New Superpower* and a managing director for Bankers Trust based in Hong Kong, writes that the rise of China is not about the embracement of free enterprise and democracy simultaneously, but about the adoption of market forces as a mechanism for raising wealth and the standard of living within the framework of a command-and-control totalitarian communist state. His argument (and it's one that seems to be supported by others) suggests that it is impossible to build a mature economy from the roots of a developing country without strong central control. The histories of Taiwan, South Korea, Singapore, and Hong Kong certainly suggest that market dynamism coupled with the absence of democratic institutions has been a successful route for growth.

This is troublesome to those of us who regard democracy as a cornerstone of civilization, but it is hard to argue against the historical evidence. The debacle in Russia in large measure is a result of granting freedoms without the necessary strength of institutions to reinforce those freedoms. The question for the long run will be whether such strategies for development are acceptable to the global community: Will the global community give China, Indonesia, and India latitude to develop in environments where democratic institutions are at least on their way to being established, if not sanctified? This is a long-term key geopolitical challenge, and it may be a mediating factor in the relative growth of these economies. It also speaks to the broader question of whether or not the western archetype of development (which is capitalism, coupled to democratically based government and accountable institutions such as stock markets) is really a model that will play out in all developed nations of the future. It seems more likely that these Asian economies will, for at least the next twenty years, and probably far longer, have a very distinct pattern of development, one that is a blend of Asian institutions and global market competitiveness, rather than an emulation of traditional North American or European democratic states.

First-Curve Countries

THE MAJOR FIRST-CURVE COUNTRIES are the United States, the countries of the European Community, and Japan. Examples of second-tier players within the first curve are the Four Tigers: Singapore, Taiwan, Hong Kong, and South Korea. The Four Tigers are virtually accepted as first-curve; the only limitation is that they are relatively small individual states. But as exporters, they are powerful. The total of the Four Tigers' 1994 exports is 10.2 percent of the world's exports, while the United States's exports represent 12 percent.

The sum of the populations of South Korea, Singapore, and Hong Kong is 20 percent of the United States's, or 4.5 percent of China's. Each of the Four Tigers opened its markets to foreign competition, forcing the local companies to adapt to very competitive markets. The Four Tigers are extremely successful, but have not as yet broken through into the consciousness of the world as part of the first-curve mainstream.

Second-Curve Countries

THE KEY EMERGING SECOND-CURVE COUNTRIES include China, India, Indonesia, Brazil, Russia, and South Africa. Some, like China and Russia, are newly open to market forces and have pent-up demand for the fruits of the market. Some, like Brazil, are shifting gears from decades of political volatility and rampant inflation. Protectionism has also played a role, as it has in Indonesia. South Africa is a "redeveloping" country, trying to build a new economy with a sophisticated but protected white economy in a fully integrated society. The markets of all of the second-curve countries share the following characteristics:

THEY ARE EXTREMELY LARGE MARKETS

With the exception of South Africa—with 45 million people—all of the second-curve markets have enormous populations. The global PC industry has discovered the second-curve countries. According to *Forbes*, emerging economies accounted for 25 percent of the almost $100 billion global PC market in 1995. Hewlett-Packard went from virtually nothing in emerging markets in 1980 to $3 billion in sales in 1995.

THEY ARE COMMITTED TO GROWTH
ON A WORLD STAGE

All of the emerging second-curve markets seem committed to growth through competitive participation in a global market. Some analysts argue that this is the direct result of the demise of the complex and inefficient trade arrangements in the communist bloc. When the wall fell, the market opened. Once opened, huge populations get exposed to the fruits of market, and there's no turning back. The power of cumulative causation sets in: growing trade fuels incomes fuels domestic consumption fuels competitiveness.

THEY ARE RUNNING HUGE TRADE AND
FOREIGN EXCHANGE SURPLUSES

These countries are now running large positive trade and foreign exchange balances which will increasingly put them in the driver's seat in the twenty-first century. They will be able to save, invest, and, in some cases, jump ahead to a leadership position through investment in R&D. For example, China has made a commitment to grow its high technology sector over the next decade.

China

CHINA IS WITHOUT A DOUBT a second-curve country, but it is a country with an important link to the first curve of capitalism. Three of the Four Tigers—Singapore, Taiwan, and Hong Kong (which, in 1997, will become part of China)—are actually market-oriented outlets for overseas Chinese, bridges from mainland China to the West. China as a state has made it clear that it is going to become a world player, but it is more realistically the Chinese people—extended Chinese families throughout Asia and North America—who are the real second curve.

There is only one China. Across Asia, the Chinese people have shared a common culture that crosses borders and millennia. For thousands of years China has been at the center and the forefront of the global economy. Emperors of China held sway over the largest, most powerful economy up until the time of the Industrial Revolution. For more than a hundred years China has been a struggling giant, first as a colonial backwater, then as a communist state trying to feed its millions. Since 1978, China has been on a new path combining the power of market forces with monolithic communist control. Today's China is a vibrant and uneasy combination of new market dynamism and old communist command and control, in the process of evolving from a third world state.

The market is fueling growth. The creation of wealth and new consumers is increasing the desire for freedom of all sorts. Beijing has felt it necessary to reassert economic control periodically to cool down the overheated growth spots. It has done this recently in the special economic zone of Hainan Island, where the central government basically halted construction to stop a rampant speculative real estate boom. What is often missed by Western business leaders is a critical understanding of the extent to which politics takes precedence over economics. The latter is definitely subservient to the former, clearly illustrated by the willingness of Chinese authorities to put their relationship with the United States at risk by directing missiles against nearby Taiwanese for varying political reasons.

Paradoxically, this uneasy blend of command and control coupled with market forces is culturally compatible with Chinese history and Confucian philosophy. For the Chinese, there are five key levels of relationships that govern behavior and beliefs. In descending order of importance, they are emperor to subject (read boss to employee), father to son, brother to brother, husband to wife, friend to friend. An understanding of these relationships explains difficult facets of Chinese culture, such as the acceptance of control by seemingly despotic leaders, the power of extended families, and the incredible difficulty experienced by non-Chinese in trying to break into the Chinese economy.

China may be difficult to understand, but ignoring it in the twenty-first century is myopic, dangerous, and just plain stupid. Sometime early in the next millennium, China will be the largest economy on the planet. It will *be* the second curve. The greater China economy of Hong Kong, Taiwan, and China itself is already an enormous economic bloc that rivals the economy of Europe in its scale of economic interdependence. For example, the top five investors in mainland China in 1994 were Hong Kong and Macao ($20.2 billion); Taiwan ($3.29 billion); the United States ($2.49 billion); and Japan ($2.08 billion). Hong Kong and Taiwan together account for ten times the U.S. investment.

While Taiwan and Hong Kong have enjoyed rapid economic growth for thirty years in the 5-to-10-percent range per annum, over the last decade—and most particularly in the last five years—China has experienced double-digit real economic growth on a very large population base. Not only are the scale and rate of growth impressive, but knowledgeable sources inside and outside China believe that the size of the China economy is understated by anywhere from 40 to 140 percent. There are three reasons for this:

The Iron Rice Bowl

China is still a communist country trying to feed and house its 1.2 billion-plus citizens. China's basic agricultural economy, like that of many developing countries, is undercounted in official statistics. In addition, workers in state-owned housing pay nominal rents. For professionals in China's bureaucracy, these rents can be as low as a few dollars a month. The real value of these rents is not accounted for. As real incomes rise for these families, they can't afford to leap to private real estate, which is as pricey as anywhere in the world, but the impact on the disposable income of these households is enormous. Chinese department stores are full of consumer goods catering to the basic consumer needs of an increasingly affluent Chinese population, one that's most dramatically present not just in the special economic zones of coastal China, but in Beijing, Shanghai, and the other major cities as well.

The Wild East

Those special economic zones have to be seen to be believed. Shenzhen is a city of about 3 million people on the northern border of Hong Kong's New Territories. It didn't exist fifteen years ago, but today you see huge skyscrapers, fancy hotels, and a myriad of factories. And a strip some 80 miles long in the Pearl River Delta, an area that extends far beyond the boundary of the special economic zone, is experiencing similar growth and development. Fueled by capital and know-how mostly from Hong Kong, but some of it originating in Taiwan and the U.S., Shenzhen and the Pearl River Delta have a Wild West flavor. The smell of growth is everywhere: BMWs make U-turns on the freeway, factories couple sophisticated manufacturing technology with labor drawn from the poorest regions of China. In many of these factories, unofficial production runs generated outside the gaze of the ministries or the joint venture partners take place for local consumption, making these new Chinese entrepreneurs rich.

Statistical Management of Growth

For all the economic dynamism, China is still a communist country and a planned economy. Planners need to be right. Therefore, they'll manage the statistics to ensure that what they said would happen actually happens. Chinese statistics need to be taken with a grain of salt and always with the realization that overall statistics are meaningless to a decision to invest in an economic market hot spot such as Shanghai, which may be growing manyfold faster than the national average.

China is committed to a growth path not only to improve the lot of its citizens, but to take its place as a major economic force in the global community. When looking at the future of China, you have to do it from three perspectives:

The Perspective Outside China and Asia. To Westerners, China is both an enormous opportunity and an enormous threat—a classic second-curve situation. On one hand, China is moving to a stage where it will become fabulously wealthy in terms of gross consumer products, just because of the sheer weight of numbers. On the other hand, its potential as a competing producer of those products is staggering. The area outside Shanghai has grown from almost nothing in the space of the last ten years to be one of the largest economic forces on the planet. Lord Young, former chairman of Cable & Wireless, describes it as the engine room of the twenty-first century.

The Perspective of the Hong Kong Chinese. The entrepreneurs of Hong Kong, many of them former Shanghai residents, have been instrumental in providing capital and know-how to help build the special economic zones of coastal China. Some of the money has flowed from the U.S. and even from Taiwan through Hong Kong to help build a viable modern industrial base. Since 1985, when all of the major dislocations took place on the anticipation of the deal to restore sovereignty over Hong Kong to China, people have made adjustments. They have chosen sides and locations, and they have made peace with themselves as to how they'll deal with the uncertainty. There is no uncertainty, at one level, about Hong Kong after 1997. The uncertainties have to do with the degree to which Hong Kong will be the central gateway to the Western world and the global market, and whether or not Shanghai and other coastal cities will take a larger and more prominent role vis à vis Hong Kong. These are key questions for the leaders of business, academia, and government in Hong Kong and Beijing, although it is clear that the colonial government's role is to ensure transition. Its role in future governments is already minimal. There is no uncertainty that the Chinese are taking over. What is uncertain is how much emphasis Hong Kong will have in a country of two systems, and what the degree of Beijing's commitment will be to the agreed fifty years of Hong Kong's lifestyle.

The Perspective of the Chinese Themselves. We have to start by stating that there isn't only one Chinese view. On one level there is only one China, but on another level there are many Chinas, made up of many factions, regions, ministries, and families vying for position in a complex (and polyglot) economy. It's difficult for everyone, even high-level Chinese, to predict how such a complex society will unfold. And it isn't that they're not telling; they just don't know.

All of these factors help to make China a classic second-curve player. It is, and will continue to be, important. Nobody knows exactly how large or how important, although you don't have to get too specific on growth rate numbers. Across a wide range of assumptions, China is a big deal. The economy could slow to high single digits, or it could accelerate; either way China becomes a major powerhouse within ten to fifteen years. It cannot be ignored.

India

LIKE CHINA, India is a population giant; it has close to a billion people, and higher population growth than China. As with most second-curve countries, India's uncertainties are political. The country has experienced numerous political turnovers of ruling parties with marked ideological differences, and will most likely continue that way, although most parties are spending less time criticizing the reforms, and are beginning to accept the fact that India needs private investment—including that coming from foreign sources. Political parties are still a long way from complete agreement; there are many different ideas about how far to go.

The country has been a protected market, with its economic growth constrained by its basic distrust of market forces. From the 1950s through the 1970s, the government took it upon itself to oversee lending and industrial planning. The country has tried to present itself as a country that is relaxing its restrictions, but that's difficult to believe. There are, for example, still limitations on foreign ownership. While the liberalization in 1991 did away with the majority of India's industrial and trade licensing—a move that fueled the private sector significantly—it is the public sector that holds about 50 percent of the industrial capacity, and that sector has been neither privatized nor given more autonomy.

With liberalization under way, the sheer scale of India has attracted infrastructure investment, but the country remains a difficult place to do business, for several reasons:

Uneasy Alliances: The Indian Government and Foreign Investors

India doesn't make things easy for foreign investors. While it's true that foreign investment has increased at an incredible rate—1994 saw $950 million, while the first four months of 1995 alone brought in $700 million—foreign investors say that although getting approvals at high levels is becoming easier, there are significant obstacles further down, obstacles that often involve bribes. Politicians have, at times, seemed inclined to transform an Indian uneasiness about foreign capitalists into a more general anger at foreign evil; the government itself seems to have mixed feelings about allowing foreign investors to take a role in India's economy. The government of Maharashtra, for example, which claims almost one-fourth of India's incoming investments, canceled a $2.8 billion power station project to which the previous administration had a firm commitment—this after Texas gas company Enron, which was contracted to build and run the power station, had invested about $300 million. The reason that the state's Hindu Nationalist ministers gave was that the government had to block foreign attempts to corrupt and take over India, an explanation that was met with widespread support, as there were some legitimate questions about the manner in which the contract was granted. In September of 1995, as a result of local businessmen's concerns that the cancellation would damage Maharashtra's power security and discourage potential investors (the state depends on industries that are energy-intensive), the government of Maharashtra announced a willingness to reexamine negotiations, and Enron has identified areas in which it could consider change. But as a result of the government's ambivalence, investors are increasingly wary.

The Complexity of Culture

Cultural differences have dramatic effects on market success. A political party in Bangalore threatened to destroy Kentucky Fried Chicken locations, saying that KFC forces an unhealthy diet on naive Indian citizens. As a result of objections by environmentalists and social activists, Dupont moved a nylon plant; similar voices are arguing against a paper plant built by Indonesian Sina Mas.

Whom to Trust?

Like most second-curve economies, India is known for corruption. There have been accusations of underworld financing of politicians, and Maharashtra's Bharatiya Janata Party says they have evidence of phone calls made to smugglers in Dubai by former Congress state government ministers. A 1993 West Bengal explosion initially attributed to a terrorist was subsequently found to be the result of an accident in a small bomb factory run by a member of the ruling Marxist party, and it is known that gangster types have commandeered polling booths and stuffed ballot boxes, causing politicians to fight back with their own respective gangsters. The "practice" eventually found its way into the patronage network and even secured government contracts and agencies in some states. Some of the neophyte gangsters have even ended up as politicians.

Shaky Institutions

The country has also suffered a judiciary erosion. Delays in the legal system are more than common; murderers are more likely to die of old age than by execution. Known crime lords become community leaders and potentially political forces. In 1991 police arrested two people suspected of running an illegal foreign exchange transaction ring. The suspects' diary noted payments from several prominent politicians—including Rajiv Gandhi—as well as top bureaucrats. And yet nothing was done; no one was arrested, no one protested. Finally, when, in 1994, the Supreme Court had been advised of the incident, the police were ordered to take action. A minor politician has been questioned, but no one really believes anything will happen to him, and certainly not anytime soon. The belief seems to be that police action is linked mostly to political expediency far more than it is to guilt or innocence.

There are signs of change, however, and while India certainly has evidence of the problems of an emerging second-curve giant, there are signs of growth as well. The automotive market is an area that is seeing a lot of activity. American and Japanese companies in particular are eager to enter the Indian automotive market, and are doing so successfully. The question is often how much their stake is. In September 1995, both Ford and Honda announced plans for joint ventures with Indian companies. Ford, whose planned venture is with Mahindra & Mahindra, a large Indian engineering group, waived its usual call for a majority stake and settled for a fifty-fifty split with Mahindra, purchasing 6 percent of the family-controlled group's main company as well. Ford hopes to begin assembly of 25,000 Escorts in 1996 at an existing Mahindra plant, then open a new fully integrated factory by the end of 1998 to produce 100,000 Fiestas a year.

Education and Competing Claims

Fueling the rise of India as a second-curve power is education. While the percentage of secondary school–aged children in school increased by 18 percentage points from 1970 to 1991, from 26 percent to 44 percent, there are concerns that education is not a high enough priority for the mass of the population. Recent elections saw competition among political parties to promise increased subsidies (for farmers, for example) which leave less money for education, health, and the basic infrastructure.

The competing political claims from the traditional first curve of rural India will inhibit the emergence of India as a second-curve competitor. But they will be only a delaying factor. India will be an important second-curve actor in the twenty-first century.

Indonesia

INDONESIA HAS ENJOYED an open economy for longer than China, and the percentage of eligible children enrolled in secondary education increased by 29 percentage points in eleven years, from 16 percent in 1980 to 45 percent in 1991. China's percentage in 1991 was 51, suggesting the possibility that Indonesia is another Asian giant poised for second-curve success. But it hasn't taken off yet; there have been several false starts, and there are several explanations as to why.

Politics and Family

The dominance of family-owned firms and corruption is a key constraint. The Suharto family rules firmly with strong support from the government, with human rights reportedly less protected today than they were under Dutch colonial rule. Suharto's family owns the large companies and controls foreign contracts, a situation that some label "crony capitalism." The country has tried to encourage and help some winners, such as aerospace. This protectionist, import-substitution approach has been the downfall of many second-curve wanna-bes in Latin America. But overall a traditional group of economists has established a framework for growth, focusing on macroeconomic stability and opposing subsidies.

Monopolies and Nontariff Barriers

Many monopolies and nontariff barriers protect basic products. Sugar, for example, sells in Indonesia at 17 percent above the world price. Migas, the Directorate General of Oil and Natural Gas, is trying to change legislation that controls downstream oil and gas operations in the hope of encouraging private and foreign participation. As of March 1995, there were only 1,490 gas stations throughout the archipelago, so that drivers often had to buy low-quality gas mixed with kerosene from street vendors. According to a U.S. embassy report on the oil industry, domestic refinery capacity can no longer meet demands, and imports of liquid fuels are increasing rapidly; 45.3 million barrels of oil were imported in 1993, an 18.3 percent increase over the previous year. The government forecasts consumption of fuel oils to be at 54.6 million kiloliters by 2000, and at 67.5 million kiloliters by mid-2004.

The marketing and distribution of oil products is controlled by Pertamina, the state-owned oil company. Oil prices are set by the government, which keeps them artificially low. Kerosene costs $0.12 a liter in Indonesia, $0.31 in Thailand, and $0.23 in the Philippines. Diesel fuel costs $0.16 a liter in Indonesia, while in Malaysia and Thailand it costs $0.23 and $0.27 respectively.

While private and foreign investment in refining is allowed, it's not very appealing to private investors without the ability to set market prices. And, according to regulations, privately owned refineries can only produce for export or sell to Pertamina, although foreign companies are involved in some of the process upstream, such as drilling and exploration. In anticipation of deregulation, more than thirty companies have applied to build refineries, although not one of the twelve approved since 1993 has gotten very far. The government continues to make clear its opposition to opening up the retail sector to foreign investment. Changing Pertamina's status and phasing out subsidies are both politically sensitive.

But despite these constraints, there are signs of growth. A new gas field off the Natuna Islands, which could be operated for up to thirty years, is being developed, but some feel that increasing real wages will make Indonesia's labor-intensive industries such as textiles uncompetitive, and will slow down investment in medium-density industries like electronics. What the country needs, the technologists say, is a new comparative advantage in high technology products like aircraft. The ministers known as technocrats disagree; they want government out of industry. The World Bank agrees, stating recently that nonmarket investments in technology, such as Indonesia's airliner, have been expensive and ineffective.

Indonesia has let foreigners invest in its stock market, which, having been developed early in the country's larger economic development, is strong. That strength has let companies raise money without heavy borrowing. In September 1995 Indonesia's central bank announced new regulations intended to increase accountability in banking, after the release of figures that showed that bad debts at state banks increased between April and June.

Indonesia has a large population base, a wealth of natural resources, and some of the key underpinnings for second-curve market growth, such as an increasingly educated workforce and a strong stock market. But, like most second-curve economies, Indonesia is vulnerable to political intervention in the market and to the corrupt practices of a tightly controlled political regime.

Brazil

LIKE INDONESIA, Brazil is a country rich in natural resources, but its political and social systems are weak. The country has been unable to set up a constitution that will last longer than ten years, and has historically been unable to control inflation. Since 1979, Brazil has had five currencies, thirteen finance ministers, twenty-seven austerity plans, and fifty-nine price-control measures.

In Brazil there is, again, a distrust of foreigners and a discrimination

against foreign investment and ownership. Tariff barriers protect domestic business—a strong contrast to the very different and very successful approach of the Four Tigers. High local-content laws mean
that Brazil has difficulty producing cars, and the computer industry
lags behind the rest of the world, which means that businesses use
outdated technology.

The country has witnessed huge social inequalities and dramatic
ideological clashes between government turnovers. While land reform has been promised since colonial times, estimates of the non-
landowning poor are as high as 12 million. But whatever the number,
the government's promise to settle 280,000 families on 27 million
acres can't help much.

In Brazil, the issue of education is still a minus rather than a plus.
The percentage of eligible secondary school–aged children enrolled in
education was 39 percent in 1991, the lowest of the countries discussed
here, although the education minister is working for improvements.
He's requested an additional 12 billion reals (approximately $11 bil-
lion) from congress for elementary education, and he has plans for tele-
vised training (by satellite) for teachers at 46,000 schools.

In terms of health care, Brazil spends $80 per person annually on
public health, less than a third as much as Argentina. The health
minister has gained backing from some of his colleagues for a 0.25
percent health tax on banking transactions.

Brazil's taxes are high and difficult to understand. There are fifty-
six separate taxes levied by federal, state, and local authorities, with
some hitting goods all along the production and distribution line.
According to Marcus Pratini de Moraes, head of the exporters' association, taxes are Brazil's biggest export, passing coffee and rolled
steel, and representing $8.5 billion on top of the $43 billion of goods
exported. The total tax burden is at a record level of 31.5 percent of
GDP, up from 24 percent in the mid-1980s. Tax evasion is very popular, so that those who do end up paying, such as large companies,
tend to feel that they carry more than their fair share.

And yet there is change. Inflation is more or less under control. In
mid-1994 prices were rising at 40 to 50 percent a month, but toward
the end of 1995, they were hardly rising each month. Brazil's currency, the real, was a year old in July of 1995 and it's still going
strong. There are other signs as well:

President Fernando Cardoso's government is attempting to open up
the economy by trying to pass constitutional reforms that would free
up the market and that are needed to keep inflation down and to en-

courage growth. And congress is examining proposals that would reform government monopolies and privatize other sectors. Taxation and social security reforms are also in the works. In June 1995, amendments that would open telecommunication to private sector franchisees and move to end Petrobras's oil monopoly made progress. Petrobras runs all of Brazil's oil business "above the gas pump," meaning before the gas reaches the pump, and including exploration, production, and refining. Set up forty years ago to defy the oil majors, using the phrase *The oil is ours*, Petrobras gives good service and is still an emotive issue.

Another sign of opening up the economy is Brazil's participation in Mercosur, the customs union that Paraguay, Argentina, Uruguay, and Brazil are trying to develop. But the trade account went negative for seven consecutive months during 1995, and Cardoso responded by curbing car imports. These actions followed large rises in tariffs, on cars and many other consumer goods, imposed earlier in the year.

There are signs of more confidence in the economic prospects of Brazil. Persio Arida, governor of the central bank and one of the designers of the antiinflation plan that brought Cardoso to power, resigned in May 1995. He was a scourge of the ill-run banks owned by Brazil's constituent states. Pressure from São Paulo state provoked his fall, and there was sufficient confidence in Cardoso that the markets did not move. Twelve multinationals are planning to spend $8 billion by 2000, and in July 1995 Volkswagen decided to build a new factory close to Rio de Janeiro. The plant will build trucks and buses and will bring the state $250 million in direct investments and 1,800 jobs.

Like China, India, and Indonesia, Brazil has a huge population and some of the key conditions for long-term economic success. It will be a key second-curve economy in the twenty-first century—unless it shoots itself in the foot through political mismanagement.

Russia

RUSSIA HAS LARGE AMOUNTS of natural resources, particularly oil and gas. Its territory is huge, and the country is well placed geographically. But it has many hurdles in terms of growth. The legal system is disorderly, taxes are huge and unpredictable, and the country suffers from political instability: in October of 1993 parliament and the government were unable to come to agreement without military intervention—tanks fired into the parliament building. Obviously, there is much work to be done.

One of corporate Russia's first tasks is the shift to real business, where companies meet customer demands and finance themselves; so far, the model has been more along the lines of production associations. Efficiency isn't yet a characteristic of Russian manufacturing: Russia's largest automobile maker—and unfortunately its most efficient—Avtovaz, manufactures its Lada (in essence an old Fiat) in 450 man-hours; to put that in perspective, it's important to know that Toyota produces a car in less than 15 man-hours. Reliability is lacking as well; it's said that you should be sure that the gear box is attached to the gear shift when you buy a new car. Part of Avtovaz's problems is too much, too little, too late: too many workers, too few models, and too little factory improvement.

The news is not much better in the banking industry, where liquidity is a question—a serious question, as evidenced in August 1995 when Russia's Interbank loan system shut down, thanks to a faulty modem, which caused a reputable bank to miss a payment. In response Russian banks frantically tried selling treasury bills as a way to increase cash, but all that did was to increase yields—and the central bank took a while to respond. There were around 2,500 banks in Russia prior to this crisis, but they will probably lose around 100 banks as a result.

The Russian stock market is a bit of a bumpy ride. In September 1994, the ROS index (the Russian equivalent of the Dow Jones) of Russian shares hit its high, then dropped 75 percent by February 1995 (though it did start a gradual recovery). Political unrest can take the credit for some of that fall, but there was more to it than that: a certain laissez-faire attitude of Russian firms toward their investors. Being a shareholder can be a little iffy: payment on dividends is uncommon, in part because managers like to hang on to the cash because of the high taxes. And some firms don't bother getting their shareholders' okay before issuing new equity. In 1995, the Primorsky Shipping Company made an unauthorized issue of shares to a subsidiary—and doubled its share capital.

Buying shares is no easy task for several reasons. First, there is no market in the shares of 90 percent of privatized firms. Foreigners must receive a bank's permission before they are able to invest. The same is true of Gazprom, a large energy company, only Gazprom takes things a bit further: if shareholders want to sell, Gazprom can deny that. No wonder that its shares aren't traded much. The prices of shares in other companies fluctuate dramatically, with bid offers even as far apart as 100 percent. The process of buying shares is a little unusual: men holding a sign indicating that they will buy shares stand outside factory gates, and there are no share certificates. Proof of ownership resides with the company's share register, which is, of course, company domain, and no sure thing. An aluminum smelter in Krasnoyarsk simply removed a shareholder the company viewed as less than desirable from the books, and that was that.

The oil industry is one that would seem to invite foreign investment, and while it's true that Western oil companies are interested in Russia's large known oil reserves, there are, once again, problems. Russian oil fields are in parts of the country that are difficult to work in, for example. And state-owned Transneft, which operates Russia's oil pipelines, is known for graft, with bribes for pipeline access at around $2 to $3 a ton early in 1995.

And yet, there is change. Manufacturing is seeing both growth and progress. In 1994, former Soviet minister Nikolai Pugin was given charge of Gaz, which used to make mobile launches for Soviet missiles. Under Pugin's direction, the company now produces the Gazel, a 1.5-ton truck, with 14,000 sold by the end of 1994, and 1995 projections at 75,000. Gaz manufacturing runs six days a week, three shifts a day, and the company estimates that demand for the trucks could soon be as high as 300,000 annually.

There are changes in other areas as well. In 1995, Russian companies were required to issue audited accounts for their annual general meetings, a move that enabled investors to compare accounts. A new securities law gives the Federal Commission for Securities and Capital Markets increased authority and clarifies shareholders' rights and violations. And the National Registry Company, a joint venture between the Bank of New York, the European Bank for Reconstruction and Development, the International Finance Corporation, Unexim, and Nikoil (a subsidiary of Russian oil company Lukoil), operating since August 1995, is handling Lukoil's registration and is negotiating with seventy other companies.

While obviously primitive, the Russian stock market is slowly becoming more sophisticated. Selling and buying shares is getting easier, and more orderly. Stockbrokers quote firm prices for buying and selling shares from screens in Moscow. Their maximum bid offer spread is 20 percent, but trade is growing. The system has been improved to help it process higher volumes and it is being used outside of Moscow.

Liquidity will be improved by the creation of a government-sponsored clearing body, the Deposit Clearing Corporation, which opened during the summer of 1995. A trial scheme has been operating. All DCC participants will have their shares registered in its name, providing they trade with each other, and there will be no name changes at company registries, a policy that saves time and money. The DCC will also reduce risk by transferring shares when it receives payment.

Foreign investors can now bypass Russia's settlement procedures. In March 1995, ING, a Dutch bank, started issuing RDCs, Russian Depository Certificates, the value reflecting the shares by which they are backed. The shares are held in trust by a depository. As of the end of June, seven companies had launched such programs. The home loan market is being expanded. In many other countries, home construction has fueled economic growth.

Russia is carrying out the second phase of the mass privatization program. The first phase, launched in 1993, involved handing shares to ordinary citizens at token prices. The main objective of the second phase is to raise money to help cover the budget deficit. With the concerns about the banking system's liquidity, some analysts wonder if the banking system can support the government-debt market and the privatization sales.

Russia is a classic case of uncertainty about the second curve. It has all the pent-up demand that seventy years of communism brings, but it also has communism's lack of motivated people and appropriate institutions such as stock markets and legal and accounting systems capable of supporting second-curve growth. However, its major weakness is political. If Russia can develop some political stability to support these market institutions over the next decade, Russia will emerge as a true second-curve market.

South Africa

AS A RESULT of the end of apartheid, South Africa is entering the world economy. In April 1994, South Africa's central bank gained constitutional independence from political leaders. Inflation dropped to 9 percent in 1994, the lowest since 1972.

Despite South Africa's membership in the World Trade Organization, numerous trade barriers keep both African and other products from the South African market. South Africa, for example, imposes 90 percent tariffs on Zimbabwean textiles, despite its free access to the Zimbabwean market. Industry is, for the most part, controlled by large conglomerates. An American consultancy estimates that the hourly wage of an assembly worker on a South African automobile line is $5.60, just under the $6 an hour of a Mexican. The problem is that the South African factory requires two and a half times as long to build the car.

Foreign investment by South African companies is restricted by exchange controls, which, in March 1995, were lifted on foreigners but not residents, the result of a concern about money leaving the country. This is hardly the case: mid-1994 to March 1995 saw a net capital inflow of 13 billion rand, a statistic that makes South Africa's economy appealing to investors.

The government's treatment of monopolies is also problematic: it attacks white-run private monopolies, but does not privatize state ones, which are white-run. Blacks control less than 0.5 percent of the stock market, and less than 4 percent of management is black. The lager market is held almost entirely (about 90 percent) by South African Breweries. Pallo Jordan, the minister responsible for Telkom (the state-run telecommunications company), disallows competition between foreign telephone companies and the state-run telephone company, his reason being the protection of black consumers.

The government sends conglomerates mixed messages, alternately complaining about them and hinting at forming new ones. Close examination reveals that five conglomerates control almost 80 percent of the Johannesburg stock market. Control of more than half can be traced to three families.

Violence continues to be a major problem. While majority rule brought a significant decrease in political violence (generally understood to involve black political problems, and occurring in the townships), criminal violence has grown rapidly—and political killings continue. Carjackings increased by a third in 1994; the murder rate in Johannesburg is higher than that of Washington, D.C. In an extreme example, the province of KwaZulu-Natal suffers the murders of tens of people each weekend. Although the crime rate continues to be highest in the townships, urban whites as well as blacks are affected by crime.

There are areas of change, however, including a move toward the equalization of education. In 1994, less than half the black students who took the national school exit exam passed it—although 97 percent of the white children did. State schools, which used to be segregated, are now open to all races. School lunch is provided for small children, and the government has set aside money for emergency repairs.

South Africa is a participant in the Southern African Development Community, an organization of twelve southern African countries that, among other things, hopes to foster a southern African economic community, including free trade by 2000, free movement of people, and a single currency. The organization—specifically South Africa, with its high tariffs and illegal alien policies—has its work cut out for it. But it is a move in the right direction.

A new labor bill, agreed on by business and black trade unions, is encouraging as well. The agreement of the two groups was no small feat: labor was known for its militancy, management for its authoritarianism. It's hoped that the bill will help to make the labor environment more appealing to investors. Commercial banks, while trying to provide banking services to the "unbanked" and depending on technology to lower the costs of banking services, for the moment offer fairly restricted services—mostly savings accounts and home loans.

While not nearly as large in terms of population as the other second-curve economies profiled here, South Africa is an interesting second-curve player. With the demise of apartheid, South Africa will open up to be a new economic force, with an economy that exhibits much of the infrastructure for second-curve growth. With strong political leadership, South Africa can become a key second-curve economy.

The New Global Marketplace

THE COMBINATION of the rise of the middle class in emerging markets and the increased global competition leads to a third dimension of changing geography: the emergence of a new global marketplace. This second-curve global marketplace is characterized by four key dimensions: interdependence, the global value chain, global work, and global scale and scope.

Interdependence

ANY WAY YOU CUT IT, goods and services will be produced in an interdependent way in the future. Knowledge, skills, people, capital, financing, and marketing—all of these components will increasingly come from sources all over the world, with the help of global expertise, and will then be marketed to a global clientele. It's more and more difficult to characterize a product as French or American or German or British. Not only are the national companies of these countries increasingly sourcing, operating, and manufacturing on a global basis; the markets financing these companies and their shareholders are increasingly globalized as well. The dimension of ownership and control hasn't been as advanced in terms of the global marketplace, but, as financial services markets increasingly operate on an interdependent global basis, it probably will be further advanced by 2010.

Evidence of the global dimensions of the second-curve marketplace are all around us, in all three aspects—the rise of global consumers, increased global competitors, and the global marketplace. Herewith a few examples.

My Visit to Prague

A FEW YEARS AGO, the World Health Organization asked me to attend a meeting in Prague. The only snag was that the meeting was scheduled for the day after I had to be in Mexico City, which meant that I had the delightful experience of flying on Air France from Mexico City via Houston. Now if you've never flown Air France before, there's something you have to understand: they won't let you on unless you agree to smoke. So I got on, and I was sitting next to a lady who had a poodle in her lap, and even the poodle was smoking, and we had a very nice flight and got to Paris and changed planes to what I thought would be another Air France flight, but turned out to be Czechoslovakian Airlines.

I arrived in Prague at 1 A.M. and I figured I was going to have the border guard experience: this was my first visit to Eastern Europe, I carry a British passport, I live in America, and I'd just come from Mexico. I guessed that these facts would probably warrant my being taken into a room and questioned.

The line to get through immigration was relatively short, and within a few minutes I was in front of the immigration official. He had a Toshiba laptop. He punched in my passport number and said, "You can go." I said, "Is that it?" and that was it—very straightforward. I went outside to get a taxi and there was a line of Mercedes taxis. I got in the first taxi and as we drove away from the airport I saw a sign: "Price Waterhouse Welcomes You to Eastern Europe."

That really says everything about the global marketplace. We think about these countries as being so very different, so very strange, and yet once these markets start to emerge, the familiar apparatus of capitalism quickly follows.

Winners in China

WHEREVER YOU GO IN CHINA, you notice two things. The first is that Volkswagen has been incredibly successful: in Beijing it seems as though every car is a Volkswagen Santana or an Audi 100. And the second is the ubiquitous cellular phone—you see it in offices and among businesspeople and leaders. Motorola has been extremely successful in providing products for the wireless marketplace, which enables telecom services to be provided in the absence of a well-established, land-based infrastructure. Motorola China Electronics Limited (MCEL) is one of the emerging giants of the new China, with $2 billion in sales. MCEL expects to triple its workforce from 1995 to 2000, from 3,500 to 10,000.

The Spaceman and the Brain Surgeon

DICK WONG is a forty-something, bespectacled guy dressed like a Chinese Marlboro man, friendly and affable. He lives in Toronto and works in China, commuting on a regular basis to his apartment in Hong Kong, where he spends three to four months at a time without seeing his family. They join him in the summertime, when the kids are out of school, and he makes periodic visits back to Toronto and his wife accompanies him to Hong Kong for a month or so. He's what Hong Kongers call a spaceman.

Every morning, Dick takes the ferry from Hong Kong beyond the second border, which separates the special economic zone of Shenzhen in Guangdong Province from the rest of Guangdong Province. Dick runs a factory in a place called Sianjing, about a twenty-minute car ride from the ferry terminal. The factory is a modest four-story building, and produces about $500 million annually of final product.

What's remarkable about this factory is that it is a leading-edge example of computer-integrated manufacturing. The production lines are making NEC 486 computers, cutting-edge cordless telephones for

Futjitsu, Sega/Genesis 16-bit game machines for the European market, and various forms of consumer electronics. (This factory shares
the passion for quality. Sega has an on-site quality control office in
the factory. Everywhere you looked on the walls there were different
total quality systems: ISO 9000—the European standard, the House
of Quality, and all the different Japanese and European systems of
quality control and quality assurance.) The lines are staffed almost
exclusively by young women, with male technicians and supervisors.
Most of the lines are run using secondhand equipment from Japanese
or other production facilities, but they're tied together in computer-
integrated manufacturing systems, which enables operators to change
the lines in fifteen to thirty minutes. Within half an hour, they can be
making a telephone instead of a computer. The high technology
emerging from a modest four-story building in what appears to be a
developing country is remarkable.

While I was there, one of my colleagues had hurt her leg in a bad
fall in a subway in Hong Kong. Dick Wong turned to his secretary
and asked her to help, then told us that she was a doctor. As it turned
out, not only is she a doctor—she's a brain surgeon from another
province in northwest China. The attraction of the special economic
zone is so great in terms of an opportunity for a better life that it's
better to be a secretary in a factory in a joint-venture private sector
enterprise than a brain surgeon in a remote part of the country.

Global Think Tanks

ONE OF THE WAYS in which large companies can deal with these
second-curve technology, consumer, and geographic markets is to
develop listening posts around the world, which help to synthesize
societal, technological, and economic trends in the global marketplace and bring them to bear on corporate strategy. Cable & Wireless and Daimler-Benz are two of the Institute for the Future's client
companies that have very similar approaches. Each company has established a Silicon Valley outpost in Menlo Park or Palo Alto, close
to our offices. Daimler-Benz has a group of about thirty based in
Berlin who are part of the company's massive thousand-person research department. Every three months, two or three researchers
come to spend time in Palo Alto to work with a core staff based
there. The group is part of a team called Technology and Society,

and they investigate the key aspects of tomorrow's society relevant to Daimler-Benz customers. The leader of the group, Dr. Eckard Minx, and his colleagues are trying to develop alternate scenarios of the future that may be of significance to the various business units within Daimler-Benz. The Institute for the Future has worked with them, trying to think through the twenty-first-century organization, and the ways in which information technology might affect their business, their customers, and the use of transportation systems.

Cable & Wireless has established a similar group, Cable & Wireless Innovations, based in Menlo Park. This group brings together a core staff, with people released from the various business units around the world for various periods of time, anywhere from six weeks to six months. This system enables these up-and-coming managers to be exposed to some of the technology, customer, and global trends that are likely to affect the telecommunications business in the long run, and to have an opportunity to live and work in Silicon Valley, then return to Hong Kong or Britain or the Caribbean with the ideas they've been exposed to, and infuse the business units of their organizations with them.

In both cases, the point is to infuse the organization with the second curve by rotating their researchers or managers, thereby creating a global mentality, an understanding of emerging technologies, and an appreciation of the new consumer among the researchers and future strategists of the organization. For Daimler-Benz, this means rotation through the home office in Berlin, the facility in Palo Alto, and their proposed facility in Singapore. Cable & Wireless is reaching between London, Menlo Park, and Hong Kong to provide a flow of ideas across three continents and many different business cultures. The Institute for the Future has also acted as a Silicon Valley outpost for client companies, in particular for Telia, the Swedish telephone company, as well as for numerous large, U.S.-based organizations that have sought to have an outpost in Silicon Valley connected to the technology communities and to be exposed to ideas, thinking, and trends across a number of different dimensions.

The Rise of the Middle Class in Emerging Markets

THE RISE of middle-class consumers is critical to continued economic growth for the planet. Allowing the wealth to be concentrated

among the few elite simply won't sustain a global economy, in terms
of its capacities for exchange, and in terms of political stability. The
rise of middle-class consumers is a signal of success, both economic
and political, and that rise will be dramatic in the next twenty years.
The net increase in middle-class households will occur on a disproportionate scale in East Asia, which presents enormous opportunities. The second curve here is one that requires careful planning to
participate in because it is difficult to enter these markets without
appropriate relationships, which take time to build.

Economic growth in and of itself isn't enough to signal the rise of
a middle class. If the income distribution (as it has been in many developing countries) is substantially skewed toward a few people making enormous amounts of money and the vast majority of people
living in poverty, significant economic growth really doesn't translate
into consumption and the rise of standard of living for all. The key to
an emerging market's becoming a true second-curve player is the rise
of the middle-class consumers.

First, we need to define "middle-class consumers." The Institute
for the Future uses a definition that has two criteria. Middle-class
consumers means households that have annual earnings of at least
$25,000 (1995 dollars), and that are in countries with potential
groupings of more than one million of these consumers. (See *Future
Tense: Preparing for the Business Realities in the Next Ten Years*, an
earlier work, for a discussion of the growth in these markets over the
next twenty years.) This definition doesn't include all the rich, or
even everyone earning over $25,000. Using this definition, industrial
countries and emerging areas have approximately 181 million households earning more than $25,000 a year. Of these, 79 percent are in
the industrial countries, with 36 percent of the total in North America, 32 percent in Western Europe, and 11 percent in Japan. The rich
industrial countries' middle-class population is growing fairly steadily
over the long run; at current growth rates, it's expanding about 2 percent per year, so that by 2010, the total number of middle-income
households in the industrial world will rise from 143 million to 211
million (IFTF 1992 forecast).

But the real growth will be elsewhere. Each year, the emerging
market areas of the world will have an increasing portion of the
world's middle-income households. Today the emerging countries
have approximately 21 percent of such households, but the numbers
are growing close to 5 percent a year. By the year 2010, if current
growth rates continue, the emerging areas of the world will have 37

percent of all middle-income households, totaling 122 million, almost what the industrial countries have today. As a result, the new emerging middle class from the countries of Asia, Latin America, and Eastern Europe will play an increasing role in the global market in years to come.

The most rapid growth will take place in the countries moving away from socialist restrictions in China, Russia, and Eastern Europe. Fewer restrictions on property ownership, more rewards for entrepreneurial skills, and greater encouragement for wider discrepancies in incomes will open opportunities for the revival of the old middle class and the emergence of new ones. The enormous increase in China, India, Brazil, Indonesia, and Russia has to be a key focus. These countries alone will add significant millions to the rolls of the middle class. With the majority of South Africans rising out of poverty, a new middle class will emerge there, too.

The Global Value Chain

THE PRODUCTION of goods and services isn't the only area that increasingly is globally sourced; you have to think of the value chain on a global basis as well. This creates particular difficulties for companies where the distribution parts of the value chain are so variable. For example, distributing a product in the United States is a very different proposition from distributing a product in Japan. The patterns of retailing, wholesaling, and physical distribution logistics are very different in these countries. Increasingly, then, corporations trying to deal with the second curve of emerging markets have to think about how the value chain operates on a global basis, but also about how it has to be customized for specific markets. This presents very interesting dilemmas for corporations that are trying to standardize globally. Some companies have been extremely successful in building a global value chain, one that overcomes the variations in each country—Coke, Pepsi, and McDonald's, which have become cultural icons in all countries, are leading examples of this. In Beijing, there are twelve McDonald's; the largest is awe-inspiring. Even in the middle of the afternoon, between meals, lines of twenty to thirty customers wait to be helped by perhaps thirty servers, who hand over Big Macs and fries that taste exactly as they do in Milwaukee.

Global Work

AS PRODUCTION AND CONSUMPTION become more interdependent globally, the value chains span the globe, and increasingly the challenge for individuals and organizations is to work on a global basis. This affects everyone and everything from the jet-set businessmen of Hong Kong and the nomadic executives of the popular business media to the practical fact that frontline customer service people are increasingly having to deal with customers and partners from foreign countries. Mary O'Hara-Devereaux and Robert Johansen of the Institute for the Future discuss this in *Global Work*, where they lay out the challenges and solutions of bridging distance, diversity, and time on a global basis. The lessons from their work suggest that greater sensitivity to cultural differences has to be a hallmark of second-curve global businesses as those businesses deal with emerging markets, and that in the future companies will increasingly have to build, as a core competency, their global capacities. The other dimension of global work has been the creation of the information infrastructures for global organization.

Global Scale and Scope

IF THE GLOBAL MARKETPLACE and the emerging markets of the second curve increasingly present the best opportunities, this suggests that in the future corporations will have to be able to operate on a global scale. The question is, does this mean that sheer size matters? In some dimensions, scale will be a factor. In the health care industry—specifically in pharmaceuticals—one of many strategies being adopted is that of global consolidation. In the entertainment business, the megaplayers are starting to concentrate horizontally in anticipation of global scale. And in banking, a good deal of the concentration of financial services will provide global and local efficiencies.

But it would be wrong to suggest that the only logical response to second-curve emerging markets is horizontal integration of global competitors. Rather, global scale and scope really speaks to the need for companies to behave, think, and conceive of their futures in global terms. This is different from sheer size. From its inception, CNN banned the word "foreign" from use by its correspondents, and its international and global reach is evident in every hotel room in the world. The success of companies like Applied Materials, companies that have embraced the global marketplace, is testimony to the fact that sheer scale doesn't mean being global, and, conversely, to be global doesn't mean you have to be huge. It's really an orientation, a mind-set, an understanding that the second curve is going to be out *there*—not necessarily *here*—and that you have to think in global terms.

Levi Strauss is a company that's been good at thinking globally in a couple of ways. Levi's sells their products in more than sixty countries under several kinds of agreements. There are wholly owned and operated businesses, joint ventures, licensees, and distributors. By 1994, the international business accounted for almost half of the company's sales, and more than half of the revenue. Levi's employs individuals in approximately twenty-three countries; the company has fifty-three production facilities and thirty customer service centers in forty-six countries. Generally speaking, the company produces their goods in the countries in which those goods are sold.

But there's more to their story than the numbers, impressive as those are. In an industry that is fraught with ethical dilemmas and misconduct—the apparel industry, known for pursuing cheap labor like the pot of gold at the end of the rainbow—Levi's acts responsibly, exhibiting a sort of *moral* global thinking. The company will not do business with suppliers who violate Levi's Global Sourcing Guidelines, company standards (written in 1992) that specify that companies with whom Levi's contracts must run their businesses in a manner that's compatible with Levi's values. The company has put its money where its mouth is, withdrawing $40 million worth of business from China in protest of human rights violations—a decision that was reached by a unanimous vote. And Levi's enforces International Labor Organization standards, which disallow employing children under the age of fourteen. When two of Levi's Bangladesh contractors admitted hiring children and agreed to fire them, the contractors also explained that working children—usually the oldest children in large single-income families—are often a family's chief source of income. In response, Levi's worked out a deal that said that if the contractors continued to pay wages and consented to rehire the children when they turned fourteen, Levi's would send the children to school and pay the associated costs (e.g., uniforms, books, and tuition). The actual monetary cost to Levi's is fairly small, particularly when you think about what they're gaining in terms of PR. Levi's operates globally with high ethical standards in a world of uneven ethics, managing to play on the second curve without compromising on its principles, and deploying second-curve technology to facilitate its global presence.

A Look at Some Global Players

THE TACTICS AND APPROACHES of global players are as diverse as their businesses and playing fields, from telecommunications in Hong Kong to Swiss chocolate.

Cable & Wireless

WHAT CABLE & WIRELESS is trying to do is really second-curve. They were founded over one hundred years ago, and, despite their name, were instrumental in wiring the British Empire. They radically transformed the planet by laying cable across the Atlantic to enable transatlantic telephone communication, and, similarly, by allowing India to be connected to the British Empire not in a matter of *weeks*, but *hours*. More recently, it's become clear that their strategy is to build a network of telecommunications companies specializing in emerging markets. The model is of interest not only as a model of the twenty-first-century organization, but also as a model of engaging second-curve emerging markets.

The company's origins were in developing a telegraph system that would link Britain with its empire in the second half of the nineteenth century. The company was first known as Eastern Telegraph, and when founder John Pender died in 1886, Eastern and associated companies owned one of every three miles of telegraph cable in the world, and operated over 30,000 miles of submarine cable. The twentieth century brought a change in focus, as telecommunications expanded to include wireless radio communication. In 1929 Eastern merged with Marconi Wireless Telegraphy, and was renamed Cable & Wireless. By World War II, the company was operating in 146 locations, and during the war Cable & Wireless facilities were often the targets of the Luftwaffe. Axis forces took over stations such as Athens, Hong Kong, and Singapore.

In the early 1960s, Cable & Wireless moved into satellites. The company built an earth station on Ascension Island in the South Atlantic to support communications for the Apollo space program, and, in the Caribbean, Cable & Wireless used tropospheric-scatter radio transmissions to provide expanded telephone, telegraph, and telex services. That system was later supplemented by microwave links. In the 1970s, Cable & Wireless expanded its satellite facilities and laid a 300-channel telephone cable from Hong Kong to Canton. They also expanded into Europe and the United States.

Over the next decade, profits grew at an annual rate of 27 percent and the company was able to shed its colonial image as the engineering arm of the Foreign Office. The company began building its global digital highway, an international fiber-optic network that connects the business capitals of North America, Europe, and Asia. In 1982, Cable & Wireless, British Petroleum, and Barclays Merchant Bank formed a company called Mercury Communications as a competitor to British Telecom. In 1984 Cable & Wireless bought out BP and Barclays, and in 1985, Mercury won the right to interconnect with British Telecom, thereby establishing itself as a strong competitor for business-based services.

Cable & Wireless is not, in terms of pure technology, a product business; it's in the business of managing services. Its unique organizational style, which combines loose and tight control, is a very flat organization—a network of peers, not a hierarchy—something that's very much at odds with traditional telephone companies. Telephone companies have historically been the ultimate "machine bureaucracy"—to use a term coined by Henry Mintzberg, Canada's leading organizational theorist—but Cable & Wireless is trying to combine a set of stable, well-run telephone companies in various regions of the world with a corporate parent that can help make strategic investments and help drive innovation through these existing systems. The various members of the network, such as Hongkong Telecom and the Caribbean telephone companies, are first-curve monopolies who often feel, *What do we need them for?* But as telecommunications becomes increasingly competitive, this model of providing independent first-curve business units with autonomy and a chance of global innovation to the second curve simultaneously is a key insight about how to manage on two curves and deal with a second curve in the emerging marketplace. Since 1992, the company has moved from individual operating companies having a great deal of autonomy—which led to a lot of duplication of management functions—to a group style. Head Office provides strategic direction, allocation of resources, and fulfillment of the legal obligations of a holding company. Special expertise, such as Hongkong Telecom's experience with video on demand, and Mercury's experience with wireless communications, should flow to where it is needed. For example, when Optus, a new service offering, was launched in Australia, it benefited from input from Hongkong Telecom's billing system as well as the Group's experience in rolling out national networks.

Cable & Wireless's business is broken down as follows. Cable & Wireless Business Networks develops global products and services and combines them to create managed solutions for multinational companies. Cable & Wireless Marine installs and maintains submarine cables with a fleet of fifteen ships, more than double the size of the fleet of their nearest competitor. These two groups are supported by Cable & Wireless Network Services, which manages the group's investment in international cable and satellite capacity. Cable & Wireless Mobile Directorate manages the group's mobile interests, and is involved in twenty-six countries. This organization will draw on the skills of the entire Group to help local companies in their own market improve earnings through exploiting synergies and sharing best practice. It will focus resources and expertise to support the Group in winning new licenses.

With operations in over fifty countries, Cable & Wireless claims to be the most international of the world's telecommunications companies, providing international communications for more than thirty countries and domestic services for over twenty, with the strongest areas being Britain, Hong Kong, and the Caribbean. Cable & Wireless's Innovations Group has the challenge and opportunity of infusing the relevant learnings through its global network of operating companies.

Hongkong Telecom

THE JEWEL in the Cable & Wireless crown is Hongkong Telecom, one of the most profitable companies in the telecommunications business, with a very good chance of playing an instrumental role in the development of telecommunications in China. Cable & Wireless owns approximately a 60 percent stake in Hongkong Telecom, which contributes about 80 percent of Cable & Wireless's operating profit.

Hongkong Telecom doesn't really produce anything; it does not make telephone equipment—it runs the telephone company's network using other people's systems and equipment. As a key pilot in innovation for all of Cable & Wireless, Hongkong Telecom is trying out a full broadband, real-time video on demand service to four hundred households. What Hongkong Telecom has in mind is *not* the kind of interactive trials that have been conducted by Time Warner in Orlando and other parts of the United States, where the technology of video on demand is being simulated by somebody loading remote VCRs. The technology that Hongkong Telecom is piloting is one where signals are compressed and sent from a video server over cable or fiber optics to homes. It's a real service, and one that will provide some key opportunities. Many at Hongkong Telecom feel that the Time Warner and other trials in the U.S. have been bound to fail simply because of the economic structures required to support the technology. Video on demand just isn't a good deal unless the price gets well below the video store price threshold (despite the fact that the Blockbuster Entertainments of the world are really making money off enormous video rental late fees and exploiting the lack of discipline and procrastination of human beings like me). Hongkong Telecom's trial will present a very interesting option and view of the future world of online interactive services, with a lot of growth potential.

Feedback from the participants in the pilot was positive. Initial results indicate people in Hong Kong will accept this new technology and be willing to pay a small premium, 20 percent, compared to video rental. People will pay for the convenience of not having to go out to rent the movie, actually finding the movie they want to see available, and no late charges, while still being able to control viewing (rewinding, fast-forwarding, and pausing). Hongkong Telecom also found that the usage of video on demand was inversely proportional to income. The lower segment watched three times more than the wealthier one. As a result, Hongkong Telecom will target the middle-income segment, since people in that segment have more disposable income than those in the lower segment, are known to adopt new technology earlier, and spend more time at home than the wealthy.

The video on demand system has simple menus that lead consumers through the process of finding the service they want—although participants in the study wanted to skip the introductory sequence after the sixth time, despite the fact that it lasts only fifteen seconds. Hongkong Telecom sees video on demand as satisfying consumers' needs for convenience and entertainment, without requiring any behavioral changes. The only thing customers need is a TV connected to a set-top box for decoding video and audio signals transmitted along the telephone line. They plan to have about eighty movies available, approximately a hundred hours of programming. And once they have a customer base established, they'll add other services: Interactive Multimedia Services (IMS) is planned for 1996, and will start with video on demand, payment services, cross merchandising (purchase of a soft toy character from a cartoon, or a pizza to eat with the movie, or a CD after listening to some music), and infomercials. Next, in 1997, comes home shopping, home banking (balance inquiries, payment services, fund transfers, personal financial planning, and loan applications), electronic yellow pages, and TV on demand; in 1998 games and educational services will be added.

Where Hongkong Telecom doesn't see growth is in home shopping (for clothes, fashion items, consumer electronics, and so forth), because of the enormous availability of these things in Hong Kong. The company believes instead that growth is more likely to be found in home delivery of groceries and produce, transactions that can be conducted fairly readily. The key advantage Hong Kong has as a site for such trials is its enormous density on both the Kowloon and Hong Kong sides. Hong Kongers are concentrated in a very densely populated strip—six million people live in 1,000 square kilometers—where one cable could pass in front of millions of users. Add to that the vertical nature of Hong Kong's development—90 percent of the population lives in high-rises, which average 174 households per building—and one vertical cable through a building could link many families to a very broadband pipe. In the United States such densities exist only in Manhattan and a few other downtown cores, in cities like Chicago or Philadelphia, but certainly not in Los Angeles or San Francisco, where the densities and high-rise Manhattanization have been kept to a minimum.

Another advantage of Hong Kong as a site for the trials is that it has a 100 percent digitized communications network, which facilitates upgrading the structure to a broadband network. More than 85 percent of the high-rise buildings are within five kilometers of one of the eighty-three exchanges. And the population is affluent, spending more than twice the average of other major cities on entertainment. They also accept new technologies. Hong Kong has one of the highest per capita penetrations of pagers, cellular phones, and personal computers.

The Hong Kong experiment is worth close scrutiny. While Hong Kong is obviously a unique place, it will still give some early signals as to the types of mechanisms and price points that might work—at least in Hong Kong. Cable & Wireless is reaching out to emerging markets, linking its global past to an innovative future.

Applied Materials

APPLIED MATERIALS has probably been one of the most successful high-tech, rapid-growth global players. CEO Jim Morgan deliber-
ately organized Applied Materials so that it operated across the
globe: departments, functions, and activities were conceived and ex-
ecuted on a global basis, rather than separated into geographic activities. This has reinforced the global nature of the market and the
company's quality, organization, and customers.

Founded in 1967, Applied Materials initially built its business on
producing and selling electronic materials. The company moved into
producing semiconductor manufacturing equipment in the mid-
1970s, and made its first profit in 1972, when it also made its first
public stock offering. Jim Morgan was named president and CEO in
1976, and he immediately began to focus the company on equipment used in semiconductor manufacturing. Until then, the company had been considerably diversified, not dominant in any one
field, and it was losing money. In an attempt to turn things around,
Morgan steered the company toward its niche. His belief was simply
that the semiconductor industry (his customers) would be global,
they would continuously innovate, and they would be passionate
about quality. Serving them with new fabrication technology would
be both profitable and fast-growing. It is this vision that has steered
Applied over the last decade.

Applied's global expansion began in 1979, when the company
bought Linott Engineering Ltd.'s ion implantation business. The
new subsidiary, named Applied Implant Technology, developed the
first fully automated implanter, the Precision Implant 9000 system.
Japan was next: that same year, to make their presence known in the
Japanese market, Applied established Applied Materials Japan Inc.,
an organization that has remained very Japanese, the American technical approach as its surface. Applied Materials Japan has been impressive: Japan was the source of more than 30 percent of Applied's
corporate sales in 1983. Applied expanded, and in 1984 opened the
Japan Technology Center in Narita, built in part with a loan from
the Japan Development Bank, an agency of the Japanese government. This was a first: the bank had never before given a loan for a
facility that was completely American-owned.

The expansion continued at an impressive rate: that same year
Applied entered into a cooperative venture with the government of
China. The result was the Applied Materials China Service Center in

Beijing, a Chinese company jointly run by codirectors from Applied and China's Ministry of Electronics.

Applied continued to see its global market grow. By 1989, company revenues from Applied Materials Japan were up to 40 percent, and two years later Applied Materials Japan finished the construction of new facilities in Japan and announced its entry into the area of thin film transistor liquid crystal display manufacturing equipment. A new wholly owned subsidiary, Applied Display Technology Inc., was formed in Japan to manage the development. In 1993 Applied and Komatsu, Ltd., formed Applied Komatsu Technology Inc., equally owned between the two companies and headquartered in Japan, which develops, manufactures and markets flat panel display–producing systems.

And it has all added up: in 1993, Applied became the first independent company in the semiconductor equipment industry to produce over $1 billion in revenue. It took Applied twenty-five years to produce that first billion; the second billion will have taken only two years. Applied is truly a global presence, which allows the company to keep in close contact with its customers as well as its operations, and helps the company to develop products that meet the needs of its customers. Applied has more than fifty sales and service offices, situated in close proximity to key customers, in the United States, Europe, Japan, Korea, Taiwan, Singapore, and China. Research, development, and manufacturing sites are in the U.S., Europe, Japan, and Israel, and include technology centers in Santa Clara, California; Narita, Japan; Horsham, England; and Tel Aviv, Israel. New technology centers are being constructed in Chun-An, South Korea, and Hsinchu, Taiwan.

Applied's revenues geographically follow those of the worldwide market, a remarkable testimony to the company's global presence. This diversification of Applied's revenues across the four main regional markets, each with its own economic cycle and product mix, has protected Applied from major downturns. You can look at 1992–1993 for an example: in that period, U.S. growth was steady and the Asian Pacific market was growing rapidly, while the Japanese market registered a marked downturn in their investment in new equipment. But Applied registered a 40 to 50 percent growth in revenue.

Applied's reputation is as one of the fastest innovators of new technologies in the industry. It is determined to improve its products as fast or faster than its speedy customers, companies such as Intel and Motorola. That approach coupled with Applied's ability to move resources and staff between projects ensures that technical developments are disseminated through the organization. Applied also includes customers in its development process; it was one of the first companies to do this. And since 1985, Applied's R&D has averaged 15 percent of the company's sales revenue. With the largest installed base of any chip equipment manufacturer, Applied controls more than 17 percent of the market. Its wafer fabrication business is more than double the size of its nearest competitor, Tokyo Electron Ltd. Applied's reputation for reliability—a more crucial factor all the time, as the industry moves to 8-inch wafers, where an error can affect a huge number of chips—is extremely high. By focusing on bringing quality to a global marketplace early on, Applied has grown into a true second-curve champion. As its business matures, Applied has built Applied Global University, whose mission it is to ensure that Applied's people continue to be innovative in building new second-curve products and services aimed at their sophisticated global clientele—the Intels, Fujitsus, and Motorolas of the world.

Nestlé

NESTLÉ IS A COMPANY that is globally owned, managed, and deployed. It is the world's largest packaged food manufacturer, coffee roaster, and chocolate manufacturer, and one of today's most multinational companies. It is the largest company in Switzerland, but derives less than 2 percent of its revenue from there. The company's manufacturing operations are worldwide, with 494 factories (most of which are in Europe—221—and North and South America—174) in 71 countries on six continents.

Global expansion and acquisitions have played a huge role in Nestlé from the company's beginnings. Henri Nestlé, the founder of Nestlé, made a formula for a baby who was unable to digest his mother's milk and was dying of malnutrition. Nestlé combined concentrated milk, sugar, and cereal, and the baby not only got well, he thrived, and was still drinking the formula six months later. Nestlé introduced the formula—he called it Farine Lactée—into the commercial market in his native Switzerland that same year, 1867, and it was a success, so much so that eight years later, Nestlé's company was operating in sixteen countries. Nestlé was sixty-one, and he sold the company to three Swiss industrialists.

This was in 1875, and another company, called Anglo-Swiss, had just begun producing infant formula. Anglo-Swiss was founded in

1866 by Charles and George Page, two American brothers who called their company, located in central Switzerland, the Anglo-Swiss Condensed Milk Company. The "Anglo" was misleading—there was no English connection—and was simply an attempt at marketing, and one that paid off. The Page brothers imported American canned milk technology, and began production in 1867. In 1872 Anglo-Swiss opened a factory in Chippenham, England; two years after that, the company purchased the English Condensed Milk Company, which was based in London. Those acquisitions made Anglo-Swiss the leading condensed milk manufacturer in Europe, and the company expanded by producing cheese and infant formula.

When Anglo-Swiss entered the Nestlé market, Nestlé in turn entered the condensed milk business. Both companies expanded abroad, with Anglo-Swiss's opening of a plant in upstate New York, and Nestlé's purchase of a condensed milk factory in Norway as well as locations in the U.S., Britain, Germany, and Spain. Nestlé also invested in the Swiss General Chocolate Company. In 1905 Anglo-Swiss and Nestlé merged and immediately held a strong position in the food industry. Because of Swiss neutrality, the company was able to continue its expansion during World War I, particularly in Latin America. After the war, Nestlé resumed its international expansion, acquiring Peter Cailler Chocolats Suisses—the first company to mass-produce chocolate bars—in 1928, and later establishing locations in Argentina, Chile, Cuba, Mexico, Denmark, and Czechoslovakia. In 1938, Nescafé—a Nestlé brand—introduced instant coffee. World War II disrupted operations and sources of raw materials, but the company was still successful at selling instant coffee, milk powder, and chocolate bars to the military. After the war, Nestlé merged with Alimentana S.A., producer of Maggi dehydrated soup, bouillon, and seasonings.

Since then the company's expansion has continued at an astonishing pace. The list of acquisitions is impressive and international, and includes Crosse & Blackwell, a British producer of preserves and canned goods, in 1960; Locatelli, an Italian cheese producer, in 1961; Findus, a Scandinavian frozen foods company, in 1962; and Buitoni-Perugina, the Italian pasta and candy producer, and Rowntree, the British chocolate maker, in the 1980s. Nestlé also acquired several large U.S. companies: Libby, a fruit juice bottler, in 1970; frozen foods producer Stouffer's (the company also has interests in hotels and restaurants) in 1973; Beech-Nut, the baby food manufacturer, in 1979 (which was later divested after some executives were found guilty of intentionally selling adulterated apple juice); Carnation, a producer of milk products, in 1985; and coffee producer Hills Brothers. There were acquisitions outside the food industry as well, including L'Oréal, the French cosmetics company.

In 1990 Nestlé formed an alliance with Coca-Cola to market ready-to-drink coffees and teas under the Nescafé and Nestea brand names, and they bought the Curtiss Brands chocolate division of RJR Nabisco, maker of Butterfinger and Baby Ruth candy bars. Nestlé consolidated its U.S. operations into a single holding company. In 1991 Nestlé and the French food group BSN took a majority position in Czechoslovakia's biggest food producer. In 1992 they acquired Perrier, the French bottled water company. Nestlé has recently emphasized emerging second-curve markets, especially the Far East/Pacific, with its forecasted growth in population. Of eleven new factories opened worldwide between 1993 and 1995, nine are in emerging markets.

Nestlé tries to match their products with the tastes, purchasing power, and desire for convenience of particular markets. In China Nestlé started with milk, went into instant coffee, then coffee creamer. Now they are going into frozen foods, also for export from China, and into infant formula, yogurts, noodles, and ice cream. That's how they grow: with the market. The company feels that foods are distributed and consumed differently in less industrialized countries and they have no interest in trying to change habits if that means going against the grain, preferring to adapt their products to local markets. In Japan, where breakfast typically consists of fish and rice, Nestlé developed cereals that tasted like seaweed and papaya.

Nestlé has thrived on a culture of global aggressiveness that continues to this day. The key to the company is the fact that they are a diverse global business team. The company builds second curves around the world by following the market on the second curve, not jumping ahead of it. By matching their investment to the emerging hierarchy of needs in the second-curve markets, they make sure they don't live in the future before it happens.

Lessons Learned

THERE'S A LOT to be learned from the second-curve global marketplace.

TAKE THE LONG VIEW

When it comes to the emergence of second-curve markets and new geographies, it is incredibly important not to focus on activities over a week or month. It takes *decades* for these markets to emerge, not months. The investment entry strategies may take decades because of cultures that have much longer time constants and may take a great deal of care in building the appropriate relationships to support long-term business. The difficulties Americans have in dealing with Japan are legendary, and those entering markets in countries like China, Vietnam, and Brazil will face similar ones.

The long view is essential in planning for these emerging markets, and one of the things it tells you is that you can't postpone entries into these markets. For example, Applied Materials had a joint venture in China in 1984, well ahead of the large-scale integrated circuit market in that country. The only way to participate in the long term is to start now, and this will call for a wait-and-see attitude when it comes to Asia. These are cultures that have long time constants, places that have complex sets of relationships, where relationships matter a great deal. To simply wait until an opportunity arises and you think *you're* ready may not be a time when *they're* ready. You have to get out and start building those relationships now, recognizing that they may not yield second-curve returns for a very long time.

ANTICIPATE DIFFERING STAGES OF DEVELOPMENT

While it is important to use the logical historical progression of developmental stages as a benchmark in terms of where these economies may emerge over the next twenty years, you can't assume that you can simply transfer Korea's experience to China, or Thailand's to Vietnam. These are different countries with different cultures and different histories, which means that their trajectories will most likely be quite different from one another, under the rule of thumb that they're moving up the developmental path and that their GNP per capita is likely to rise on a pattern not dissimilar to the predecessor's but will not match the exact configuration of the economy in terms of the relative emphasis between heavy and light industry, the growth in particular segments of their consumer market, and the relative concentrations in specific cities or regions from a distribution point of view. All of these dimensions are going to be very different depending on the history, geography, and culture of each of the countries looked at. For example, in the case of China, the Chinese authorities skipped the classic industrial development wave of heavy industry, choosing to focus investment instead in the light manufacturing area and in building a financial services infrastructure in Shanghai. This seems a much more sensible way given the hand they were dealt than to try and emulate Korea's or Japan's forays in heavy manufacturing such as steel, shipbuilding, and heavy engineering. It remains for countries such as Vietnam to select their development paths, but it is likely they may be different again. Initially absorbing the spillover from South China, they may be the beneficiaries of relatively lower labor cost and less hectic economic competition, but in time they may seek alternate development trajectories.

EXPECT STUTTERING STEPS

Not only will the path of the second curve be uncertain in terms of which of the possible development trajectories each country might take, but we must expect that along the development path over the next twenty years many of these countries will falter. Not permanently, but periodically. And this is extremely confusing for investors and corporations driven by quarterly timetables. Most of the stuttering steps result from political uncertainties and immature institutions to support democracy and markets. Earlier we reviewed how such problems existed in all the big second-curve markets we identified. The recent events in Mexico suggest that even the most rapidly developing and seemingly maturing economies can falter in both their political and their economic development. Two years ago Mexico was the darling of the stock market, with the North American Free Trade Agreement ushering in a period of growth and global competitiveness. Over the last two years its economy has faltered badly in the wake of political assassinations and uncertainty over the stability of future directions. Similarly, Russia, with the fall of communism, seemed to be ripe for full participation in the global economy but has stumbled badly in its attempts to build anything approximating a European or North American economic base. It's cowboy country. China under the leadership of Deng Xiaoping managed to orchestrate a fairly methodical but dramatic rise to economic prominence throughout the 1980s and early 1990s. What possible stumbles will there be on the path to greater economic greatness? Brazil and the other Latin American economies have flirted dangerously close to oblivion with the perils of inflation, political instability, and corruption. So one must fully expect in taking the long view to find not a smooth path but rather a faltering one. And that these stuttering steps to a second curve superseding the first are indeed both uncertain and volatile.

DON'T UNDERESTIMATE THE POWER OF THE U.S.A.

The second curve belongs to the emerging markets. But this does not imply stagnation of the U.S. market. Whereas Europe, particularly Northern Europe, is in at least stagnation if not decline in terms of growth in both population and labor force (and in turn therefore its economy, since economic growth is a function of both population growth and productivity), America does not suffer from a lack of dynamism. It is true that our economic growth in the United States is unlikely to exceed 3 percent per annum, taking a long view of the economic potential of the U.S. over the next twenty years, but that is significant because of the continued attractiveness of the United States to people from around the world. One of the key questions will be the degree to which continued immigration is not only allowed but encouraged. The current political climate is one in which politicians are increasingly exploiting racial divisiveness and whipping up anti-immigration fervor, in some senses blaming economic malaise on the rise of the number of immigrants in the United States. This is not a new phenomenon. Throughout America's history, when things got tough, the immigrants were blamed. But if one takes the longer view of immigration as a positive contribution to the American economy, it is clear that having more people willing to come to this country for a better life is a good thing, and provided we build infrastructures to fully harness that human capital it augurs well for the future of the U.S. compared to other nations.

In particular, in California we have a unique opportunity in that the connections—cultural, economic, and in many instances familial—with the rapidly emerging economies of South Asia and Latin America provide us with a unique cultural and economic bridge to those nations. The political posturing that Governor Pete Wilson has done in recent years has probably damaged some of those relationships, certainly with Mexicans. Proposition 187, which denies schooling and medical services to illegal immigrants, was viewed as hostile toward our neighbors to the south.

Overall, however, the U.S. has exhibited an enormous capacity to reinvent itself. It is likely that it will continue to do so. The combination of markets and freedoms in the United States, despite the deep inequality and divisiveness that will be aggravated by many of these global trends, gives it a tremendous capacity to produce jobs, to produce new enterprises, and to spawn opportunities and ideas for the world.

It is clear that America is the dominant nation on the planet at least in terms of popular culture. While American culture is likely to be modified and embellished by global influences, it is astonishing to travel the world and see the MTVing and CNNing of the planet where, literally in every hotel room I have ever been in, there have been *Married . . . with Children* reruns. Larry King is seen in more countries than probably is any other human on the planet. The pervasiveness of American cultural icons, Madonna, MTV, Marlboro cigarettes, is everywhere, and for right or wrong American cultural exports have an enormous place in the emerging economic base in the countries we've described. So the U.S.A. should not be underestimated as an emerging second-curve player in and of itself. Within the U.S., new dynamic markets will emerge, spawned from the rich mix of cultures that have been drawn to this country. For example, the Latino market (part of a worldwide market of over 300 million Spanish-speakers) is large and growing larger in numbers and affluence. Similarly, the Asian American population is a powerful bridge to the second curve and a dynamic market in and of itself.

THE SECOND CURVE MAY BELONG MORE TO CITIES THAN TO NATIONS

Whereas the unit of analysis of the first curve is countries and corporations, the unit of analysis of the second curve may be cities and individuals. New world cities are emerging—Shanghai, Singapore, and Bangkok are perhaps the best examples. It may be more important to think about the future of what happens in Shanghai rather than of what happens in China. It's more important to think about the future of a group of individuals, rather than that of one particular corporate entity. It's where does Steven Spielberg end up, rather than what happens to a particular corporate entity. Increasingly, those changes in unit of analysis will become significant in a global second-curve world.

Second-Curve Industries

TO FULLY EXPLAIN the impact of the second curve, it's important to select a few areas of the economy and examine them from a second-curve perspective. We will look at retail and distribution, health care, and financial services for a couple of reasons. First, these sectors represent a significant proportion of the economy, one that touches many individuals. Second, each of these sectors illustrates different ways and combinations of driving forces and the emergence of second-curve phenomena; they also offer many examples of companies trying to deal with two-curve type problems. Together these industries account for approximately 50 percent of industry in general. All three are obviously key industries for the future in terms of both employment and the well-being of the average American household—though this is not a uniquely American situation. These sectors of the second-curve economy are undergoing fundamental structural change around the world. And while it's true that you'll find examples of the second curve in many industries, it's particularly useful to consider these three areas because their examples expose many of the alternate strategies you can use in playing the first curve, the second, or both. These are industries rich in examples of two-curve strategic choice, of frustration among those trying to manage on two curves, and of people who've started out on one curve, assuming it was the second curve—only to find it was a blind alley.

But the most striking reason for examining these three industries is that each of them is at a very different place in terms of the second curve. The second curve has already happened in retail and distribution; its tracks are pretty clear. Here's where the second curve has already hit. The distribution and retailing sectors are being fundamentally affected by new consumers, new technology, and global orientation, and are perhaps the simplest and most visible example of the two-curve phenomenon in action. Retail and distribution are the first place that consumers have seen the emergence of the second curve; the rise of mail order and the growth of new channels of distribution are directly observable to people. This has been an area where some of the most profound changes have occurred in terms of the emergence of a second curve and it is reported daily in the newspapers: consumers are finding new ways to interact with suppliers of consumer-oriented products and services. The innovation of the second curve is everywhere, from Starbucks Coffee to Wal-Mart to Intuit, causing fundamental shifts in the ways consumers view products and services.

In the United States and around the world, health care is in the midst of fundamental structural changes, but the question is, do those changes add up to a second curve? The health care industry is a huge global industry, employing anywhere from 8 percent to 15 percent of the workforce, an absorbing share of the economy in most of the countries of the developed world—and the subject of major debate in most countries. When I visited Hong Kong recently, the daily newspaper, *The Hong Kong Standard*, carried the banner headline "Health Care in Crisis." That headline has very likely been replayed in Canada, Germany, the United Kingdom, and the U.S. in the last three years, although nowhere is the nature of the crisis or the level of the stakes as high as in the United States.

One of the reasons why this is a very interesting example of the second curve is that it is not clear yet whether the second curve is really the one offered in the popular business press. The second curve of health care probably has yet to be invented. Nevertheless, we are observing some fundamental shifts—but false starts—toward a satisfactory solution. The true second curve of health care is not here yet. But clearly, many health care organizations are in two-curve transitions and are managing as if the second curve were well known and clear, which leads to probably some shortsighted if not dead wrong behaviors. The other reason this example is interesting is that it provides an opportunity to begin to confront some other technologies apart from computers and communications which—although they too will have an enormous effect on health care in creating the second curve—aren't the only important technologies. In particular the role of biotechnology could have a fundamental effect in creating a truly new second curve in health care out of the rubble of current systems.

Since the late 1980s, health care has been going through a period of fundamental structural change. For the last ten years, the Institute for the Future, its partners Louis Harris & Associates, and the Harvard School of Public Health, Department of Health Policy and Management, have worked closely with a consortium of fifty leading health care organizations. This program has focused on assessing the structural change in health care (both in the United States and abroad) to determine the pace and direction of change and the implications for key decision-makers.

Financial services is on the edge of a highly dramatic precipice of change, a fundamental restructuring both here in the United States and in other countries, a stage in which change is only beginning, where the second curve has yet to emerge. Once again, the boundaries are blurring in this industry. There are major shifts under way which will change the rules of who does what to whom, but the fundamental shift comes not only through globalization and more sophisticated consumers, but through the realization that on a basic level, financial services is all about the movement of information— the manipulation of electrons. And as such, the traditional structures that have served the financial services industry—the salespeople, the institutions, the physical buildings—are all under assault as new mechanisms and channels are developed for distribution of financial products. New players emerge almost overnight to vie for market dominance; new concepts emerge; and new technologies enable very different ways of interacting. Some of the oldest, most profitable organizations on the planet are being forced to confront the reality that major shifts are upon them and that there has to be a clear focus on where those shifts will take them.

Retail and Distribution:
The Death of the Middleman

THE SECOND CURVE is very present in the transformation of retail and distribution. Retail, perhaps more than any other area, has
seen the emergence of second-curve players, and has become one of
the earliest and most evident transformations of a new order. The
second curve has come because of new consumers, new technology,
and new geographic markets. And the transformation of the consumer market, in turn, has reapportioned power within the distribution system. The key to the second-curve transformation in both
areas—retail and distribution—is the elimination of the middleman.

The Great Transformation

POWER IS INCREASINGLY SHIFTING down the distribution
chain to those who own the customer. Unnecessary impediments in

the middle between producer and consumer will be eliminated, but this doesn't mean that stores will disappear. Rather, stores (or the entity that really touches the customer) will reach back into the manufacturer and increasingly dominate the entire distribution chain. Conversely the manufacturer will embrace new channels and reach directly to the consumer. The power of the retailer can be enormous, as we've seen with private label.

Large manufacturing firms and the middlemen who served them have lost their preeminent position as de facto leaders of American business. Driven by the growing role of the new consumer and the inability of downsized manufacturers to keep a monopoly on critical information about these new consumers, a variety of players along the distribution chain have gained specialized access to the consumer. As a result, these new players are participating in critical business decisions as they never have before.

The Industrial Firm as King

FROM THE LATE NINETEENTH CENTURY until the past few years, large industrial enterprises in the United States made virtually all critical business decisions about the production and distribution of products: what new products were developed; when they were introduced; and what their style, design, quality, price, labeling, and packaging were. Large companies also determined the appropriate distribution chain, oversaw advertising and promotional activities, decided on warranties and guarantees, and provided after-sale service. They were the bastions of the first curve.

Large industrial enterprises carried enough in-house expertise in all of these areas to control the decision process. They conducted their own R&D, designed products and labels, set production schedules, controlled advertising campaigns, kept the pulse of the public through their marketing research departments, and often handled their own trucking, distribution, and servicing. They were truly the center of decision-making in the U.S. business world.

During the 1980s, the large manufacturing firms took a big gamble. International competitive pressures were forcing them to become leaner and more flexible in their approach to the market. They attempted to farm out many tasks to suppliers, distributors, and service firms while keeping control of the key decisions themselves. By increasing productivity, they were able to cut back on the number of production workers. By leveraging their internal resources with the right consultants and service firms, they were able to cut back on the size of internal staff. As a result, in the 1980s, the Fortune 500 industrial firms held on to most of their share of final sales while achieving a dramatic decline in share of the workforce.

The New Democratic State of Business

BUT FROM A STRATEGIC PERSPECTIVE, large manufacturing firms may have lost the gamble. The leaner, meaner industrial corporations may not be able to maintain their preeminent role in the business world. Indeed, they no longer make the decisions alone but now share that power with a whole spectrum of actors in the distribution chain. A good measure of this shift is the increasing market value of large service firms, including media/communications firms such as Time Warner, Disney, and MCI and retailers such as Wal-Mart and Price/Costco. Over the past ten years, but especially in the past few years, large service firms have moved ahead of industrial firms in market valuation.

The increased valuation of the service sector in the U.S. reflects a fundamental shift in favor of those organizations better placed to interpret and influence customer needs directly. Those who have closer ties to the consumer are moving into positions of control. A point-of-sale terminal in a White Plains shopping mall creates a more informed response than a focus group at corporate headquarters.

This consumer focus has brought on a new democratic business world in which manufacturers participate in the decision process with many other actors: supermarkets, department stores, discounters, interactive media, cable TV purveyors, phone companies, international firms, catalog companies, and stores that can market their own brand of goods. This transformation will change forever traditional assumptions about distribution, thereby affecting how we think about vertical integration, channel systems, consumer tracking, product valuation, branding, wholesalers, retail outlets, and company profitability.

Drivers of the Retail and Distribution Second Curve

WHERE DID THIS TRANSFORMATION come from? New technology, new consumers, and new geographic markets have played huge roles—most notably the new consumer, which is what really sparked the distribution revolution. New technology has also been a big factor, largely in respect to the emerging electronic infrastructure that has allowed electronic data interchange (EDI) to occur between manufacturers and retailers, lubricating all of the elements in the distribution chain. The electronic infrastructure also includes the web of point-of-service networks, which have provided consumers with many more choices in the way in which they purchase goods and services. The range of payment mechanisms has expanded significantly, so that even in the most humble retail outlet multiple forms of payment have become acceptable. But part of the electronic infrastructure is invisible, an infrastructure that the consumer doesn't see or even necessarily interact with, but which is key to much of the transformation. That infrastructure includes the following:

Logistics. Some have argued that the reason the allies in the Gulf War prevailed so quickly and so decisively was really a triumph of logistics. The U.S.-based logistics systems were highly computerized, extensively coordinated, and technologically sophisticated. Increasingly, logistics systems help get goods to the right place at the right time with a minimum of inventory.

Inventory control systems. Logistics systems are coupled to inventory control systems, extremely sophisticated market-tracking mechanisms that combine point-of-service, point-of-sale terminals and technologies, scanner systems with bar codes, readers, and the integration with computerized manufacturing processes, so that increasingly it is possible to build a retailing electronic infrastructure which links all of the elements in the value chain together into a seamless system.

The new geography has also played a part in the transformation. The most prominent source of new competition is the unending onslaught of firms from abroad. Overall, the share of sales of foreign-owned firms in the United States has more than doubled in the past decade. The striking thing about the growth of foreign enterprises is that it covers the whole gamut of businesses, not just the traditional manufacturing industries as in the past. Foreign firms' sales in the U.S. service sector (including computer services, consulting, research, accounting, law, and advertising) are growing the fastest. The

presence of new competitors from abroad in sectors such as manufacturing, retailing, and advertising is promoting new ways of doing
business, introducing new financial clout, and bringing new ideas
into the market.

Another factor has been maturing economies. The underlying rate
of growth in the richer consumer markets has slowed by about half in
the past twenty years. In addition, retail expenditures are declining as
a share of personal income because more and more spending goes into
ongoing purchases—housing, health care, savings, recreation and
travel, and so on. The marked slowdown in the inflation rate over the
last decade has also had an effect. Together these trends mean that retailers have less room for maneuvering. With slow growth in household income, new products have to compete with old. With little
consumer-price inflation, higher prices for one product leave less income for spending on other products. Overall sales increases in a new
store come increasingly out of the sales of a neighboring store.

And last, but certainly not least, is deregulation, which, with privatization, has swept the globe in the past fifteen years. In the United
States, industries intimately involved in the distribution of products—telephones, wireless communications, cable TV, trucking, airlines, pipelines, energy generation, banking, insurance, financial
services—have been exposed to the hurricanes of open competition.
This has affected every local market. Other countries have experienced the same changes, compounded by the privatization of government monopolies in everything from telecommunications and
utilities to chemicals and steel production.

The Industry Responds:
Trends in Retail and Distribution

HOW HAVE RETAIL AND DISTRIBUTION RESPONDED to the
transformation? Information technology has had a tremendous impact on how businesses distribute their products and services, and the
obvious and well-publicized examples, such as EDI and home shopping, only hint at the potential for dramatic changes in the underlying models of distribution. At the same time that technology is
enabling new business relationships, increasing competition is forcing
companies to reconsider distribution and supply. We're seeing four

emerging distribution models: virtual vertical integration, the new logistics, convenience meets labor savings, and network-based businesses.

Virtual Vertical Integration

UNTIL RECENTLY, companies have been able to convince themselves and their customers that they add high value to their products and services, with the result that they have commanded high prices for them. Increasingly, as aggressive competitors find low-cost ways to enter new markets, distributors end-run upstream manufacturers, and information technology makes available new information about the characteristics and availability of products and services, premium prices are getting squeezed, and more products are looking like commodities. Customers will no longer pay premium prices for products or services that they have to integrate themselves in order to get all of what they want. An obvious value-added strategy for the future, then, is for companies to integrate vertically.

But companies in many manufacturing industries are confronting the dangers of actual vertical integration, which requires large capital resources, where the economics of the other business are not always well understood, with embedded management and information systems often incompatible, and cultural differences between partners making it difficult to reach a common vision. An emerging model we expect to see increase in the next few years is virtual vertical integration. Enabled by information technology, companies will engage in close partnerships with suppliers, customers, and even competitors to produce economies of scale without the risk and rigidity of actual acquisitions. For example, I flew on a plane with an executive who was building a $900 million business to supply paper for laser printer users, using a network of alliances from the paper manufacturers to regional distributors.

The New Logistics

THE PHYSICAL DISTRIBUTION OF GOODS has undergone a revolution with the use of information technology. What used to be an inexact art—experienced dispatchers making educated guesses at what delivery schedules would be most efficient, then tracking their units in the field on large wall maps, never sure about where goods actually were at any time—has given way to a new science. Linear programs that plan delivery routes and schedules now run on desktop PCs instead of mainframe computers. Geographic information systems, global positioning satellites, and wireless data communications give a real-time picture of vehicles and goods. Information systems now give even small companies global reach and almost microscopic local accuracy.

Several trucking companies are at the leading edge in using satellite-based communication to direct the distribution of their trucks. In December 1994, Landstar System Inc. signed a multimillion-dollar contract for one thousand OmniTRACS Satellite Fleet Management Systems to be installed in two of Landstar's owner/operator fleets: Ranger Transportation, a dry-van carrier based in Jacksonville, Florida, and Independent Freightway, a drop-deck and platform fleet out of Rockford, Illinois. The OmniTRACS system is a geostationary (meaning that the satellite remains over the same spot on earth) satellite-based mobile communication system that provides two-way data and position reporting services. Qualcomm, which produces, operates, and licenses advanced communications systems and products based on its proprietary digital wireless technologies, has sold more than 99,000 OmniTRACS units worldwide, with systems operating in the U.S., Canada, Europe, Japan, Brazil, and Mexico, and implementation under way in Malaysia. M.S. Carriers, a Memphis trucking company that runs a fleet of 2,344 trucks primarily within the eastern two-thirds of the U.S., uses its state-of-the-art satellite communication equipment to constantly track its drivers.

At the Volpe Transportation Research Center in Cambridge, Massachusetts, Federal Aviation Administration researchers have built the Pit, a large room loaded with satellite communications and computer equipment including a 16-by-20-foot electronic map of the world. On that map, hundreds of dots correspond to commercial airplanes actually in the air. The operators can drill down to show the identification number, flight number, altitude, direction, and air speed of any plane on the screen. They can zoom in to show the United States, California, the Bay Area, or the approaches to San Francisco International Airport, Runway 28 L. They can select all flights bound for Newark International Airport. And eventually the means will exist to link information from the passenger manifest to the display. The Pit provides an integrated view of a large, complex system. At the same

time, it facilitates technicians' efforts in analyzing and examining
the details under the big picture.

Under European Commission sponsorship, REDAR, GmbH, a
small German firm, recently demonstrated a portable radio-frequency
transponder system that provides an active electronic identification
signal for vehicles and containers. Sounds reasonable, but what can it
do? Here are some important applications:

- A truck loaded with several containers pulls into a warehouse. As
  it clears the door, detectors identify the truck and each of the containers on board. The information is automatically entered in the
  receiving and inventory computer.
- A forklift drives toward a stack of containers. Guided by the electronic signal from the containers, it automatically identifies and
  picks up the correct container.
- A cart slowly cruises the aisles of a warehouse, taking information
  from each container along its way. When it finishes its rounds, the
  business has a fresh inventory.

None of the information gathered by the technologies in the scenarios is new. What are new are the ability to connect the big picture
with the real world, the speed with which data is available, the global
reach of the communications and information systems, and the ability to rapidly consolidate information from diverse sources into an
integrated information system. What first appears to be just a difference in amount or speed of information turns out to be a difference
in kind. Implications include:

Turbocharged customer service. The new logistics permit distribution companies to reach new levels of customer service—to give more
reliable information on delivery schedules, inventory, and so on. The
ultimate result in many industries is likely to be a shift of inventory
risk up the supply chain. As business customers grow more capable of
forecasting with precision the availability of products (with information provided by their suppliers), they can shift the burden of carrying
inventory back onto the same suppliers. Baxter International (formerly American Hospital Supply) was able to gain incredible competitive advantage by being the first to place an online ordering system
on the desks of hospital purchasing managers. This made it easier to
order from Baxter than from any other supplier. Then Baxter linked
the ordering system to an inventory management system. Now, typically, hospital pharmacy and supply rooms carry little stock—they're

linked electronically to their suppliers, who hold the inventory and make deliveries twice a day. As a result, the level of customer service is significantly higher than ever before.

Just-in-time supply. Ultimately, if the dynamics of purchasing, distribution, and supply are well understood and coordinated, companies and their partners can move beyond shifting inventory cost to actually reducing it. Just-in-time supply reduces the amount of goods in the supply chain at any time.

A *higher service threshold.* Enhanced logistics will follow a pattern we have seen in other customer service businesses. The first companies to use an innovation will gain an initial competitive advantage. Then other companies will imitate them, changing the landscape completely. Soon after, this level of service will become necessary for any company to compete at all. Ultimately, the proliferation of competing systems will complicate rather than simplify life for the customers, who in response will demand that suppliers standardize their systems. Baxter found that as dozens of its competitors imitated its ordering and inventory system, hospital purchasing managers complained of too many different ordering systems. Customers demanded, and Baxter provided, a standard EDI-based method of ordering from all suppliers. Similarly, Federal Express gained an initial competitive advantage when it introduced real-time package tracking. Now United Parcel Service has imitated it, and this service will spread to other shipping companies as well. Both companies provide this service online through their home pages on the Internet, as well as through proprietary software systems that run on customers' PCs. Ultimately, customers could demand a single tracking system common to all shipping companies.

Higher technological risk . The new logistics rely heavily on complex software systems, wireless communications, global satellite systems, and other advanced technology. Technological risk comes in several forms. As increasing numbers of systems are linked up, there is a growing risk that they won't interoperate. And forcing them to work together by composing standards for communications, such as the EDI or the uniform product code, carries its own risk—putting a technological straitjacket on systems that are just beginning to evolve.

A *global view of your business.* The new logistics will permit businesses with a large geographical scope to gain a more comprehensive, real-time assessment of the business. Schneider National, a trucking firm in Green Bay, Wisconsin, bases its success (it has doubled its revenue since 1989 and now is the largest hauler of full-truckload freight) on the use of sophisticated information and communications systems. Each truck is equipped with a satellite link and a computer that sends drivers to their next delivery, warns them of road hazards, and tracks their speed and driving time. The company's information system permits a high degree of control and economy of operation. A measure of the company's success is that it recently won a contract to manage logistics for General Motors's automotive parts business.

Where Did Everybody Go?
Convenience Meets Labor Savings

TRADITIONALLY, people—clerks, tellers, checkers, gas pumpers, attendants, sales agents, telephone representatives—have been the primary link between companies and consumers. People were the first curve of customer service. When companies eliminated these positions in the past, they did so to improve efficiency and productivity, not customer service. Indeed, the customer often suffered, with longer lines and overloaded and underinformed salesclerks. Now customer service technology is closing the loop between customers and companies, improving customer service without the intervention of humans.

Why Am I the Only Person in This Picture?

Systems—not people—are becoming the second curve of customer service. At your ATM, not only can you deposit, withdraw, and transfer money, you can also print a bank statement, check market rates on CDs and other instruments, buy and sell mutual funds, buy stamps, and even pay bills. When you pump gas, you swipe your credit card through the pump's card reader. After it gives you authorization, you pump the gas, replace the nozzle, take your receipt, and go. At some gas stations with convenience stores, you can enter an order for convenience store items from a keypad on the pump. When you're done pumping gas, you pick up the items in the store. And when you go to a first-run movie, you can now call in to a touch-tone-operated telephone system, select the movie and screening, and enter your credit card information. When you arrive at the theater, you bypass the ticket office and go directly to a kiosk that reads your credit card and dispenses a ticket. As you get ready to take your car from a parking lot, you now run the ticket through a machine that tells how much you owe. You pay up and get your ticket back. At the exit, you simply insert the ticket and drive through.

These systems are only the beginning. As user-interface and networking technologies improve, and customers become more accustomed to dealing with machines, the use of customer service automation will increase, especially in areas where it is now used experimentally, such as in the United States, Europe, Japan, and Singapore. It could expand to include automated toll taking; travel and entertainment applications such as reservations and ticketing for airlines, sporting events, and plays; and government information and transactions, such as welfare payments, food stamps, and driver's licenses. These developments have several implications:

The productivity paradox may be resolved. One of the recent key business dilemmas has been the difficulty of documenting the payoff from information technology investment. As Nobel economist Robert Solow has said, "You see computers everywhere except in the productivity statistics." White-collar productivity always has been difficult to measure, and returns on investment in information technology have been hard to find. As companies reengineer, restructure, and reduce their workforces substantially, the productivity payoffs are becoming more evident.

Customers are ready for technology. An estimated 50 percent of workers now routinely use a computing device for their jobs. Despite common horror stories about voice mail (or voice jail), many people now leave substantive messages rather than just hanging up. Consumers, too, have begun to use electronic technology, such as ATM and point-of-sale terminals at banks, grocery stores, gas stations, and restaurants, more routinely. Today, almost 60 percent of households use ATM cards, compared to 40 percent in 1980. Even elderly households are becoming more comfortable with ATMs. The consumer's new readiness will make the shift to other uses of electronic technology smoother.

Again, the service threshold goes up. Just as with new logistics, successful applications of customer service automation become widely imitated and soon turn into competitive necessities. No consumer bank today, for example, would consider staying in business without access to an ATM network.

Real-time data becomes available. Customer service technologies give customers a new role: data entry. If the interfaces are designed properly (and correct data entry is rewarded, for example, with a cash withdrawal), customers can become a source of real-time data. When combined with the type of presentation techniques developed for the "Pit" scenario described earlier in this chapter, that information can give companies a unique perspective on the dynamics of their businesses. Combining supermarket scanners with credit or debit cards, for example, permits consumer packaged goods companies to get real-time assessments of the performance of different products. By linking geographic and demographic information with knowledge about advertising and promotions, they can measure the effectiveness in real time of different sales strategies.

Network-Based Businesses

AS MORE PEOPLE AND BUSINESSES are computerized and connected to a global information network, the opportunity to use that network for commercial activities increases. You can make money using the network in three ways: by selling more existing products and services as you reach new customers over the network, by servicing existing customers better over the network, and by selling new services over the network.

The network is not yet fully evolved, either in its reach or capacity. As it connects a growing number of people with high-bandwidth communications channels, many different services may arise that can replace existing transactions. Until then, network-based businesses will be oriented toward computer users. Some services will use a hybrid of the network and other technologies, such as CD-ROM. Among some of the commercial experiments under way:

CommerceNet. An $8 million experiment in electronic commerce in Silicon Valley. The goal is to reinforce public computer networks, such as the Internet, for business use. CommerceNet will support a range of commercial network applications such as online catalogs, product data exchange, and engineering collaboration. It will also offer outreach services such as technical assistance to small and medium-size businesses that want access to public networks.

In April 1994, CommerceNet launched its version of Internet client-server software for search and navigation. This software will incorporate encryption and authentication technologies to make business transactions secure.

The FAST Electronic Broker. A prototype automated broker for standard, off-the-shelf items like electronic and optical parts and components and laboratory and test equipment. FAST's customers send quotes and orders electronically by means of the Internet or commercial networks. FAST automatically analyzes the request to identify appropriate vendors, then it electronically requests a quote from them. With this information, FAST buyers negotiate with vendors to get better prices. If customers agree to purchase the merchandise, FAST produces an electronic purchase order.

New channel—selling software on CD-ROM. Microsoft, Adobe Systems, and Apple Computer are all using a new business model to sell software products. Instead of packaging different software programs separately, they're bundling a wide range of software on a CD-ROM. Free demonstrations of all software are available. To buy software, purchasers phone an 800 number, give credit card information, and receive a code that releases the use of the entire software program. Documentation is available on the disk or is sent separately.

Because networks are such a new tool for distribution, there are significant issues about how to develop network-based businesses to be resolved:

Appropriate pricing and payment mechanisms. To get access to a network-based business, consumers must use online information, communications, or transaction services. Those services may be billed in any number of ways: by subscription, time connected, volume of information used, number of transactions or messages, or as a share of the value of transactions. And how do you pay for products or services sold on the network? Typically, services use credit or debit cards, but these add an extra step to the process. A key element missing from the current electronic infrastructure is electronic payment. In the near future, we expect to see new consumer interfaces for electronic funds transfer.

Transaction support. If the network comes to encompass cable television, online services, telephony, and the Internet as it is forecasted to, there will be substantial opportunities to transact business both on and in support of the network. Conventional marketing concepts like charging mass advertising costs based on a set fee per thousand heads reached will be replaced by more tangible and targeted measures that charge for each actual lead generated. New mechanisms will have to be established to create and manage a profile of users' tastes in goods and services to steer advertising material. Profiles of users' media preferences also will have to be created and managed to present the right information in the right media. Sophisticated linkages will be possible between products shown in entertainment programming (you see a Ford Explorer on your favorite video on demand) and online advertising (once the show is over, you signal that you want information on the Explorer and you are connected to Ford's online information and ordering system). Ford pays for the movie; you signal your preference and Ford knows it.

Future Trends

IN ADDITION to these models, there are some general trends we're seeing in response to the changes:

Deregulation Continues

By increasing competition, deregulation and privatization have created a new level of awareness about consumer desires and have brought new players into the markets, players with fresh ideas about how to reach consumers and how to package products and services. For example, banks now sell mutual funds, while mutual funds companies offer home or ATM transfers. Telephone companies allow you to choose the movie you watch on TV, while newspapers are delivered by TV. And cellular phone services compete with the Bells for local calls, while electronic messaging eliminates secretaries and receptionists.

Businesses Harness New Technologies

With a more sophisticated consumer in the catbird seat, a whole slew of new communications technologies—interactive TV, shopping channels, multimedia kiosks, PC-based shopping services, point-of-sale linkages to inventory and manufacturing sites—promises a continuing transformation of distribution roles and responsibilities in the next decade.

Brands Make a Comeback

Nowadays, brands are competing with private labels for market share, but with the emergence of new electronic distribution channels, brands could make a comeback in the short term. Consumers are not completely comfortable with these new distribution systems and will look for familiar indicators of quality, reliability, and reputability. A participant in a recent focus group said, "I'm more leery about what I buy than I was in the past. Now, with all of the home shopping channels, it appears that they are trying to talk you into buying something. I feel like I'm being tricked a lot." Traditional brand names can comfort these inexperienced electronic shoppers. Another consumer said, "For most products, especially for things like toys or tools or consumer electronics and things like that, if it's name brand stuff . . . you don't feel like you're taking that big of a chance." As consumers become more comfortable with alternative shopping experiences, the battle of the brands and private labels will intensify again.

Customers Replenish Rather Than Acquire

Many electronic shoppers say that they are uncomfortable with not being able to touch their merchandise before they buy it. As a result, consumers may be reluctant to buy new things electronically, but they might feel different about items they have bought before and need to replace. Consumers might welcome the convenience of electronic shopping for replenishing items. Assurance that an item can be returned easily and painlessly is critical for consumers who order remotely.

Big Retailers Have a Head Start

The increasing mobility of consumers, their desire for a wide range of choice, the emergence of new delivery and back-room technologies, and the cost of financing expansion favor larger players. Technology allows greater economies of scale, more efficient tracking of consumer preferences, and more effective inventory and delivery systems. Look for the larger retail units to continue to hold on to a bigger share of the retail market. This will fuel consolidation of retailing on the first curve.

Retailers Seize Customers

Consumer market research shows that the placement of the product (by brand or by product line, with one price alternative or several, or associated with a promoted product or not) can affect consumer choice. For example, whereas two fairly similar products (Brands A and B) with only one different characteristic may split the market, the addition of a third choice with a clearly inferior alternative to one of Brand A's characteristics will materially improve the sales of Brand A. Brand A can enhance this kind of advantage through sales pricing, shelf positioning, and comparative pricing.

Three factors give the retailer the upper hand in product placement:

Information on sales. The growth of point-of-sale technology (scanners, ATMs, point-of-sale terminals) gives the retailer the most up-to-date information on customer sales and the profitability of particular products.

Inventory control. The just-in-time delivery systems introduced in the 1980s give retailers the power to order products as they need them rather than on the basis of regular deliveries.

The scale of the store. The movement to large stores has given the retailer access to a much larger group of customers and a much wider range of products. In this context, the retailer has a wider range of choices, and the success or failure of any single product has less of an impact on total sales.

These attributes mean that in many cases the retailers have taken control of the placement and pricing of items on their shelves. This gives them the upper hand in promoting their own store brands. Their placement in the new information stream has increased the retailers' power in the customer relationship and over the manufacturer.

Wholesalers Up the Ante

Wholesalers are fighting to keep their special role in the distribution chain. Despite the squeeze on them from both manufacturers and retailers, wholesalers are focused on adding value for the smaller retailers in order to bring them some of the advantages of big players. To do this, they provide their clients with a number of value-added services, everything from overnight delivery to increasing the number of products they handle to special financing or technical services on hand. They may also assist customers in reducing handling charges, and tailor their product lines to their customers. And they may carry customized products, items specially designed, labeled, and packaged for their customers.

Sophisticated wholesalers are helping small retailers act more like their bigger competitors. They are willing to drop their margins as well as provide extra services to keep competitive. Still, these steps will only help slow the longer-term decline in the amount of gross domestic product that goes to wholesalers.

Small Manufacturers Find a New Life

The new retail distribution channels are making it easier for small manufacturers to play a competitive role in the battle for the new consumer by building relationships with the discount retailers. Recently, for example, one small company came up with a major process innovation that provided a new (and much cheaper) way of producing sanitary products for seniors. Until then, the company had focused on the nursing home market because retail distribution required very large marketing expenses for third-party distributors.

Its innovation enabled this company to go directly to the sales managers at Wal-Mart and Price/Costco. The latter allowed them a four-month trial in twenty stores. Satisfactory performance (good quality at lower prices) led to a permanent place on the shelf and an in-store promotion. Price/Costco's only requirement was a continuing standard of quality and a request that packages be large (thirty-two to a single package rather than four or six) because Price/Costco makes its profits on volume. This experiment resulted in a happy small supplier (that became a medium-size supplier); a happy store with another way to attract the smart, value-conscious shopper; and happy customers who had more money left at the end of the month and more confidence in their store of choice. The only unhappy player was the national brand whose margins continue to shrink.

A Global Perspective

ON A VISIT TO TOULOUSE a couple of years ago, my wife and I were struck by the degree to which the stores on the main street were really an exposition of global retailing. Benneton, the Body Shop, Victoria's Secret, the Nature Company—it was as if we were at the Stanford shopping center in California. Even the quaint sidewalk cafés seemed like a French caricature of the caricatured French sidewalk café in the Stanford shopping center. One of the trends that this reflects is the homogenization of a retailing culture, or perhaps more accurately, the emergence of a default global standard of retailing. Whether you go to Hong Kong or Beijing or Tokyo or Toulouse, you see the same stores. And increasingly that's not just a function of the economies of scale, but the emergence of a uniform set of global tastes and preferences.

A more sophisticated and demanding consumer is emerging not only in the United States but around the world. As a result, distribution channels worldwide are undergoing the same revolution as those in the United States. The rich consumer markets of the North Atlantic are opening rapidly to the global marketplace. The Asian high-income markets, despite great institutional resistance, also show signs that they are undergoing a distribution revolution. And even in the emerging middle-class markets of Asia, we are seeing significant changes in the way goods and services are distributed.

Many of the institutional changes originated in the rapidly changing U.S. markets. U.S. firms introduced to the world many of the key distribution mechanisms, including mail order, self-service supermarkets, TV shopping, discount stores, warehouse clubs, factory-outlet malls, and fast food restaurants. As they spread throughout the world, these alternatives to traditional retailing and distribution systems are changing the global economy. To understand the changing distribution system worldwide, it is helpful to examine the global players that will have great impacts on international distribution.

The International Retailer

THE LOWERED INTERNATIONAL BARRIERS accompanying the emerging global economy are enabling international retail firms to enter many local markets heretofore closed to them. This is changing local distribution systems. Big manufacturers have dominated multinational markets by selling branded products to the world from their home bases. But increasingly over the last few years, retailers themselves have moved aggressively across borders to reach and hold the middle-class consumer directly. Big retailers can bring many advantages with them across borders: strong brands, buying power, high-powered finance, effective sales systems, widespread distribution systems, staying power, style and design, and familiarity with key technologies.

In the past few years, many big retailers have found that international earnings are as important for them as they are for the big manufacturers of multinational brands (table 1). Many key retailers are truly international firms, and, in general, retail distribution companies are speeding up the process of globalization, becoming the preferred niche for bringing products or services to customers around the world.

TABLE 1: LEADING INTERNATIONAL FIRMS

COMPANY	COUNTRY	TYPE OF STORE	SALES ($ BILLION)	INTERNATIONAL SALES (%)
Retailers				
Ahold	Netherlands	Food	11.6	50
Aldi	Germany	Food	13.3	40
Carrefour	France	Food	20.2	30
Ikea	Sweden	Furniture	4.1	75
Ito-Yokado	Japan	Department stores	22.3	40+
Marks & Spencer	United Kingdom	Department stores	8.6	11
McDonald's	United States	Restaurant	24.0	34
Promodes	France	Food	14.5	40
Sainsbury	United Kingdom	Food	12.9	11
Manufacturers of Consumer Products				
Cadbury Schweppes	United Kingdom	Beverages	6.0	53
Coca-Cola	United States	Beverages	13.1	67
Kellogg	United States	Food	6.1	43
Kimberly-Clark	United States	Consumer products	7.7	32
RJR Nabisco	United States	Food	15.7	19
L'Oréal	France	Cosmetics	5.7	65
Procter & Gamble	United States	Consumer products	29.4	50
Philip Morris	United States	Food	50.1	28

Source: IFTF, 1994

The United Kingdom: Adapting to the Opening Rich Consumer Markets

INCREASING COMPETITION FOR RETAILERS is rapidly changing the distribution system in the United Kingdom. Retail margins
in the United Kingdom have traditionally been very high, averaging
from three to five times those in the United States and Europe. One
reason has been that market share is concentrated among large retailers. For example, the grocery sector is dominated by the Big
Three: Sainsbury, Tesco, and Argyll.

Traditionally, the Big Three have met threats of competition by
using their financial clout to build large new stores in middle-class
districts where they can offer a wide selection of high-value products
(on average, about 20,000 in a store compared to the discounter's
600). In addition, the Big Three control the product mixes and competitive conditions in their own markets: more than 50 percent of all
items sold in their stores are their own brands. Selling their own
brands gives them a 15 percent price advantage over national
branded products of similar quality sold in competing stores.

The changing U.K. market shows the power of the new consumer.
The internationalization of this maturing market has produced a
major fight for position. Profit margins are coming down, and the
central position of the Big Three supermarket retailers is under challenge: both Sainsbury and Tesco have laid off workers, their share
values are down, and they are having a harder time getting capital to
build new stores. Every manufacturer or provider of services to the
U.K. market must decide the extent of the hold domestic retailers
have over the customer and how this affects the distribution of their
own products.

As in the United States, however, the consumer, with rising levels
of education, income, mobility, and sophistication, is leading a distribution revolution. The United Kingdom's fairly open economy has
attracted increasing interest from foreign multinational firms with
their eyes on the United Kingdom's large margins. The United Kingdom is seeing more competition from both foreign and domestic
firms in a variety of new formats:

Discounters. Discounters, who accounted for 9 percent of the market in 1990, are expected to have 15 percent in 1995 and 20 percent
by the year 2000. Examples of the more aggressive discounters are
the big German retailer Aldi, Denmark's Netto, and France's Ed.

These are large and powerful multinational firms that have made long-term commitments to the U.K. market, with the strategy of building large discount superstores that offer prices well below the standard supermarket fare.

Retail warehouses. The number of large specialized stores in areas other than food (such as furniture, carpets, electrical goods, and hardware) has exploded in the last decade, growing from about 100 in 1980 to more than 1,000 today.

Warehouse clubs. Price/Costco recently received final court approval for the first warehouse club store in the United Kingdom. The Big Three opposed the deal vigorously because the environmental and permit process had been less rigorous for warehouse clubs than for retailers, but the courts allowed the distinction between retailers and warehouse clubs to stand. At least five other stores immediately applied for warehouse club permits. The warehouses will bring much larger stores to the United Kingdom than pure discounters, offering up to 3,500 products.

Factory outlets. U.S. developers are exporting another idea new to the United Kingdom—malls of factory-outlet stores. In the United Kingdom, only about 10 percent of all clothing is sold in discount stores, whereas the proportion in the United States is 50 percent.

Japan: A Traditional Retail System Forced Open by a Changing Consumer

TRADITIONALLY, THE JAPANESE RETAIL SECTOR has consisted of a huge number of small retailers (along with some very large stores) and a complex and highly structured distribution system built on the *keiretsu. Keiretsu* are formal and informal alliances between manufacturers, distributors, retailers, and banks that own each other's stock and exclusively buy and sell each other's goods and services. This system is certainly the most inefficient distribution system among those of major consumer countries, and it is increasing international tensions. The formal relationships within the *keiretsu* make it very difficult for foreign products to break into the domestic market. Under this system, sales outlets are determined not so much by customer needs as by protection of traditional channels. It is estimated that, as a result, Japanese retail prices are 13 percent higher than they should be by measurement of GDP.

Traditionally resistant to change, the old distribution system is being challenged by innovators taking cues from the global marketplace and reaching out to the new middle-class consumer. A number of such trends portend a shift in the domestic market significant not only for Japan but for the international trading scene as well. Nine changes that will help to break the old *keiretsu* mentality include:

Retailers take control. Ito-Yokada (which controls 7-Eleven Japan as well as other retail outlets) has begun a team-merchandising project designed to develop products for groups of manufacturers, wholesalers, and retailers. The key innovations in this approach are that it circumvents the *keiretsu* and that it is led by the retailer.

Daiei develops its own products. Daiei, the number one retailer in Japan, is moving rapidly to develop its own store brands and currently has over three hundred in place. New agreements with manufacturers promise that this number will go up dramatically over the next few years, giving Daiei much more control over product distribution and consumer relations than any other Japanese retailer.

A *manufacturer gives up control of distribution.* After thirty years of holding back its products from Daiei stores, Mitsubishi Electric, one of the biggest producers of electronic products in the world, signed an agreement to distribute its products through Daiei stores even though Daiei will discount these goods and hurt Mitsubishi's 24,000 mom-and-pop stores that have been its traditional outlet in Japan. Control of pricing is passing to the retailer.

The salaryman looks for a new suit. The Japanese businessman's traditional uniform is an expensive business suit purchased at one of the big department stores. The Aoyama Trading Company is changing this. It has opened discount suit stores all over Japan that sell suits from Hong Kong, Taiwan, and China at about 60 percent of the department store price (it plans to have 80 stores in Tokyo and 110 in Japan by the end of the year). In addition, other discount clothiers like Rothmans from Hong Kong now have a number of shops in Japan.

Larger stores grow like mushrooms. The size of the average Japanese store is increasing. Under pressure from the United States, the Ministry of International Trade and Industry (MITI) modified the rules for opening large retail stores. Traditionally, stores of over 500 square meters had to get approval from local governments, which meant that influential local retailers had some say in who was approved or not. The process usually meant long delays—if approval came at all. Recently MITI has raised the limit for local control to 1,000 square meters and speeded up the approval process so that it would take no more than one year. As a result, the number of large stores being built in Japan has doubled in the last four years. A leading player in the game is the U.S. discount retailer Toys "R" Us, which was instrumental in initiating international pressure several years ago. It now has 15 large outlets in Japan and is building 15 more.

Foreign consumer goods do exist. Traditionally, foreign companies have found it very difficult to break into the Japanese distribution system. But breakthroughs in the distribution system, the rise in the value of the yen, and Japanese overseas investments in consumer goods production are changing that. During 1993, for the first time ever, more washing machines, color TVs, refrigerators, and vacuum cleaners were imported than exported. Markets are now being driven by consumers rather than producers.

Discounters look abroad. The aggressive discount chain, Jonan Denki, is looking to increase the penetration of foreign products in Japan. The president of the chain, Toshio Miyaji, sponsors an annual fully paid shopping trip to Paris for one hundred Tokyo women to purchase women's apparel and cosmetics, and uses the publicity generated by the trip to favor its foreign goods at cheaper prices. The price difference is partly due to tariffs, but is mostly due to Japanese cosmetics firms that will not allow the distribution of products through any shop that discounts prices below a very high set rate, giving them a monopoly power over distribution. Jonan Denki is also challenging the Japanese law that says only 10 percent of lipstick sales can be imported. "I'm prepared to go to jail," says Miyaji. "It's bad to violate laws, but I'm resolved to fight an inappropriate one."

The domestic supply market is opening. The major manufacturers in Japan have long relied on secure sources of supply from captive companies or members of their *keiretsu*. The need to reduce model variation and get to better levels of scale is breaking this down in the auto industry. Tokai Riba has signed contracts to build gearboxes for both Toyota and Nissan, while Taiyo, which was set up by Matsushita as an exclusive contractor, now does only 30 percent of its work for them.

Even MITI is willing to look to a more open market. MITI has long been the advocate of a strong supportive industrial policy for Japanese producers. It seems to be shifting its stance: aside from easing the rules on retail space, MITI is adapting rules that foster greater opportunities (and potential failures) for venture capital, easing restrictions on financial regulation, and favoring the use of product liability laws rather than preemptive bureaucratic rules. In addition, Nippon Telegraph & Telephone recently dropped its support for the Japanese analog standard for HDTV (high definition TV), thereby admitting that the European-U.S. digital standards would prove superior in the long run. This is causing confusion and concern among Japanese firms that had committed billions of yen to the development of both the analog high-definition technology and programming in a battle that has been lost.

The Japanese market is still a closed market compared to other industrial countries, but there are signs of significant changes. The results of these changes may be more significant for foreign firms hoping to get their products into Japan than all the government-to-government negotiations over tariffs, quotas, and numerical targets. For producers of goods, it means the opening of a major route into the wealthy and underdeveloped Japanese market.

Emerging Asia: The Moth and the Flame of Third World Growth

THE REAL GROWTH in the number of middle-class buyers is not taking place in the rich consumer countries but in the rapidly developing countries of the world such as Thailand, Malaysia, China, and Taiwan. The upper-income segment within these countries (the number of households earning over $25,000 per year) is growing at more than 5 percent per year. This means that in fifteen years the number of such high-income households will double in these areas. (It will grow even faster in China, where the restrictions before 1990 on the right to own private property kept the number of high-earning households artificially low.) In just five of the emerging nations of Asia, the number of high-income households will rise from about 12 million in 1990 to 47 million in 2010 (table 2). This total will almost equal the number of high-income households in the European Community in 1990 (about 51 million).

TABLE 2: GROWING MIDDLE-CLASS POPULATION IN ASIA

(Millions of Households with over $25,000 in 1990 Dollars)

	1990	2010
China	2	24
South Korea	3	7
Taiwan	3	7
Indonesia	3	6
Thailand	1	3

Source: IFTF; historical data from World Bank, 1994

With the rapid growth in an affluent middle class, these Asian countries are going through a distribution revolution of their own. Ten years ago, traditional distribution outlets were the rule throughout many of the emerging countries of Asia. This meant that neighborhood markets, informal stands along major roads and avenues, and streets lined with shops were the primary locations for buying and selling goods. But as households cross higher income thresholds, they change their shopping behavior dramatically—this has been a notable trend throughout Asia. In 1987, for example, only 3 percent of Taiwanese purchased groceries in large supermarkets; by 1993, 50 percent did. In Thailand, where two thirds of consumers under forty-five years of age and over 95 percent of current shoppers have completed primary school, the growth of department stores has been phenomenal both in the city centers and in surrounding suburbs. Thai retail shopping space doubles every five years. Other Asian markets are also moving quickly from a distribution chain relying on millions of small local stores to a rapid increase in large, centrally located stores and shopping centers.

Urban markets are moving rapidly to develop distribution patterns similar to those in the rich consumer countries. Much of the development involves international firms seeking to get in on the ground floor. Big international retail firms are increasing their presence in all of the markets: Sogo (Japan) has been in Thailand for a decade and has major operations in Indonesia, Singapore, Hong Kong, Taiwan, and Malaysia as well. Sales at Thailand's 7-Eleven convenience stores increased eightfold from 1991 to 1994. Besides Sogo, Singapore's Orchard Road has many major stores, including Isetan (Japan), Takashimaya (Japan), Lane Crawford (Hong Kong), Marks & Spencer (United Kingdom), Toys "R" Us (United States), Galeries Lafayette (France), and Giordano (Hong Kong). In fact, competition is so hot among the international retailers in Singapore that prices and profits are falling dramatically.

As the new retailers come into a country, they force changes in the domestic distribution system: they bring international branded products with them; they purchase local products (while demanding very high quality for those products that will carry their store labels); they are large enough to have a big impact on the size and scale of local producers' runs; and they often eliminate layers of wholesalers that connect small producers and small retailers.

The competition brought about by these changes means that the emerging Asian markets are not plums ripe for the picking but very hard competitive nuts that might be difficult to crack. Newcomers with sometimes chaotic relationships with producers will have to wage battle in markets that are just opening and still small. On the other hand, these are the second-curve markets, and their size will soon be rivaling the more mature markets of North America and Europe. Enter these markets at your own peril: false steps, wrong partners, or a slack organization will lose you lots of money. But ignore the second curve and you will lose the future.

South Korea: Conglomerates and the Captured Customer

WHILE A PART OF EMERGING ASIA is rapidly opening to international distribution trends, another part has been particularly resistant to change and has caused problems for both the international trading system and their own consumers. These are the countries—Japan and South Korea are the most notable—where the distribution system is driven by interlocking ties among producers, distributors, and retailers.

While the conglomerate or the vertically integrated company has a long history in the United States and is still common in many European countries, it has been strongest in Asia under local names such as the *keiretsu* in Japan or the *chaebol* in South Korea. These national conglomerates are large diversified enterprises that form in one of two ways: either they contain a large number of vertically integrated firms that link raw material extraction, production, distribution, and sales into a seamless whole, or they consist of firms more loosely associated by financial and corporate ties with other firms up and down the distribution chain. These are tied together in bonds of interdependence (I will distribute my product only through your outlets if you sell all your other products at higher prices than the relatively high prices I set for my products). These interrelationships can take the forms of direct ownership, large holdings of each by a common bank, or relationships built up over the years that the national government is willing to tolerate for reasons of policy (for example, stable employment, a strong export position, personal ties, or growing investments). For both Japan and South Korea, the goal of building large and well-financed companies that can afford high levels of R&D expenditures and compete on the international stage has been of particular importance.

These key corporate relationships are changing. In South Korea, for example, the *chaebol* are under attack by the reformist government of President Kim Young Sam for being too rigid to compete in the new world of flexible international corporations. He is attempting to force the *chaebol* to be more flexible by providing inducements for them to focus resources on areas of concentrated interest. Those *chaebol* in the top ten that pick three areas to concentrate on will be freed from government controls over borrowing and will receive government subsidies for research and development. Each of the *chaebol* has responded: Hyundai (the largest, with $52 billion in sales) has chosen motor vehicles, electronics, and petrochemicals, leaving out holdings in heavy industries, textiles, semiconductors, financial services, insurance, hotels, and shipbuilding; Samsung (the second largest, with $47 billion in sales) has chosen electronics, heavy machinery, and petrochemicals, leaving out trading and distribution, textiles, semiconductors, financial services, and car making. The goal is to encourage competition, to foster small business, to break the power of the old industrial dynasties, and to stem the growing conflicts of interest in interlocking businesses. But the policy has not worked out as cleanly as hoped. While some areas have been targeted for separation, no action has been taken yet and the government is seeking to modify the move. It is forcing companies to reconsolidate some of the lopped-off units to avoid excessive competition. The recent grant of a cellular license to a consortium of *chaebol* to meet foreign competition also shows that the Korean government remains tied to protecting and nourishing their big companies at home.

Second Curve Sightings in Retail and Distribution

RETAIL AND DISTRIBUTION have become a highly competitive marketplace, one that's forced new responses from second-curve players. How have second-curve players responded? Creatively and diversely.

New Strategies, New Markets: Black Cat

BLACK CAT is the trademark of a company in Japan called Yamato Unyu. The logo shows a black cat carrying a kitten in her mouth, with the intent of the visual imagery being to suggest a product that is carefully delivered. Black Cat is the Japanese equivalent to UPS, and in fact has a joint venture with UPS outside of the United States. They provide door-to-door service anywhere in Japan, and will pick up just about anything—items as small as an envelope and as large as you like. And they'll pick that something up anyplace and deliver it anyplace. They started by being simply a transportation company, then saw the increasing potential in the parcel and small package delivery business. The mail-order share of their business isn't big at the moment, but it's growing at 30 to 40 percent annually, and while the company anticipates that may slow to around 20 percent annually, that's still a fairly healthy click.

Part of the reason for the growth in their mail-order fulfillment business is that they offer C.O.D. service, which is great for mail order. The mail order generation in Japan tends to be the younger generation, meaning forty and younger. Older people tend to want to see and touch the product, but younger people believe if they can see it in a catalog, that's good enough. CDs are an important part of this.

A few years ago McKinsey tried to encourage the use of mail order in Japan, but the perception at that time was that the products offered were both cheap and inferior. But this has changed. Increasingly, Japanese mail order products are perceived as high-quality. And the interesting thing is that the source of Black Cat's major area of growth isn't durable goods like CDs or clothing, but food— perishables like groceries, natural foods, and local foods. The company is exploiting its Kool Service Refrigerator Cars as the fastest way of getting fresh products without damaging the goods. People routinely order specialty seafood, from as far as 50 to 100 miles away. In a sense, Black Cat is exploiting the enormous traditional distribution systems in Japan, the number of different people who are involved in production, distribution warehousing, retailing, and so forth. And they're capitalizing on the increase in two-income households and the lifestyle changes that implies. The company can add some of these very specific specialized services because their trucks are passing by the homes or offices of every Japanese, almost on a daily basis. And obviously they are exploiting the density of Japan, where having a truck visiting a neighborhood of Tokyo puts them in contact with far more of the population than in a typical American city. They deliver 600 million items annually, an average of about 15 per Japanese household.

The company assigns a driver to a specific area, so the Black Cat man is almost as familiar as the mailman. And delivery is always face-to-face. He hands you the parcel, and you're reminded of the company's credo: *We're not just delivering goods, we're delivering our heart.* If no one's home, they leave a message card. When you call, they redeliver between six and eight in the evening.

Some retailers are obviously concerned that Black Cat is end-running some of their business. Others have tried to partner with Black Cat, which so far has not agreed. But the company does see that they could become a second-curve distributor with the Internet or the online services in Japan—the Nifty System, the CompuServe of Japan, which has a joint venture with CompuServe in the U.S. Electronic mechanisms for ordering coupled with Black Cat's reputation for quality, reliability, and service could result in a very new distribution system for daily, weekly, and monthly purchases. Black Cat could be a physical distribution system of the future. A similar thing may be happening in the U.S.: an increasing number of companies offer products on the Internet. Those orders can be delivered by FedEx, or in some cases UPS, within twenty-four to forty-eight hours.

Black Cat's revenue in 1994 was 547 billion yen, around $700 million to $800 million, 83 percent of which was from the delivery service. The company has made forays into electronic services, but was unsuccessful with their version of Zap mail (an electronic hybrid mail service), just as Federal Express was, and has since focused more heavily on the traditional delivery business. The company believes it has a real advantage because of its brand name loyalty and its reputation for customer service, although it knows that can go overboard, as it learned when it began delivering refrigerated melons. Melons need to be warm for their best flavor, and customers complained.

Distribution at Arm's Length: Pharmaceuticals

IN THE U.S. PHARMACEUTICAL INDUSTRY, manufacturers have moved farther away from their end customers. In the past twenty years, the share of products distributed through wholesalers rose from less than 50 percent to more than 70 percent. As a result, manufacturers have lost access to information about where and why their products are dispensed. More recently, as insurance coverage for prescription drugs has increased, third-party payers have begun to exert more control over the prescribing behavior of physicians.

In a move toward actual vertical integration that stunned the industry in the summer of 1993, the pharmaceutical giant Merck acquired Medco, one of the largest prescription drug mail order and pharmacy benefits management firms. By gaining access to information about patients, prescribers, and dispensers, Merck hoped that the combined firm could integrate its manufacturing, distribution, and management more efficiently. Moreover, access to detailed information on treatments and outcomes is presumed to help guide upstream research to discover new and more cost-effective products. For this type of integration to work, the parts must learn to compete together against the outside world, not compete within the firm.

Other smaller drug companies with less capital and greater risk aversion are pursuing virtual vertical integration (VVI) strategies. To create a full line of drugs, some are entering contractual relationships with other manufacturers that have complementary drug portfolios. Together, these partners then seek relationships with independent pharmacy benefits managers (PBMs) to offer integrated pharmaceutical services that emulate the Merck/Medco arrangement, offering a full drug portfolio, a network of pharmacies and mail order distributors, claims processing, and other information and distribution services. Many PBMs themselves are virtually vertically integrated. They typically link a network of pharmacies together by contract and by computer to distribute prescription drugs and collect claims data. They often contract with independent software providers for the drug utilization review and quality assurance software they use to monitor prescriptions.

As with all new relationships, however, there can be a rocky period of adjustment after the glow of the honeymoon wears off. Companies that look to VVI to rescue their fortunes must face a number of potential hurdles:

The mutual disrespect problem. The natural tendency in many businesses is to think that the other guy's business is simple. Resist that temptation. Understand the difficulties of each part of a vertical business. Realistically assess where value is added in the entire business.

The compensation problem. This is a corollary of the previous point. Because it is difficult to measure added value across a vertical business, each partner in a VVI venture tends to undervalue the other partners' contributions. They will have to negotiate creative approaches to find satisfactory compensation arrangements.

Getting the incentives right. For VVI to succeed, each partner must provide a piece of a complex product or service. Assuming that the capabilities of the partners are well matched to operate economically, it still will be necessary to provide incentives for each company to perform as expected. Transfer pricing discounts may make it more profitable in the short run for alliance partners to deal with outside (retail) customers, rather than within the alliance. Companies will constantly face a dilemma: Should we place a higher priority on servicing customers that are ours alone or customers that belong to the alliance? Each company must have incentives to service both.

Info tech due diligence. Many VVI ventures are based on the expectation that the information resources of one firm will enable all partners to operate more efficiently. This strong assumption requires extensive due diligence about the actual information resources of the partners. These assumptions have two sides: the compatibility of the information systems and the actual value of the combined information itself, which must be analyzed. One exercise to conduct is to mock up a report that would be available from the new venture. Put hypothetical data in the report and ask whether any business decisions would change as a result.

Forward, But Not Too Fast: Electronic Shopping

FOR A LONG TIME, shopping was the same for everyone. Retailers communicated with you, the consumer, through mass advertisements in newspapers and magazines or on radio and TV; then you went to the store to make your purchases. That may not be true for long: technology may change the way goods are bought and sold so much that these activities may seem quaintly nostalgic, like dialing a rotary phone, or getting up from the couch to change the TV channel.

Alternative distribution systems are emerging to meet the needs of the sophisticated consumer, systems that promise convenience, quality, and customized shopping. These new channels will also change the relationships among manufacturers, retailers, and consumers. Current alternative shopping experiences include home shopping channels and infomercials on TV and computer online services. But technology and telecommunications vendors promise even more, including additional specialized shopping channels and online services, interactive television, CD-ROM catalogs, interactive kiosks, and virtual reality.

Shoddy customer service is driving customers away. According to a MasterCard International recent survey, over 60 percent of its respondents, in the last six months, had left a store without buying anything after being unable to find a salesclerk to help them make a purchase. But customer service isn't all shoppers want. The survey showed that almost nine out of ten shoppers make price comparisons. They want product variety and detailed, unbiased information. To meet customer needs, new distribution channels will have to offer that variety and that information, and the information must have more validity than that offered in a traditional store, where shoppers recognize that salespeople, because of inexperience or the lure of commission, aren't objective. These new systems will have to meet consumers on their own turf—in the home or office or anywhere else they may be standing.

Many kinds of new distribution channels are striving to meet these sometimes variable consumer needs:

Home shopping programs. In recent years, QVC (Quality Value Convenience), Home Shopping Network (HSN), and other home shopping channels have hit the airwaves. Nearly 13 million adults have been inspired to order merchandise such as jewelry, clothing, consumer electronics, toys, and personal care products. And this number is bound to increase: For example, QVC has launched a second shopping channel, Q2. But while the number of shopping programs is growing, the programs are not fulfilling all consumers' needs. According to MasterCard's study, home shoppers perceive that these programs give them only limited selection and variety. And only 40 percent of consumers rate these channels as excellent in terms of convenience. The future of home shopping programs lies in their ability to provide better value, convenience, product variety, and information.

Interactive television. The answer to greater consumer convenience may be interactive television, which has several potential players. One of the most publicized is Time Warner, which is running a test in Orlando, Florida. Over 4,000 households are equipped with a set-top box and a color printer that together provide a range of applications including movies on demand and automobile and grocery shopping. Consumers can select a movie by title or category and even stop, start, and rewind the movie. But the most interesting feature for business is a dialogue box, which appears on screen and asks the consumer to view a commercial and answer a few questions in exchange for a free movie, allowing the manufacturer to build a customer database of lifestyle and interest information. Whether or not consumers are willing to answer the questions remains to be seen. They tend to be very vocal about their right to privacy, but they're also often lured by the free gift. When they are tired of watching movies, potential shoppers can browse the Auto Mall by category or manufacturer. Color samples, interior views, and full-motion clips of test runs are available, as well as product literature that can be printed on the attached color printer.

Another program Time Warner is exploring in Orlando is Shopper Vision, a grocery shopping experience. Using a joystick, shoppers can move down the grocery aisles, pick up an item, view it three-dimensionally, and even check the nutrition label. (This attribute will be critical to Shopper Vision's success. Many earlier grocery shopping packages provided shoppers only a long list of products with the options listed numerically; shoppers had trouble visualizing what to buy.) Once shoppers have decided on an item, they place it in their grocery cart, proceed down the aisle, and check out at the front of the store, then indicate whether they want the groceries delivered or whether they'll pick them up.

The basic assumption of interactive television is that consumers want full interactivity of entertainment, shopping, and information.

Yet the TV is a symbol of entertainment and has bred several generations of couch potatoes who watch the tube to escape. The most powerful and empowering technology of the late twentieth century is the remote control. Historically, users have had a low degree of control over the content provided by television, and as a result, interactive television is not likely to emerge broadly until after the year 2000, because even given greater sophistication, it will take a great deal of time to change consumer behavior.

Online services. Four percent of all households have online access, and many of these are now subscribing to online services. The total online services market was almost $16 billion in 1995, but only 6 percent of revenues were from consumer online services, according to Online Services 1995 Review, Trends and Forecasts. The rest were from business services. The four major consumer service providers are America Online, CompuServe, Prodigy, and GENIE, which account for 90 percent of the 4 million consumer subscribers. They have had tremendous growth in the past few years. America Online alone added 70,000 subscribers in December 1993, but ironically the compelling driving force is access to the Internet.

Online users have access to up-to-date news and information, electronic messaging, chat lines, reference sources, magazines, software programs, Internet gateways, and electronic shopping. Users can also buy or sell products and services. Typical purchases include consumer electronics, clothing, toys, tools, home improvement and personal care products, and hotel and plane reservations. Currently, most of these services provide a vehicle for communication and information dissemination and do not cater to electronic shoppers. Prodigy has tried to position itself as a shopping service, but has had poor results and suffers from high turnover rates. One problem is that most of these online services offer graphics that have to be downloaded to the shopper's hard drive, which can be tedious and frustrating for shoppers, who generally have the slower 2400- or 4800-baud modems. Another problem is that some services, such as America Online, offer no graphics for shoppers, just text.

Interactive CD-ROM catalogs. As alternatives to stores, traditional catalogs have been successful distribution channels. In 1993, catalogs generated $36 billion. Now efforts are under way to take catalog shopping into the twenty-first century by making it electronic. The hope is to make catalog shopping more entertaining and to match the electronic experience more closely to the way consumers shop in person. An early version was En Passant, a CD-ROM of twenty-one catalogs that Apple, Electronic Data Systems, and Redgate Communications tested in 1994. While browsing individual catalogs like Tiffany, Lands' End, Williams-Sonoma, L.L. Bean, and Patagonia, customers could double-click on any item to get information such as sizes, colors, and return and exchange policies. In addition to text, both audio and video (full-motion and still images) were available.

CD-ROM catalogs, like online shopping, will in all likelihood continue to be a niche market into the next decade. Only a small fraction of CD-ROM drives are estimated to be in U.S. households; most are in businesses, a factor that will slow the growth of electronic catalogs for the next several years unless people decide to shop at work. But with the price of computers dropping, CD-ROM drives are being bundled with new computer packages, and as that installed base grows, consumers will become more comfortable with this channel.

Mobile shopping. Information appliances, often called personal digital assistants (PDAs) or personal communicators, are creating new experiences for many business professionals and some consumers. They not only track addresses, send and receive e-mail, and download data and spreadsheets from the office; you can also use them to shop. The cross-platform electronic shopping software package called eShop allows users access to personalized stores and malls by means of their PDAs. The software simulates a street lined with storefronts. You choose a store, enter, and are greeted by an intelligent agent. Products are displayed in the same fashion as in a retail store, and you can view different items by browsing up and down the aisles. When you've decided what you want to buy, the virtual agent totals your purchases, charges your credit card, and tells you when you'll receive your purchases.

Interactive kiosks. Companies are beginning to offer interactive kiosks in public areas such as shopping malls, convenience stores, and train stations. The kiosk market grew from $112 million in 1991 to $252 million in 1993, an annual increase of over 50 percent, most of which was due to falling prices and better technology that boosts the cost-effectiveness of interactive kiosks. In addition, kiosks are being used in new ways. In 1990, most of the kiosks were used for providing information; now almost half of all kiosks are for sales and services.

The Minnesota Twins baseball team has been one of the more successful organizations at using kiosks for sales and services. In 1993, the Twins installed thirty ticket vending kiosks in supermarkets and discount stores throughout the Minneapolis metropolitan area. Twins fans can check seat availability, see the view of the field from their intended seat, pay for the ticket, and have the ticket printed at the kiosk. Not only was this convenient for the fans, but the team found that many fans upgraded to higher-price seats once they discovered that they could get a better view and that about 10 percent of the fans who bought tickets through the kiosks probably wouldn't have gone to a game otherwise. Currently, only 2 percent to 3 percent of the 2 million total ticket purchases are conducted by kiosk, but the team hopes this will increase to between 10 percent and 15 percent.

Unlike the Twins, the U.S. Postal Service has had bad luck with kiosks. The U.S. Postal Service partnered with the Postal Buddy Corporation to install multimedia kiosks to streamline the change-of-address system. The system allowed consumers to change their addresses; purchase personalized products such as return-address labels, business cards, and stationery; and notify catalog and magazine publishers. After rolling out almost two hundred kiosks, the Postal Service canceled the contract because the kiosks were not generating a return on investment (only $15 to $30 in revenue each day compared to the projection of $35 to $55). There were two major problems: the kiosks often ran out of stamps, and they didn't give change—only credit for future purchases.

Financial services companies are also considering the use of kiosks. One company is exploring the idea of using interactive kiosks that allow customers to obtain information about its products and definitions of unfamiliar words and concepts. Another provider, Wells Fargo, has a bill-payment service that allows customers to pay recurring bills electronically from Wells Fargo ATM machines and kiosks placed in public locations such as the post office.

Kiosks do have their limitations. Most are installed in public places, which means that the information shown on the screen cannot be sensitive, and that consumers must be kept safe. In addition, only one person can interact with the system at a time. So far, the low volume of usage and high capital costs for the video device, computer, input device, and software make kiosks a risky investment.

Virtual reality. Retailers are beginning to use virtual reality (VR) to bring consumers into the store and, once they get them there, to close the deal. Using tools like computer-assisted gloves and headgear, VR generates three-dimensional images that create the illusion of real-life events. The biggest applications have been for training (particularly for physicians learning new surgery techniques and military personnel learning to use expensive, high tech systems) and entertainment. But consumer applications are also emerging. VR can help consumers visualize end products, especially those that involve complex elements of design, as in building or remodeling houses. Silicon Graphics and British Gas are testing a system they call Kitchen Reality, a desktop-based VR system that lets you see exactly how your redesigned kitchen will look. You can wander through the proposed kitchen, opening drawers, shrinking down to child-height to check for safety, trying out different work-top veneers and tiles, and rearranging appliances and cabinets. In the short term, VR and other visualization systems will help consumers to visualize end products to promote rather than facilitate sales. It is unlikely that this type of system will allow consumers to purchase remotely. Rather, it will reassure buyers that the product is what they want, enabling retailers to close the deal more quickly and easily.

The Rules of the Second Curve

EVERYBODY IN THE DISTRIBUTION CHAIN is entering a new arena to play a new game. So that they don't lose before they begin, participants should take a strategic approach to learning the new rules—or should define their own. The new rules include the following:

LOOK PAST THE HYPE

From the sounds of the press, electronic distribution systems will be available and used by nearly everyone in the very near future. Look again! In the early 1980s, consumer computer online services emerged to account for a market of under $100 million. Industry experts stated that by 1990, the online market would reach $30 billion. By 1995, it generated only $1 billion, one of the reasons being that for this new revolution of interactivity to flourish, many different players will have to cooperate.

RECOGNIZE THE NECESSITY OF
MANUFACTURER COOPERATION

Television distribution channels such as home shopping and interactive television generated over $3 billion in 1993, an increase of 20 percent annual growth since the early 1990s. Yet they still account for less than 0.1 percent of U.S. retail sales, which totaled over $2 trillion in 1993, or 5 percent of nonstore retailing. It may still be the second curve, but it's going to take a while to take off.

When IBM and Blockbuster decided to introduce a make-your-own CD technology, they commanded lots of press attention. But they forgot to involve the record publishers, a big mistake because, as it turned out, the record industry didn't want to give up the rights to the music. So IBM and Blockbuster had to pull the plug.

CONSIDER THE QUESTION OF PRICE: WILL CONSUMERS PAY?

Many businesses, including Blockbuster, are getting shoppers to make purchases with their pocket change. As a result, most consumers don't tally how much they spend on rental movies, for example. A full third of video rental store income comes from late fees. In the electronic world, consumers may suffer from sticker shock when they get their bills at the end of the month. This sticker shock could slow the adoption of interactive applications such as movies on demand and home shopping until consumers change their behavior and learn to live with the new costs (as many have done for cable TV).

MAKE A COMMITMENT TO THE CUSTOMER

Keeping pace with consumers and dealing with their increasing need for choice, access, and service will be expensive and time-consuming. Yet rapid adaptation to changing consumer needs will be essential to success. Pick the relationship that best suits your needs, find the right partners or channels for the long run, and make your commitment.

MANAGE THE CHANNEL

Large producers often must use third parties to distribute their products, and sometimes they must bundle them with other products to capture the myriad of small shops and distributors that make the final sales. Second-curve channels are emerging. Computer sales, for example, are often made to individual users or to small departments or working groups and are tied to sales of software, networking capabilities, and servicing support. Thus computer makers must build relationships with distributors that provide mutual benefit. They must ensure that both partners profit, that competition with the distributor is kept to a minimum, and that areas of mutual self-promotion are found.

For example, Compaq, a very successful desktop computer manufacturer, built its success by first agreeing to sell only through distributors and to cooperate with Microsoft in packaging hardware and software with easy connections to other peripherals (so-called plug and play). Compaq has moved ahead of the early market leader Dell, which sells only through its own network.

Companies are learning that it is the channels that have direct ties to the customer: those in the channels are there to answer customers' questions, to show them alternatives, to set a final price, and to establish confidence in a continuing relationship. In such a position, they can develop their own brands or find substitute products that promise them a greater cut of the final product. Companies are learning that it is in their interest to make the manufacturer a commodity and to put themselves in the value-added seat. Keep your eye on the final customer at all times and find channel partnerships where mutual benefits are clear to both sides.

FOCUS ON TIME-TO-MARKET

Time-to-market is getting shorter, a key result of second-curve consumers meeting second-curve technology. This means that products have less of an opportunity to establish themselves in the marketplace before substitute products replace them and that information about the customers and what they need is all the more important to manufacturers and their R&D activities. Look at some of the striking changes in the time it takes to bring products to market:

Autos. In the 1980s, Japanese firms were able to take an increasing share of the global auto market by being more flexible and adaptable to the consumer market. While European and U.S. firms took 5 years to deliver a new car to market, the Japanese could do it in 3.5. This is changing, however. In recent years, Chrysler delivered the Neon to the market in thirty-one months, and Ford redesigned the

Mustang in thirty-six months. Chrysler has introduced five new basic chassis platforms between 1992 and 1994; it had only three in the previous twenty years.

Auto parts. AEPP, an English automotive parts firm, used to take twenty-six weeks to develop, test, and deliver new pistons. With computer-assisted designs, it can now do it in six weeks.

Semiconductors. Intel, the market leader in microprocessors, is speeding up the time to deliver sophisticated new chips to keep competitors at bay. The total development time for the newly introduced Pentium chip was four years. The next generation chip will move to market in two years. Likewise, Texas Instruments has just built a large new production plant in Texas designed to move specially designed chips to market in half the time it took its previous plant.

Customer services. In the communications industry, as elsewhere, the drive to provide specialized services to customers quickly is catching on. A few years ago, it took Bell Atlantic two weeks to connect customers to their preferred long-distance carriers; they can do it now in a few hours. A few years ago, AT&T's design-to-delivery cycle for custom-designed power supplies was fifty-three days; now it is five days. In 1992, IBM Credit took a week to approve major credit deals; now it takes four hours. Timing product innovation effectively is a key lever for controlling the distribution system. Superior customer service is a hallmark of the second curve.

PARTNERSHIPS ARE MORE IMPORTANT

Ties of mutual interdependence are growing throughout the distribution system in the form of formal partnerships or ventures that set up specific contractual relationships. Partnerships can help bridge the uncertainties between two curves. These relationships are a great opportunity not only to sell products but to develop new products together or to provide a service better than either of the partners has done alone. Still, ventures do not work as smoothly as a single integrated company can. Coordinating activities across organizations takes extra time. Half of all ventures end with one partner buying the other out or simply withdrawing. Make use of partnerships, but don't bet your firm on them.

Health Care: Doctor, Doctor, Give Me the News

IN TIMES OF CHANGE, people prematurely jump to a conclusion about what the second curve is really about. American health care is jumping to a phantom second curve. When you look at the health care industry today, you can't help but see enormous structural change in many of the developed nations. But while it's certain that the changes are real, it's questionable as to whether or not we're seeing a real second curve. It looks like one to a lot of people, but it's more likely a false second curve, an unsustainable interim stage where, as much as we'd like to believe that we've solved the problem, we're really just rearranging deck chairs on the Titanic of the first curve.

In the United States, the apparent second-curve changes involve the growth of managed care over traditional fee-for-service medicine, the increase in corporatism in health care, and the restructuring of health care into gigantic vertically integrated systems. The validity of these changes as signs of a true second curve is questionable in a couple of ways: first, whether or not the second curve we're seeing can become the mainstream solution to the American health care crisis, and second, whether or not that solution is sustainable. But the health care example is critical. It shows that people (particularly consultants) can convince themselves of meaningful change, when it's really a work in progress.

Sources of the Health Care Second Curve

THE SOURCES BEHIND the transformation of health care systems in the U.S. and around the world involve five major areas: the key drivers we have seen throughout the book, in particular new consumers and new technology. But health care has some unique features: tradeoffs in financing and delivery, the increasing power of buyers, and medical ethics.

Tradeoffs in Health Care Financing and Delivery

TO PROVIDE QUALITY HEALTH CARE to everyone, health care systems everywhere have to struggle with tradeoffs in three basic areas: cost, quality, and access. And, in the United States, there's a fourth: security of benefits.

Cost

How much is paid, and by whom? Most developed nations spend between 7 percent and 10 percent of their GDP on health care. Most health care systems in Europe, Canada, Australia, and New Zealand have managed to contain cost as a share of GDP for five- to ten-year periods. The United States, on the other hand, has, over the last seventy years, continually expanded the share of the economy devoted to health care, with little interruption to that trend. It is currently 14 percent of GDP.

Quality

Traditionally, particularly in the United States, the quality of medical care was thought to be a function of the caliber of inputs. Better-trained physicians and other professionals with state-of-the-art technology in well-organized, well-financed, highly specialized settings would produce high-quality care. But this view is being challenged. Increasingly, scientific evidence shows that the returns gained from ever-increasing inputs of resources are either negative, zero, or, at best, so minuscule as to not warrant further investment. The work of the Rand Corporation in the United States indicates that anywhere from a third to a half of medical procedures—such as coronary artery bypass surgery—in the U.S. are unnecessary, and as a result medical care is being called to task. What has it done with all the money? Where is the improved health status as indicated by factors like longevity, mobility, and the quality of life?

Access

Who gets what care and services, and under which circumstances? Developed countries that make up the Organization for Economic Cooperation and Development (OECD) have achieved universal coverage for health care for virtually all their residents, with the notable exceptions of the United States and South Africa. In the United States, more than 40 million people are uninsured at any time, and as many as 60 million are uninsured at some point in any two-year period, a number that continues to rise by almost one million per year. Inadequate access to health care is particularly acute for children: at any given time, more than 10 million American children lack access to health insurance.

Security of Benefits

Depending on their social, economic, and employment status, Americans can lose and gain health care benefits several times in the course of their lives. While the elderly enjoy guaranteed coverage through Medicare, and some low-income individuals have access to health care through Medicaid, most Americans receive health insurance through their employers, and this is the direct cause of the volatility in the uninsured population—85 percent of the uninsured are working people and their families. As people change jobs or move in and out of employment, they go on and off insurance.

The New Power of Buyers

HEALTH CARE PURCHASERS, be they government, private payers, or individual patients, are focused on containing costs and increasing the value from their investments. Whether they are health care coalitions and large employers in the United States, provincial ministries of health in Canada, or regional health authorities in the United Kingdom, power is shifting to purchasers, and they're using it. For example:

- Despite decades of inaction, employers have recently joined forces to create more effective business coalitions—partnerships that have negotiated tougher contracts, raised employee contributions, and increased their use of managed care.
- Cutbacks in the growth of Medicare and Medicaid will only amplify the trend toward the concentration of purchasing power.
- Public employee group purchasers such as the California Public Employees Retirement System (CALPERS) have emerged as public sector entities concentrating their purchasing power through a relatively limited number of managed care plans.

The Rise of Sophisticated Consumers

SOPHISTICATED NEW CONSUMERS and their agents are challenging the unique authority of physicians and insisting on a greater role in clinical decision-making. Patients can't be treated as passive fodder for medical practice; increasingly, they're as educated as their doctors, all of which creates a market that will differentiate between truly personal health care products and services, and plan-purchased products and services. For example, more drugs are likely to be placed on a restrictive formulary, while at the same time patients will increasingly have the right to trade up to other medications that enhance elements of their health and well-being. As the baby boomers age, side effects of aging like impotence and incontinence will be perceived as incredibly threatening and will warrant a premium price, paid directly by the consumer, if such side effects can be minimized. Surveys conducted by Louis Harris & Associates and the Institute for the Future indicate that a significant subset of consumers, approximately 20 percent, will trade up with their own money, particularly for health plans and pharmaceuticals that directly impact their well-being.

New Technology

MOLECULAR BIOLOGY AND INFORMATION TECHNOLOGY will transform medicine in the next century. Total exposition of the human genome will bring about new insights into disease, and possibly uncover the secrets of effective therapy for a host of diseases. But perhaps more powerful will be the application of computer and communications to the practice of medicine and the coordination of care. Medicine is an information-based activity, yet in terms of the efficient and appropriate use of information technology, medical practice has lagged behind other industries by decades. (Some would even say centuries.) The most significant transformations will come from the combination of powerful handheld computers, so-called PDAs or personal digital assistants, wireless communications, and large patient databases. Combined, these tools will support the mobile nature of medicine and provide a platform of new approaches to clinical practice in the hospital, the clinic, and the home.

The Ethics of Controlling Human Biology

NEW TECHNOLOGIES, cost pressures, and sophisticated consumers are a powerful and potentially toxic combination. As the global baby boom confronts its mortality in the next century, death and dying will become a major focus of societal debate. The legitimacy of rationing by both public and private payers on behalf of patients they serve will come under enormous scrutiny. And because debates about the ethics of rationing will not be solved easily by technical analysis, the battles will be ugly, political, and confounded by issues such as race and poverty. Enormously complex questions will be asked about the rights of human beings to control their own biology and the biology of the unborn. Deep-seated beliefs about life, disease, personality, and death will be challenged by the new biology.

The Supposed Second Curve

THESE TRENDS are affecting health care systems across the world. These driving forces have created a need for change in health care, and considerable change has occurred.

From Fee-for-Service to Capitation

THE MOST SIGNIFICANT SHIFT in the United States has been the shift from fee-for-service to capitated managed care. Fee-for-service is a mechanism of payment which involves paying physicians or hospital-based providers every time service is provided. Given that consumers have little say in determining whether or not a service is required, there is a huge tendency for fee-for-service to lead to escalation in cost. Providers obviously have an economic benefit if there are *more* procedures, tests, surgeries, and visits, rather than fewer. Capitation is a mechanism of payment whereby providers are paid on a per-member, per-month basis: reward and reimbursement are earned for being available to take care of patients on a monthly basis, rather than for specific procedures performed. Under capitation, the incentive is to do less rather than more.

At the core of the shift to managed care is the notion that providers ought to be bearing more of the risk for the care they provide. Because consumers run the risk of being overtreated in a fee-for-service system and undertreated in a capitated system, it's crucial to have mechanisms that measure the quality of care. As we shift from professional to corporate practice and as medicine confronts the demands of sophisticated consumers and powerful buyers, the need for accurate information on the value of medical care will increase, requiring systematic methods of collecting, analyzing, and reporting scientifically sound data on the cost, process, and outcomes of care. This field is still in its infancy, and considerable research and development is required to develop metrics and institutions for evaluating the cost-effectiveness of health services. And while such developments are under way, whether or not such methods of evaluation will be systematically applied and implemented in the highly pluralistic U.S. health care systems on a standardized basis is certainly questionable. There are some pioneering organizations that are trying to build a forum and a set of tools and practices that move toward such standards. The National Committee for Quality Assurance (NCQA) is a Washington-based nonprofit organization whose mission is to develop methods of evaluating the quality of managed care organizations, and to provide information to the public and to the payers of the health care bill (most notably the private sector employers). But many parties, including pharmaceutical companies, benefit consultants, hospital providers, and specialty societies, have a structural interest in making sure that evaluation of quality is highly fragmented.

From Professionalism to Corporatism

WHILE MEDICINE has historically been dominated by the self-regulated professional—doctors who take the Hippocratic oath to serve the patient and do no harm—the field is being transformed from a professional to a corporate activity across the globe. Whether they are the American for-profit health plans and hospital chains, or the British fund holders, health trusts, and regional health authorities, the key institutions of the future will be run more like corporations than professional practices. And nowhere will that rise of corporatism be pushed to the limit as in the United States. The investor-owned hospital sector (Columbia/ HCA in particular) is headed toward enormous first-curve concentration as it pursues a strategy to dominate local markets. Similarly, the managed care industry and the Blue Cross–Blue Shield plans are in the midst of both consolidation and conversion to for-profit status.

The huge opportunities in the long run will be in the health care service of the emerging Asian economies. It's unlikely that Asia, particularly countries like Taiwan, South Korea, Thailand, and Vietnam, can afford to guarantee first world medicine to all its citizens. What is likely is that a basic guaranteed service will be available to all, with private markets for those emerging middle-class consumers who wish to increase the quality of and access to medical care. Universal services analogous to the state-run British National Health Service model is likely to be a floor for all citizens, but there will be several opportunities within the country to trade up to more exclusive and expensive Western-style medicine. This will be the future of health care in a number of countries.

From Inpatient to Outpatient

THE HOSPITAL has been the key institution of health care for the
last one hundred years, not only in the U.S., but in most developed
countries. This was a historic shift; prior to that, hospitals were
viewed as repositories for the sick, and were both unsafe and unpleas-
ant. But increasingly the shift is away from the hospital as the primary
locus of health care. In the United States, there's been a successive
decline in the use of hospitals over the last thirty years, and since the
early 1980s hospital occupancy rates have fallen sharply. The number
of admissions per thousand has dipped significantly, and the rate of
use of beds per thousand population has plummeted, particularly in
those areas where managed care is most prevalent. Capitated managed care provides an incentive to reduce the utilization of expensive
services—and hospitals are, of course, the most expensive dimension
of the health care system.

The shift in the location of care has taken power away from hospitals and given it to alternate site providers, such as home care organizations, IV therapy companies, and other forms of independent
agencies such as surgery centers and ambulatory care centers. More
and more care is being provided in a physician's office and the home,
rather than in the traditional hospital setting.

Part of the transformation toward a home environment is a reflection of patient preferences. Nobody really wants to be in a hospital; if
care can be delivered in a less acute setting, most individuals will be
interested. From a cost control point of view, it's ironic that countries that have much lower health care costs than the United States
(Japan, Britain, and Denmark are examples) have higher use of the
hospital per capita in terms of number of days per thousand population spent in hospital, and length of stay in the hospital. The key to
cost is really not the length of stay, but the acuity and intensity of
servicing during a patient's stay in the hospital. The U.S. has been in
the forefront of extremely intensive utilization of technologies in the
hospital during short lengths of stay.

As managed care grows, and more and more shifts occur to the
ambulatory environment, the public increasingly questions whether
or not these lengths of stay are appropriate. The most recent example, and one that is a harbinger of future interventions, is the situation in New Jersey where the governor recently signed into law
legislation that limits the ability of managed care organizations to
discharge women in less than two days after normal delivery of a

child. This has received considerable popular support, and similar legislation is on the books in California. The intent of the legislation is to protect mothers from premature discharge from hospitals, which would be thought to be prejudicial to the health of both mother and child. Managed care organizations and some provider groups oppose the movement because they believe it to be a thin end of the wedge which could lead to further disease-specific legislation limiting the ability of organizations to manage care.

The Response from the Delivery System: Vertical Integration—or Disintegration?

BUYERS ARE CONCENTRATING their purchasing power, forcing health plans to lower rates and consolidate horizontally. In fear of becoming lackeys to intermediaries, providers are beginning to integrate. In American hospitals, health plans and physicians are reorganizing themselves in a myriad of relationships, attempting to align incentives of all of the parties to contain costs and improve quality. Similar shifts are occurring in Sweden and in the United Kingdom.

One unifying theme in the reintegration of health care is an attempt to shift the basic incentives of medical care from fee-for-service to capitation. A consequence of this is an increasing emphasis on primary care over specialty care. More patient care is being put in the hands of primary care physicians, who act as gatekeepers to the specialized care provided by hospitals and medical services. In effect, these primary care doctors become general contractors on behalf of their patients.

The creation of fund holders—groups of physicians who receive capitated contracts in the United Kingdom, or capitated medical groups in the United States—is an attempt to give providers significant financial incentives to lower the costs of treating entire populations rather than to maximize the services they provide. But because the stock of physicians in the United States is so dominated by specialists, there is a real question as to whether or not this model can provide the majority of health care services. In the United Kingdom, more than 50 percent of the physicians are in general or family practice, compared to less than 20 percent in the United States. It's virtually impossible for the United States to change this mix significantly in the short run. The argument is made that the best way to respond to the new world of managed care is to create so-called integrated health systems, vertically integrated systems of care combining hospitals, physicians, and insurance functions into one organization that provides services to the community on a per-member, per-month basis.

There are three general types of such integrated systems, each demonstrating a different balance between the insurance, hospital, and physician counterparts.

The Traditional HMO

The first and classic type is the traditional HMO, an organization in which hospitals, physicians, and health insurance work exclusively for the plan, creating a combination of shared risk in a tight triangular relationship where everybody is in it together, even though in many of these systems the physicians have a very strong voice as a group.

The typical managed care organization is supposed to be capitated. Historically, the early pioneers in managed care, the Kaiser Permanente system of California and the western states, the Harvard Community Health Plan, and Group Health of Puget Sound in Seattle, were organized as nonprofit community organizations where physicians and providers were capitated: their rewards and incentives were on a per-member, per-month basis rather than on a fee-for-service basis. These systems were culturally driven; they tended to have a kind of quasi–social democratic feel to them, and they tended to service blue-collar working families. In the 1980s and through the 1990s, the organizations that tended to grow the fastest in the managed care world were less strict or physically defined forms of managed care, or "managed care light." The growth in light managed care has been impressive and has accounted for most of the growth in the managed care industry. These organizations, including some variants of HMOs and the increasingly popular PPO (preferred provider organization), were structured on three principles. First, they used their purchasing power to negotiate contracts with a subset of providers so a restricted panel of physicians was offered, although many of these plans offered the alternative of opting out to any provider in the community, albeit at a higher cost to the patient. Second, they used mechanisms like utilization review to actively interfere in the clinical decision making of physicians. And third, they used a model known as point of service, a sort of hybrid between the PPO and the HMO, which has been attractive because it provides the illusion of choice. Conceived as a socially acceptable way of getting New Yorkers into HMOs, point of service is, at its core, an HMO with a restricted panel of physicians, where providers are reimbursed on a capitated basis, and the patient has the right to see providers in the community outside the core network. But patients face fairly steep financial penalties in terms of co-payments and deductibles with out-of-pocket costs for an episode of illness capped as high as two or three thousand dollars. Facing such incentives, patients tend to stay in the network; after a year or so of experience in a point of service plan, 90 percent of them seem to stay in the network. Such systems have been increasingly adopted by employers as a means of capping their liability for employee benefit plans.

The Medical Group

The second model is one where physicians are key in terms of bearing the risk for the care of their patients. This is particularly prevalent in Southern California, where a number of at-risk medical groups such as Mullikin, Bristol Park Medical, and Health Partners agree with several HMOs to look after patients on a per-member, per-month basis. These medical groups became general contractors on behalf of those patients, responsible for providing primary care and specialty medical services as well as hospital services. The health plan does the marketing to employers, and the medical groups organize care and subcontract the hospital dimension to the hospitals within their own network. In many instances in California, these medical groups actually own a small hospital, enabling them to capture full-capitated payment, including the hospital and physician component. This is partly due to a wrinkle in California law that forbids the corporate practice of medicine and will not allow an organization other than an insurance company to bear risks for hospital care, unless it is owned by the medical group.

This model is one in which the plans have increasing market power as they consolidate horizontally, and in which the medical groups are increasingly price takers rather than price makers, where they have less and less ability to argue for higher rates. Their margins have been squeezed substantially over the last five years. In late 1995, the typical employer would pay HMOs like Health Net or Pacifi-Care $125 per member per month for a commercial life—a typical enrolled member under sixty-five. The medical plans in turn would receive only about $75 per member per month, with $50 staying on the health plan side to cover administration and profit. Such profits are fueling the substantial salary and compensation of these health plan entrepreneurs; they also led to a run-up in the stock market valuation of these plans in the early 1990s.

What is perceived by some to be excess profit is a concern both to the purchaser and to the physicians. There is increasing concern that too much money is being taken out of the system and not used appropriately in the delivery of medical services. This will be an increasingly contentious debate over the next few years for this model.

Hospital-Based Systems

The third type of integrated system and the one that is something of a legend in the hospital community is a model in which hospitals organize an integrated system to include primary care physicians under the auspices of a hospital organization. The intent is to build a system that emulates the incentives of an HMO or medical group model, but with a hospital as the base. The problem with these systems is that the basic motivation for developing them is to preserve the income of the existing actors in the hospital, namely the hospital administrators and the high-priced specialists who are based there. But managed care really requires that these types of actors be taken out of the system and that their incomes be sharply reduced, which makes this model appear somewhat illogical. Nevertheless, it's extremely popular among consultants who are parading across the country trying to help hospitals convert from being sleepy fee-for-service-oriented to capitated, integrated systems. Establishing this strategy as the mainstream second curve in American medical care is going to be a hard act to pull off; fundamentally, specialists are fee-for-service oriented and it's difficult to organize primary care physicians into these models, first because there aren't enough of them, and second because they don't particularly want to be indentured servants supporting (through their hard work) the income of their higher-paid specialist brethren. We're kidding ourselves as a nation if we think that simply by capitating and integrating—or pretending to integrate—at the hospital level is sufficient.

The Special Threat to Academic Medicine

NO MATTER WHAT, hospital capacity will have to come out of the system, but one of the problems is that the pseudo–second curve may end up closing the wrong organizations; academic medicine in particular faces a substantial threat. For most countries, academic medical centers have been their crowning glory, the highest form of medical care. In the United States and elsewhere, academic medicine has enjoyed massive cross-subsidy from faculty practice plans. The hospital bills at a much higher rate than it pays its medical faculty for performing esoteric, complex, and expensive clinical services such as organ transplants and open heart surgery. In the United States, the 1980s were the golden years of academic medicine because of special differential academic payments they enjoyed.

But the world of powerful purchasers is a shortsighted one. No rational employer coalition or health plan or fund holder would underwrite the excessive cost of medical education. In response to the threat of powerful purchasers, academic medicine has turned to integration. Some, like Stanford University, have tried to integrate into primary care, hoping to leverage a small though very prestigious primary care base to support a very large, sophisticated institution. Others, like Johns Hopkins University in Baltimore, have abandoned their managed care base and tried to consolidate at the top of the food chain in their region by focusing on the most specialized services. Similarly, many of the prestigious New York City institutions, such as Mount Sinai, are affiliating with every local hospital that's not nailed down in hopes of building a horizontal feeder network of community-based institutions that can support the high technology medical palaces of Manhattan.

But these strategic moves ignore the key challenge. Who's going to pay for research, teaching, and service innovation in a world of powerful purchasers? If academic medical centers don't respond quickly, many could be in real jeopardy. The best approach may be for them to go over the powerful purchasers' heads to the public and demonstrate their role as centers of innovation; in so doing, they can demand separate and distinct funding for the research and teaching functions. Otherwise it's going to be difficult to cross-subsidize esoteric residency programs from service profits, when considerable competition—other provider groups—can provide the less esoteric programs at much lower cost. Ultimately, academic medicine will have to transform itself by producing fewer specialists and more generalists; by focusing on the creation of cost-reducing, not cost-increasing, technologies; and by becoming more responsive to community needs with the clinical services it provides. It remains to be seen whether academic medicine around the world can respond to these enormous challenges.

Insurance Companies and the
Transformation Toward Managed Care

SEVERAL YEARS AGO, the Institute for the Future worked for
most of the large insurance companies in the traditional indemnity
mold. Their health care businesses were a significant part of their
revenues and many of them were on the cusp of deciding whether or
not they could fully participate in managed care. We argued in 1988
that the traditional health insurance industry in the U.S. would frag-
ment into the following functions: marketing and distribution, managed care networks, data jockeys (specialized companies focused on
analyzing health care data), management of medicine, reinsurance,
transaction processing, and benefit consulting. Our belief was (and it
has proven to be correct) that this fragmentation would essentially
lead to the insurance industry's being disintermediated if it didn't
succeed in one of two areas: transaction processing, where it can
compete effectively in a commodity business, processing claims in
the traditional fee-for-service mode; or as a truly active participant in
the managed care business. The latter course required insurers to develop managed care networks: to go deep into the heart of managing
medicine, and to learn as much as anyone about being an HMO.
This helps explain why the big five insurers have had to make a
choice to be in or out of health care. Aetna, Cigna, and Prudential
are in—at least for now; Metropolitan and Traveler's are out.

The more nimble second-curve competitors, such as U.S. Healthcare, United HealthCare, and PacifiCare, have been more successful
than the traditional insurers in developing, implementing, and managing managed care networks. (Indeed, in 1995 United HealthCare
bought METRA, the block of health care business that came from
Metropolitan and Traveler's merged operations.) First, they haven't
been hampered by first-curve indemnity thinking. The original first-
curve players are desperately trying to catch up, but they bring with
them a lot of cultural baggage having to do with predispositions toward fee-for-service medicine, indemnity forms of insurance, and
sales and marketing to large employers rather than providing packages that are attractive to both employers and consumers. Similarly,
the various other functions, such as being data jockeys and employee
benefit consultants, have opened up enormous new second-curve
niches for companies providing specialized information and support
services that traditionally came under the auspices of an insurance

company. Insurers are under significant assault in such a world of transformation to managed care.

The Impact on Doctors

PERHAPS THE MOST SIGNIFICANT TRANSFORMATION brought about by all this change is the impact on physicians. Doctors used to practice as autonomous professionals, where their word was final. Increasingly, with the rise of managed care and with the growth of sophisticated consumers and patients, they are no longer in a position of such autonomy. Insurers second-guess their decisions, and doctors are subjected to "1-800" hassle, where someone (who not only didn't make it through medical school, but in many instances didn't make it through high school) questions their judgment: a certain specialty referral they made, or a particular test they may have ordered. This infuriates physicians; they've spent years learning what they do, and they greatly value the role of independent clinician looking after patients. Even though there is some scientific evidence to suggest that the variation in medical practices is not only unwarranted but unsafe, doctors are quick to preserve and defend the right to make it up as they go along. Right or wrong, managed care interferes with that autonomy.

Secondly, managed care is predicated on either a smaller number of specialists, or the reduction in specialists' income, both of which are beginning to occur in the most advanced managed care markets, where specialists' incomes are coming under assault. A 1995 survey indicates that about a third of physicians believe their incomes have fallen in the last three to five years. These are mostly procedure-oriented specialists who are seeing their incomes drop substantially because they've been left out of managed care networks, or because they've had to negotiate much higher discounts in their fees with managed care organizations.

The prospects for physicians in the future aren't as rosy as they once were. But it's important to recognize that these specialists who are being disintermediated—that is, cut out of the food chain—are not going to simply roll over and die. They're going to fight politically, and are doing so through any-willing-provider legislation—an attempt to block HMOs from excluding physicians in their networks. They'll also fight in terms of passive-aggressive clinical behavior, where they bond with the patient against the insurer, trying to upcode their bills to creatively distort their claims and to inflate their prices and practices in order to extract as much revenue as possible from the evil managed care organizations. This dysfunctionality is likely to increase, and it's one of the reasons that the so-called second curve of managed care is unsustainable in the long run.

The Institute for the Future has a joint venture with Louis Harris & Associates and the Harvard School of Public Health aimed at providing companies in the health care business with a view of the unfolding health care system. Research conducted by the partnership under the auspices of our Health Care Outlook program, as well as independent academic research conducted by both Harris and Harvard, suggests a trend toward the demonization of managed care. The public and certain physician groups, most notably specialists, are beginning to notice that managed care does indeed have an effect on the use of clinical resources. Access to specialists is being restricted, and the continuity of care between the physician and the specialists and hospitals to which he or she would normally refer is being interfered with. In addition, restrictions are being placed on the access to certain services, and those restrictions are being posed not by the doctor, but by the insurer or the managed care organization.

In surveys conducted over the last three years, Harris has documented the rising discontent among certain significant sectors of the public. Such discontent is likely to be whipped up by the media, whose general proconsumer, anticorporation sentiment these developments offend. We will likely see increasing demonization in both the Congress and the state capitals around the country in the form of legislative initiatives, such as the limitation on early discharge following the normal delivery of a child.

American physicians are facing an ugly set of shifts, and while doctors are trying to put a brave face on it, it's increasingly evident that the golden days of medicine have passed, at least in terms of physicians' economic and clinical independence. While it's true that the public still holds its physicians in fairly high regard, medicine's privileged place as the paragon of professional virtue has eroded over the last twenty years.

In a long-running Harris poll of confidence in institutions, medicine—compared to other institutions such as the military or education—was perceived to have a 15 to 20 percent premium over those institutions as a benchmark. In the early 1990s, consistent with the overall decline in confidence in the leadership in institutions that's occurred over the last twenty years, medicine fell below the average of other institutions, never to recover. Part of this may be due to the increasing perception among the public that physicians are more interested in money than in patients, although that's a general criticism of physicians as a whole, and not of individual physicians.

The Impact on the Pharmaceutical Industry

THE GLOBAL PHARMACEUTICAL INDUSTRY has been severely affected by the changes in health care in the U.S., which traditionally has generated the highest share of profits. If you look at where the pharmaceutical industry has been and where it is currently, you see fundamental shifts. In the old days—the 1970s and 1980s—the pharmaceutical industry would discover a white powder by screening thousands of chemicals for therapeutic effect. It would establish safety and efficacy of the product through clinical trials and the Food and Drug Administration-approval processes. It would then promote that product to physicians, and have consumers pay for the product. A perfect game. The final payer (the consumer) had little or no idea how to judge the value of the product, had no say in its pricing, did not control the selection of the product, and, because of heavy patent protection, was subject to monopolistic prices. In such an environment, the key was new products that maintained monopoly pricing. The pharmaceutical industry paid little attention to the distribution system or third parties such as insurance companies, because they played a very little role in paying for drugs. Indeed, consistently through the 1960s and 1970s, the pharmaceutical industry gave up the distribution system to wholesalers like McKesson and Bergen Brunswig.

Managed care has sharply eroded that world. Today the pharmaceutical industry has to design a white powder using the tools of biotechnology, coupled to the traditional screening of alternative esoteric compounds. Increasingly, the industry has to demonstrate not only safety and efficacy to the FDA, but cost effectiveness, if not to the FDA, then to other important decision-makers such as state Medicaid programs and large managed care organizations, like Kaiser and United HealthCare—all of which has given pricing decisions importance in the launch of new products in a way we haven't seen before. Similarly, when it comes to promotion, the pharmaceutical industry promotes to anyone beginning with a P: physicians, pharmacists, patients, payers, plans, pharmacy benefit management (PBM) companies—even politicians. All have a potential say in the selection of a product and the prescription and use of a product by consumers.

Many pharmaceutical companies were led to believe that with the rise in managed care, the sales forces (the first curve) would become redundant—just doing a deal with the health plan was sufficient, they thought—but this hasn't proven true. Certainly sophisticated marketing to plans has become a requirement, but in addition, because of the complexity and disintegration of the delivery system, insuring that the physician is constantly reminded to use the product when choice exists is also important. Manufacturers have to pull through the distribution chain to reinforce their products with physicians' and patients' tastes and preferences. All of this has made marketing more complicated at a time when there is also increasing pressure on margins. Powerful purchasers put pressure on health plans, and plans (particularly the pharmacy benefit management plans) put increasing pressure on the pharmaceutical companies.

Another change is in who pays for the drugs. Today, instead of the consumer paying for the product (as was true in the old days), increasingly the insurer is paying, a third-party payer—either an HMO or, more typically, a pharmacy benefit plan.

Since 1985, there have been sizable cuts in areas such as mental health insurance and drug plans. Companies like Medco, Diversified Pharmaceutical Services, and Value Health built substantial businesses in providing employers with the opportunity to manage their drug benefits, and, even more effectively, they used mail-order drug distribution as well as bulk purchasing of drugs to establish what is called a formulary. This is a restricted set of drugs that they encourage patients to use and that they list through a point-of-sale network established in each pharmacy across the country. Today every pharmacy in the United States has a PC connected to the pharmacy desk, allowing for indirect controls to be embedded in software so that when you present your drug card the pharmacist knows that there is only a certain set of prescriptions that will be available to you. As a patient of a PBM, you will be encouraged to use generics where possible. And this set of information is reinforced by incentives to the consumers in terms of the co-payments they make. For example, if you pick a drug on the formulary you have to pay a deductible of $5, as opposed to $15 if you choose an alternate therapy, or one that the physician has prescribed but that is not on the formulary.

A key question is how much control these systems have over the selection choices of physicians. It is clear that they have an enormous impact on generic substitutions; where a generic substitute exists, the pharmacist has the legal right to make that substitution, unless overridden explicitly by a doctor. What's less clear is that these pharmacy benefit management plans have the ability to effect therapeutic substitutions—the substitution of a similar kind of product, even though the chemical entity is not the same. With increasing third-party coverage through sophisticated purchasers like insurers and PBMs comes third-party control. And that's clearly a differentiation in terms of both control of price and control of volume, which the pharmaceutical industry has not been exposed to. These shifts have prompted major strategic changes by the pharmaceutical industry, which has adopted three basic models:

Big D Little r

This strategy recognizes that pharmaceutical companies are best at discovering and marketing drugs, and that straying from this core competency makes no sense. However, there is increasing risk and difficulty in coming up with a blockbuster product. Finding a blockbuster new therapeutic drug is a bit like winning the lottery. If you buy more tickets—i.e., invest in R&D—you have a better chance, but it certainly doesn't guarantee a win. So this strategy involves two dimensions: One is horizontal consolidation, to get scale in R&D, thereby increasing the probability of finding a blockbuster, streamlining marketing and development functions for this new, more vigorously contested world. The other is laying side bets on the research pipeline by investing in or buying biotechnology-based companies. Key examples of this second strategy are Hoffman-La Roche (HLR), which followed on its majority stake in Genentech with the outright purchase of Syntex Corporation. The company is now building significant California-based R&D research capacity, with both Syntex and Genentech running as separate organizations under the Roche umbrella, but with a common focus on the new biology of the twenty-first century, with close ties to the biotechnology industry of the San Francisco Bay region. Another example would be Ciba-Geigy, with its purchase of a majority stake in Chiron, another example where the pipeline is being purchased for the future, as well as providing greater horizontal scale. Similarly, Glaxco's purchase of Burroughs Wellcome provides greater horizontal firepower in the pharmaceutical market. American Home Products' merger purchase of the Lederle division of American Cyanamid is an example of another large horizontally integrated play where side bets are going to be laid in terms of the development pipeline.

Consumer Focus

Because one of the core competencies of the pharmaceutical companies is their ability to market to both patients and physicians, it may be in their interest to have powerful prescription drugs sold on an over-the-counter basis where abilities in consumer marketing can be brought to bear on product selection, even though the margins won't be as high as in the prescription drug business. While it's hard to find a pharmaceutical company that has followed this strategy in its purest form, you can see elements of it in Johnson & Johnson and in the recent activities of SmithKline Beecham, whose blockbuster drug Tagamet came off patent in late 1994 and is now being released in a lower-dosage over-the-counter form, marketed under the Tagamet brand in order to build an OTC (over-the-counter) awareness among consumers. Tagamet is a product aimed at the treatment of duodenal ulcers—this was its original FDA-approved use—but it has been prescribed as a powerful antacid.

The M Strategy

The third strategy is to buy anything with M in it: PBM, DSM, MCO. These stand for pharmacy benefit management, disease state management, and managed care organization. This strategy has been used by several large companies that have tried to position themselves for the world of managed care by vertically integrating with pharmacy benefit management companies—in particular in an effort to transform themselves into what the industry has begun to call disease state management entities. It is a strategy that has been overplayed, in that the amount of control that a PBM really has over the channel of distribution is much more limited than you might think. The PBMs do not own the loyalty of the patients they serve. They only control them by virtue of the prices they charge to employers. This is a very price-sensitive game; if another insurer or PBM comes into a large employer like General Motors and offers to cover that employer for a dollar less per member per month, it would be imprudent for the large employer not to accept such a bid. Consequently, the block of lives in a drug plan that GM might control would be transferred overnight from one PBM to another. Therefore, the degree to which the consumers are truly and permanently under the control of a particular PBM is questionable.

A fundamental assumption of a PBM strategy is that there is effective control of the channel for the product selection decisions of the individual physicians who are prescribing medication. Whereas it may be true that generic substitution is under the control of the pharmacist involved in the PBM network, it is less clear that the pharmacy benefit management companies could be particularly successful in changing the therapeutic substitution choices of physicians. This requires in-your-face integration with doctors to get them to change their opinion; in much the same way that utilization review became unpopular with doctors, as Institute for the Future surveys indicate that such interaction is indeed seen as an increasingly serious problem among physicians when you start interfering unduly with the ability to prescribe specific medications.

Another assumption under the PBM strategy was that PBMs had access to particular types of information by virtue of their large databases of claims of individual users. There are two issues involved here. First, the quality of such data is not necessarily very reliable. There is indeed a standardized coding of drugs, but the coding of diagnosis associated with each patient would at best be very spotty. Previous experience in the hospital world suggests that this information is not clearly identified when transactions such as prescriptions or pharmacy requests or lab requests are made, and that to predicate clinical decisions on the flow of such information is not only wrong but bloody dangerous. Nevertheless, there was a presumption among many in the pharmacy benefit management world that these new entities had access to some unique high-quality database. What most of the companies are finding out is that there is indeed a lot of data, but the value of it is questionable. But second, even if the data is reliable, what can you do with it? It certainly is a very large data set which potentially has value in combination with other data. However, it is very difficult to envision that data being consolidated in a way that will allow the remote practice of medicine. The vision that one can simply zap practice guidelines over the Internet to doctors and have them voluntarily paying attention so that your product is prescribed more often than somebody else's has to be challenged, both in terms of logic and in terms of the Justice Department's willingness to allow this to happen without open competition within these companies. These factors have made the PBM strategy somewhat less effective than was originally hyped by the investment bankers and the consultants who presumably reaped some great reward by putting these deals together.

Three very large deals were done: Merck paid $6 billion for Medco; Lilly paid some $4 billion for PCS, the pharmacy benefit arm of McKesson; and SmithKline Beecham paid in excess of $2 billion for DPS, which was the Diversified Pharmaceutical Services arm of United HealthCare. This is not to say that these purchases were imprudent. Most of the PBM companies are reinventing themselves to find the true second curve. Whether or not these systems succeed in the long run depends, to a great extent, on how the companies manage their way through this dilemma. But it is an example of a sort of premature jumping onto the second curve without any clear evidence that that second curve is indeed real, or that your buying delivers what you thought it would.

The Phantom Second Curve

IN TIMES OF CHANGE, people prematurely jump to a conclusion about what the second curve is really about. This is something you very definitely see in American health care, and the conclusion that capitated, integrated, communicated managed care is the answer is even spilling over to the health care systems of other parts of North America, as well as Europe and Asia. Concluding that discounted managed care or the kind of "Gong Show" that is American managed care is the answer seems not only premature, but wrong for several reasons. First, there is no clear evidence that in terms of the macro indicators of cost, access, quality, and security of benefits the shifts that have occurred in the last three to five years have been positive across any of those dimensions. Indeed, because we have no real-time data on costs, the current apparent slowing in the rate of increase may be simply a phenomenon of background general inflation. The last official statistics that we have from the Department of Health and Human Services, which are from 1993, indicated that health care was still growing three times as fast as inflation, some five percentage points in real terms, which is the long-run average for the last thirty years. The reason the growth rate is considerably less in nominal terms is that background inflation was minuscule. In terms of access, in 1995, 43 million Americans had no health insurance, and it is inconceivable that that number will go down, given the current trend toward cutting back on Medicaid growth and the shifting and downsizing of corporate America, which will take away even more jobs from the well-insured ranks of large corporations and place those jobs among the smaller corporations, where health insurance is much less prevalent. Estimates range from 50 to 60 million uninsured by 2005. In terms of quality, we've cited several surveys that have indicated that there is a considerable concern among physicians and consumers that quality, at least as measured by choice, waiting time, and so forth, is being affected. We are less clear that final outcomes have been affected because there is really no national standard of measurement yet for these, and certainly not one that applies to both fee-for-service and managed care, but nevertheless there is concern that quality may not be going up, and may even be declining. And finally, in terms of security of benefits, volatility in the workplace and the amount of change brought by managed care increase the volatility and insecurity of health benefits at least in terms of continuity with specific physicians and with specific plans. This suggests that on all four of the basic parameters and goals of the health care system this so-called second-curve solution may not be a solution, but rather an interim step toward a true second curve. But let's be clear: the first curve is dying.

We can learn three things from the changes we've seen so far:

Horizontal, Not Vertical

Despite the euphoria over vertical integration, there are very few examples of effective vertical integration, and a lot of examples of horizontal integration. Purchasers are massing their firepower and joining together in purchasing coalitions, and they are willing to do whatever it takes to use that firepower to reduce costs and improve quality. In addition there's been a huge consolidation at the health plan level, particularly in the more advanced managed care markets. Health Systems International, formed by the merger of QualMed and HealthNet in 1994, attempted to merge a year later with Wellpoint, formerly Blue Cross of California's business spun into a for-profit subsidiary. The proposed giant, had the marriage ever been consummated, would have been larger in the West than Kaiser, with more than five million lives. Similarly, Metropolitan and Travelers merged their block of health care businesses in a joint venture in 1994 under the METRA label. Because of their lack of expertise and perhaps lack of interest in the true managed care market, they sold out at a fairly discounted price to United HealthCare, which used the proceeds from their Diversified Pharmaceutical Services windfall to buy 10 million (albeit discounted fee-for-service) lives that were embedded in the block of business held by Metropolitan and Travelers. United may use this block of lives to leverage themselves into markets where they were previously not a force and give themselves a chance to build a point-of-service system with their expertise providing a hard core center to the light lives previously controlled by Metropolitan and Travelers.

A similar example of horizontal integration is the enormous increase in the Columbia/HCA giant over the last three years. Columbia, which came out of HCA-Hospital Corporation of America, has become the behemoth of hospital care in the United States. This for-profit chain is the darling of Wall Street, run by a very smart lawyer who seems intent on radicalizing the American hospital industry much in the same way that the horizontal consolidation occurred in the railway industry in the 1890s. Indeed, the parallel with the railways is striking. As I have said, the thing that killed the railways was that they were run by people who liked trains too much; the thing that will kill hospitals is that they are run by people who like big white buildings and being important. Hospital CEOs are absolutely terrified of the prospect of being taken over. They've run institutions with several thousand employees where, compared to their counterparts in other countries, they've enjoyed CEO-like benefits and salaries and the kind of stature in the community accorded to few but the leaders of American Capitalism.

Columbia is using its financial clout to enter markets where hospitals are perceived as vulnerable and indecisive. Using their seductive southern twangs to reassure the hospital boards that they'll bring sophisticated management and couple it to community service, they enter into either a full ownership or a joint-venture arrangement, whereby they get control of the institution. Once it is under their control, especially if they own two or three hospitals in the community, they can go about closing down certain hospitals and rationalizing the clinical services, which is a logical thing to do, a kind of private sector regional planning, which means that these hospitals will be running in a more effective manner.

Perhaps the most important contribution that Columbia/HCA can make is that, as a corporate for-profit entity with deep pockets and direct control from Nashville, it can exert far more decision-making sway over an institution and can do so much faster than the typical community hospital board. Whether this is in the public interest in the long run remains to be seen, but it is clear that some very good hospitals will come under their control to be closed, downsized, or both.

Virtual, Not Actual

Most integration activity is horizontal, but where there is vertical integration, it's being done most successfully on a virtual basis, rather than an actual basis. A good example is the success enjoyed by organizations like PacifiCare who have built a fairly substantial enterprise without physically owning hospitals, doctors, or any other of the hardware of health care. PacifiCare came out of the Lutheran Hospital Society in Southern California, which then became Uni-Health. PacifiCare's roots were from a chain of religious hospitals that saw the potential of managed care running in competition with Kaiser (without the baggage of actually owning hospitals or physicians). Over a five- to ten-year period, PacifiCare successfully built a very high-quality effective organization with great marketing strengths and an ability to organize networks of physicians. In particular, they became dependent on the organized medical groups of Southern California to manage the medical care on behalf of Pacifi-Care. PacifiCare has the reputation for being the partner of choice among medical groups in Southern California. This is in contrast to some of PacifiCare's competitors who are seen by medical groups and hospitals more as bullies than partners. PacifiCare and other organizations are being incredibly successful both in terms of their stock market valuations and their profitability in recent years. In the future, these organizations are likely to see their growth come not so much within California, but from exporting the kind of virtual expertise they've developed to other parts of the country, particularly in the management of Medicare. The Republican Congress sees Medicare managed care as a major opportunity to control costs in the long run, and is encouraging the further enrollment of Medicare recipients in HMOs such as PacifiCare's Secure Horizons. In Boston, PacifiCare has a joint venture with Tufts Associated Health Plan. In Southern California, more than 50 percent of Medicare recipients in certain counties are in such plans, and around a third of Americans will be in such plans by the turn of the century, an estimate that seems to be supported by officials at the Health Care Financing Administration.

Partial, Not Complete

Even if this phantom second curve were the real thing, it still offers only partial solutions to the problems at hand. Throughout the health care globe, performance measures of the entire health care system are inadequate, which causes us to find fixes in one part of the complex system that create unintended consequences elsewhere. An example is the DRG system (diagnosis related group system) of the early 1980s, which provided incentives for earlier patient discharges from the hospital. This may have caused an overreaction and encouraged premature discharges, hurting patients in the process. Similarly, the current wave of capitation may be encouraging reductions in hospitalization and use of services to a point where quality of care and outcomes of care suffer. There is no scientific evidence that managed care delivers inferior outcomes. But there is growing survey evidence that managed care limits choice of doctors and hassles doctors in ways that patients and their doctors notice. We shouldn't be surprised by this. It's what managed care does.

Patient groups such as the elderly are being exposed to managed care techniques, although there is considerable criticism. Applying capitated-type models to the elderly has to be balanced so that the health care plans do not exploit the obvious incentive: to sign up healthy Medicare recipients for whom they receive exactly the same monthly compensation as they would for sick health care recipients, without the requisite need to provide services. The best way to make money on a Medicare risk contract in America is to sign up elderly Medicare recipients with single-digit golf handicaps, since this correlates well with income and inversely with age, meaning that you get a young, and therefore somewhat healthier, subset of the elderly and assure yourself that you make money rather than lose money by entering into a capitated risk contract.

The True Second Curve

IF ALL OF THESE TRENDS aren't adding up to a true second curve, where will the real second curve come from? Most probably from the following five sources.

The Rubble of the First Curve

The first source for the true second curve is indeed the rubble of the radicalized health care delivery system described above. These changes aren't all negative; America certainly has too many hospital beds, as do most of the developed countries. These shifts will provide an enormous incentive to reduce the numbers of such beds, and will greatly change the location of care away from hospital-based institutions to sites where patients are better served at lower cost. This is not a negative; it's a positive, and perhaps in some perverse Schumpeterian bargain it is why health plan leaders and executives such as Columbia/HCA's Richard Scott are creating so much personal wealth: they are indeed doing a service to the system as a whole by radicalizing health care delivery.

Biotechnology

In the long run, biotechnology may yield a significant transformation of health care delivery in the U.S. and around the world. As the human genome becomes fully explored and the secrets of genetic predisposition to disease understood, we will have increasingly sophisticated tools that will allow for early diagnosis, including in vitro diagnosis, prior to birth. Such diagnostic tools harnessed to powerful computer tools in the emerging science of genomics will allow screening for the probability of carrying genes for various cancers, heart disease, and disorders such as muscular dystrophy and multiple sclerosis. The question remains as to whether or not this early detection can be matched by early intervention. The conventional scientific wisdom is that there will be a five- to fifteen-year lag between tools for diagnosis and tools for therapy. What kinds of dilemmas does this present if a patient knows he or she has a predisposition for a certain disease, a disease for which there is no cure? What if a couple know that their unborn child may have such a predisposition? One obvious consequence in the latter case is that abortion will be a very significant and contentious tool for the treatment or intervention or forestalling of a particular medical disaster. However, in the long run, as the tools for medical gene therapy become available, the frightening diagnosis may have a happy outcome, namely that early detection of a particular genetic disorder doesn't mean burdening the patient or family with difficult choices or a death sentence. Rather, it provides the opportunity for intervention using new biopharmaceutical products aimed at actually treating the disease at its molecular source: specific cancer-fighting tools that will become available in the next twenty years which will significantly affect the mechanisms of treating disease, for example.

Information Technology and Electronic Commerce

In the health care system, one of the basic problems has been continued escalation in cost despite the new technology. Unlike other areas of life, where technology has yielded enormous productivity gains, technologies in health care have tended to be cost-increasing rather than cost-decreasing. Part of the reason for this is the incentives embedded in the health care system. Until the rise of capitation, fee-for-service rewarded technologies which raised billings rather than lowered billings, raised incomes rather than lowered incomes; as a consequence there was a structured set of incentives to those companies that were developing technologies that essentially increased the flow of revenues rather than reduced costs. As the market shifts more toward managed care and as powerful purchasers assert themselves, it has become increasingly evident that the pharmaceutical and medical equipment industries have to adjust to a world where they must produce cost-reducing rather than cost-increasing technologies. And as rational business people, they are beginning to do so, recognizing that the market will reward technologies that do in fact reduce cost. One real hope for doing so is the role of information technology. A woeful lack of technology prevails in the physician's office. Here the physician is operating with '70s technology—1870s. The white board, the pen, and the pad are the base technologies of the physician's office. Although 75 percent of U.S. doctor's offices have computers, they are generally tools for dealing with insurance companies rather than for use in clinical diagnosis or information storage. Most of the clinical record-keeping is still done in a mixed-media format. (Think of those folders with scribbled notes, photographs, x-ray film, and typed or dictated notes from the physician that are maintained in a rather sloppy if not totally disorganized fashion.)

There has been a long history over the last twenty-five years in pursuit of the electronic medical record. It's a bit like the Holy Grail. No one has really done it, partly because of the mixed-media nature of these records and partly because of the enormous investment in infrastructure that would be required to support the compilation of these records in real time as physicians dodge about hospitals and various care sites and treatment centers on a daily basis. However, with the emergence of the hand-held devices of point-of-sale and point-of-service technology and of voice-activated and voice-controlled input devices, it is not inconceivable that in the next ten years all dimensions of clinical practice could be captured—either as part of the ongoing function, or by convenient, easy-to-use PDA-type or voice-activated tools that would involve natural language skills rather than some kind of conversation with robo-doc. The exciting potential is for these kinds of interface technologies to be coupled to the ubiquity of the Internet so that there could be real sharing of information across the sites of care in open-access networks where patients, plans, providers could exchange information securely across a secure Internet environment. The Internet and tools of electronic commerce could be a very useful backbone for health care systems, where pluralism is likely to reign for a very long time and where it is unlikely we are going to see all physicians marshalled under the sway of a large vertically integrated Kaiser-like entity. Even though that dream may be the dream of many.

Consumer Choice and the Right to Trade Up

Any health care system in the future is going to have to respect sophisticated consumers. The true second curve, as we have said repeatedly, is one sensitive to the needs, aspirations, and wants of sophisticated consumers, and the health care system is no different as a market in this regard. It is very clear that the second curve of the future will be consumer responsive. And again there are opportunities for this to occur. Customer service tools that have been applied in airlines, retailing, telecommunications, and so forth have yet to be made fully available in the health care system. As members of medical clinics, many of us are looked after by a hundred voice mail systems practicing in a group. Health care could design much more user-friendly customer service systems where patients could be guided intelligently through a system in which real people or smart computers helped them solve their problems without actually physically turning up at a site. Often a quick pursuit through an algorithm—with a little bit of coaching—might help patients reach an answer and have something prescribed without necessarily meeting with a physician (in the old fee-for-service system this was clearly not in the provider's interest, which is why such systems were never developed). In a world of capitation, however, in a world in which it is increasingly important to contain costs and improve quality, such systems may become attractive.

The other thing that has become clear from a political point of view in the United States and elsewhere is that patients equate choice with quality. Sophisticated consumers will demand the right to trade up with their own money. That right could be codified in what we call floors and ceilings. The dilemma faced in the U.S. is a dilemma similar to that in other countries, where what people really want is a basic floor below which no one falls. But they also want the right to trade up with their own money to a nicer waiting room with a nicer class of people where potentially more expensive esoteric technologies are available to them. Whether the state or employer or private insurer should be responsible for such a high level of care will be the subject of some debate. The current global trend, however, by both government and private payers, is from defined benefit to defined contribution. In other words, the employer, for example, guarantees a contribution of $2,000 per year to an employee's health insurance. From then on, it's the employee's choice to trade up. The only sustainable solution, from both an economic point of view and a social justice point of view, is to establish a basic floor for all, regardless of income, which through the state or the employer or some combined mandate is made available to all citizens. But given that floor, in a world where there are increasing technology options, there must also be some right afforded to individuals who want to avail themselves of certain types of services, such as in vitro fertilization, where they do so with their own money. The Brits, the Swedes, the Germans, and others will reluctantly come to such situations as they run out of people to tax. Americans will have already confronted this. Our problem in allowing a plethora of different standards is that trying to get a basic floor for all is becoming an increasingly difficult political prospect, given the excessive costs already embedded in the system in covering some 85 percent of Americans.

Population Health

The true second curve will involve an increasing recognition that the factors creating health have very little to do with medical care. Evidence coming from the population health literature suggests that a person's educational level, income, and job have an enormous impact on future health status, longevity, and so forth. One of the best ways to live a long and healthy life is to be brought up in a very nice family, have a very good education, and work for a good company. One of the central features in the population health literature is the recognition that people who are in positions of less authority and no control tend to have much higher death rates from cancer and other diseases than those who are in a position of some autonomy in their work environment. There will be increasing recognition that the kinds of workplaces we design will have an impact on the future health of the population, and it will also become clear that investment in early childhood development will yield enormous benefits down the line in terms of reducing health costs and improving health status. While this may sound too much like socialism for the average American, it will be such enlightened choices embedded in government policy and in business practice that will have to emerge if we are seriously going to address the problem of ever-escalating costs and concern over the ability to serve populations at risk.

The fact is that the second curve which seems to be emerging in health care is indeed a phantom that is not sustainable as the second curve, and it is a very good example of why second-curve thinking is so critically important. If you are going to work the second curve, you've got to be constantly challenging yourself that you're really on that curve. You've got to ask yourself the hard question: Is this curve sustainable? Is it solving the problem it is meant to solve? And if the answer is no, then there is a good chance it won't continue. The separation of fads and trends is always hard. In the case of health care, particularly in the United States, we've tried to convince ourselves that the managed care marketplace is the simple answer to all our problems. The likely result is that it is a very important intervening stage toward some new reform. But it is quite conceivable that we will never discover the second curve because we are so paralyzed by the cultural conflicts that health care presents. The difficulty in dealing with quality and social justice in a society which rewards and reveres independence, individualism, and incentive may be too much for us to handle, and rather than make the transformation to a sustainable second curve, we may flounder on the first curve in perpetuity. We hope that's not the case.

Financial Services:
Can I Help You?

IF YOU WERE TO CHARACTERIZE the relationship between financial services and the second curve, you could describe what's happening as a slow build to a monumental second curve. The second curve is about to hit financial services, and it's going to hit hard. Of all the industry sectors, financial services could be the one that will experience the greatest shift over the next decade. Unlike health care, where in many instances the patient has to be physically involved for a transaction to occur, or retailing, where physical goods may have to be delivered, the distribution of financial services is largely about the movement of limited short bursts of electrons. The institutions established in the United States and throughout the world to manage our money and the flow of capital have their roots in the logical extension of first-curve activities, where people physically deposited cash, and assets were kept in safe vaults. We use metaphors—a solid bank, lock boxes, safe deposit, firewalls, Chinese walls, and Wall Street—all to connote a physical presence. But increasingly, as assets become intangible and as money becomes electrons rather than bullion, these institutions have evolved to being custodians of information, rather than protectors of physical property.

The second-curve threat here is extreme, for several reasons. First, despite all the changes that have come to the financial services industry in the last forty years—and there have been many—there's still a good deal of inefficiency built into the way in which banks, insurance companies, securities firms, and other dimensions of the financial services world operate. There are extravagant sales forces, impressive but somewhat wasteful physical presences in the downtown office towers of most cities, expensive showy corner branches, the huge number of physical sites for distribution of information, and the very large and somewhat inefficient mechanisms that financial services institutions have established for so-called customer service. And a lot of institutions have managed to keep the first curve alive through regulation or sheer market power or a combination of the two. But all of these factors render financial services vulnerable to the second curve.

In short, what we don't know is what the financial services' second curve might finally look like; what we do know is that it will be massive.

Building to a Massive Second-Curve Transformation

OVER THE LAST FORTY YEARS, the financial services industry has experienced tremendous change. Joseph Nocera's perceptive book A *Piece of the Action: How the Middle Class Joined the Money Class* chronicles the basic changes that we have seen to date, namely the rise of the credit card, the money market account, the mutual fund, the ATM machine, and the discount brokerage house. All of these institutions have one thing in common: they are, as Nocera's subtitle puts it, "how the middle class joined the money class." Nocera's key insight is that each of the major innovations in financial services over the last forty years has brought the middle class closer to the kind of private banking instruments and attention once only enjoyed by the Rockefellers. But it won't stop there. Financial tools once available exclusively to corporations will be increasingly accessible by individuals. The next wave of technology, the new sophistication of the consumer, and the globalization of financial markets will build on the innovations of the last forty years in a crescendo of change.

To understand the coming second curve it is important to review the pieces that have been built to date in financial services. We will focus here on consumer-oriented financial services, but similar profound changes have happened and will continue to evolve in commercial financial services.

The second curve has been building slowly but surely in the consumer financial services sector for decades. The changes so far have resulted not only in a dramatic shift in the market share of financial intermediation between and among established financial market segments and players (i.e., commercial banks, investment banks, insurance companies), but, more significantly, a shift to a whole range of new market segments, players, products and services. Most of these new market segments and products could have been offered by the incumbents, but weren't for a number of reasons. In some cases, regulations disadvantaged the traditional players because their legal history precluded taking advantage of loopholes identified by new entrants or simply did not allow them to offer the types of products— such as mutual funds—demanded by the consumers of the day. In other cases, while fixing first-curve product problems, through user fees for example, the traditional players simply ignored long-term strategic, marketing, and competitive implications of the solution. This created opportunities for new products and competitors to eclipse the old. In other words, in support of short-term profit or risk control, traditional financial services players actually facilitated their own disintermediation, with the result being permanent erosion of market share, brand equity, and customer relationships. Frozen by the security and controls of the first curve, they now run the risk of being locked out of the second.

The vast majority of change in the financial services industry occurred because of the inattention of the first-curve players in the industry to the concerns and needs of its increasingly more educated and sophisticated customers. A fundamental disconnection developed between how the users and the suppliers of financial services perceived their business relationship and the products and services they required. In the end, this led to consumers' finding new solutions to fit their financial needs, most likely provided not by other traditional competitors, but by special-purpose companies dedicated to delivering new products in new ways, such as Fidelity and Charles Schwab. Eventually, innovations such as money market accounts and mutual funds found homes in traditional banks.

The results have been devastating for commercial bankers. While in 1955 the banking system—commercial banks, S&Ls, and mutual savings and credit unions—had a 62 percent share of the intermediary market for financial assets, that share was down to 39 percent in 1992, and to 37.6 percent in 1994. The average consumer has less than 15 percent of his or her money in bank CDs. Almost a quarter is in money market funds. Over 50 percent of home mortgages in the U.S. are held by nonbanks, and nonbank credit card issuers account for almost a quarter of the marketplace.

Sources of the Financial Services Second Curve

THERE ARE SEVERAL KEY DRIVERS that have been slowly building this massive second curve in the financial services industry:

Deregulation

Banking and insurance are highly regulated industries. The large banks have been prevented from aggressively entering insurance markets. Fostered by populism and the fears of a financial collapse of the order of the Great Depression, the various banking acts have prohibited and limited both the geographic scale of bank operations within states in terms of the emergence of national banks, and the participation in security markets and insurance. This geographic decentralization is in contrast to every major industrial country that has large national banks. In Canada, the seven or so larger banks of Canada operate as brands throughout the country. The Bank of Nova Scotia is certainly not limited to Atlantic Canada, and the signature glass towers of the Bank of Montreal and the Royal Bank of Canada are normal skyscrapers in every Canadian city. This is not the case in the U.S., where Chase, despite its national brand name as a credit card company, is a branch bank of the greater New York metropolitan area, as is its new partner, Chemical. Similarly, Bank of America and Wells Fargo are perceived as California banks, although increasingly they are banks of the West. Citicorp has been

the leading consumer bank, but its physical presence is still disproportionately East Coast.

Insurance companies, on the other hand, operate on a national
playing field and have managed to preserve their place as separate
from banks by virtue of their protected position—banks and securities firms have not been allowed to sell insurance. Much of this is
breaking down, partly because banks are now in the business of not
only managing, but selling mutual funds and other services. The
next step—insurance—may not be so far off.

Tax Policy and the Market for Retirement Savings

The purpose of most savings in the U.S. is retirement financing.
While banks and insurance companies have been the major beneficiaries of the growth in retirement programs under defined benefit
plans, as more corporations convert their programs to defined contribution plans, there has been a dramatic shift away from bank
and insurance assets to mutual funds, securitized instruments, and
the equity markets. This has created a whole new class of investors.
Furthermore, with increased consumer sophistication and participation in how their retirement funds are invested, banks have also
seen their industry and brand awareness suffer in favor of mutual
funds and brokerage firms. And because of this, when it comes to
any financial activity, consumers now know they have more choices
than just banks and often have prior experience with those alternate providers. In other words, if your 401(k) plan has a Fidelity
mutual fund, you might consider Fidelity for your discretionary investments as well.

The Regulator Made Me Do It

The changes in consumer banking have parallels in commercial
banking. During the '70s and '80s, corporations were increasingly
finding themselves more creditworthy than their bankers, and they
found they could borrow directly from the security markets more
cheaply than they could borrow from their banks. With the exception of commercial paper, federal law and regulation severely limited
commercial banks' ability to assist their large corporate clients.
Commercial paper was one of the few corporate securities that commercial banks could underwrite. These are unsecured promissory
notes of nationally known corporate firms with initial maturities of

less than 270 days. The credit quality of the paper is a reflection of the financial strength of the issuing firm. Companies can sell commercial paper either directly to investors or indirectly through dealers. By selling commercial paper, firms avoided the compensating balance requirements that many banks tie to loans and paid lower effective rates. However, commercial paper is frequently collateralized by a line of credit at a commercial bank.

The result was the emergence of investment banks as the primary bankers for the corporate marketplace, with all the accompanying rewards and risks.

In the mid-1970s, the Arab oil embargo spurred a rise in inflation and interest rates. This, plus computer technology which made the execution of complex transactions move with a speed and technical ease unimaginable a few years earlier, drove the growth in the commercial paper market. Any company with a computer and the correct software could enter the market as buyer or seller. Commercial paper grew from $35 billion in 1970 to $330 billion in the mid-1980s. This was great for companies, but not so great for the commercial banks who lost some of their best customers.

Enter Bankers Trust, a commercial bank that examined the situation and identified a second curve, then came up with a plan. In the late 1970s the bank sold their relatively profitable retailing bank business and focused their resources on wholesale banking, specifically major corporations, financial institutions, governments, and high-net-worth individuals. The result? Today Bankers Trust is a global merchant bank.

In the 1970s, the loan department accounted for 70 percent of the bank's total earning assets; by 1995 that number was trimmed to 25 percent, with over two thirds coming from liquid assets. That high liquidity gives Bankers Trust a flexibility it considers crucial; with it, the bank can react quickly to adverse factors that could affect their asset position.

Bankers Trust now bundles and unbundles different risks, selling some and keeping some and charging fees for the service. As technology improves Bankers Trust's business may yet again be at risk as companies will increasingly be able to offer many of the services that presently are performed by the bank.

Bankers Trust exited the retail business only to return in the guise of a wholesale supplier of retail services to other institutions and corporations. For example, they are one of the largest suppliers of participant processing for 401(k)s. Bankers Trust services 401(k)s for

General Motors and is currently writing loans to GM employees against their 401(k) accounts. By having online PC connections to General Motors, Bankers Trust can immediately credit employees' checking accounts for the amount borrowed. They are able to do this because when they closed their branches they did not give up their commercial charter.

Regulation Q and the Deposit Market

Prior to the late '70s, consumer interest rates in the U.S. were highly regulated, with banks not able to pay any interest on demand deposits. Meanwhile, U.S. interest rates were rising to record levels, with short-term interest rates significantly higher than longer-term rates. As inflation rose, as interest rates went up, it became increasingly obvious to consumers and regulators that consumer bank deposits were a bad investment, while large corporate deposits, the Eurodollar market, and corporate debt securities paid record interest rates. About the only way for consumers to share the wealth was to remove their money from direct FDIC-insured bank accounts and invest in money market mutual funds and other short-term low-risk debt instruments. Banks were unable to compete for these investment dollars until March 1980, when Congress amended Regulation Q, which in 1933 had placed ceilings on interest rates payable on time and savings deposits, by passing legislation that phased out interest rate caps on savings and term deposits for banks and S&Ls over a six-year period.

New Competitors

Another driver is the emergence of new competitors. Deregulation is positioning Regional Bell Operating Companies to enter financial services through nonbank infrastructures, and financial services have not worked or lobbied for broader deregulation of their industry to compete more broadly. One of the wedges that were pushed into the traditional financial services business was the emergence of new competitors, such as Fidelity and Merrill Lynch entering with money market funds; Charles Schwab with discount brokerage; and the Fidelity Magellan Fund, Putnam, and the rest of the mutual fund industry. This has transformed the way people think about managing their money as consumers; they no longer simply assume that their cash will be held in a bank where minimal interest is returned. Rather, more and more Americans have been and will continue to be investing their money in organized money market funds and, increasingly, mutual funds, where they (theoretically) can enjoy much higher returns and tolerate higher risks than they could if they kept their money in the bank. Investment in the low-inflation and high-real-interest-rate environment of the mutual fund industry will continue its spectacular growth.

Global Money

We've seen the globalization of stock markets, and the globalization of currency, equity, and debt instruments. The interdependence of the various stock and money markets around the world is such that capital flows smoothly across the globe on a twenty-four-hour, real-time, anytime, anyplace transaction basis, putting the large institutions into direct global competition. But it's also fair to say that even though these organizations work globally, there is still strong regional attachment to the people you know. Deutsche Bank handles most of its business in the U.S. not with American corporations, but by providing financial infrastructure for German corporations operating in the U.S. Similarly, many of the Japanese banks that have been successful in North America have done so on the back of, or as an extension of, their relationships with companies in Japan operating in the U.S. market. Similarly, the rise of such organizations as the Hongkong & Shanghai Bank in Western Canada is based on the relationship with the flood of affluent Hong Kong Chinese immigrants into Vancouver and the Western Provinces in the last few years as a protection and side bet against the possible negative consequences of Hong Kong's being repatriated to China after 1997. But the global infrastructure has just begun to touch consumers. Investment in global and regional mutual funds is increasing and there is more choice of financial products and services from globally competitive firms. With increased trade in services and the rise of a new middle class around the world we will see many more consumers of financial products, and new competitors will emerge.

Consumer as Corporation

It's clear that partly as a result of new innovative competitors and partly as a shift in their own preferences consumers now behave as if they are corporate entities in terms of the way they manage their banking relationships, their equity relationships, and their debt.

Consumers through the 1980s became increasingly leveraged, much in the same way that corporations have been, by using debt. The rise of home equity lines was substantial in the 1980s. This was a parallel to the increasing use of debt by corporations in the prior decades. The leverage of the household began to emulate the corporate style.

How Financial Services Has Responded—So Far

THE FINANCIAL SERVICES INDUSTRY has responded to the second curve in a variety of ways. Many of the responses are first-curve consolidations. Others are attempts at jumping to a second curve. Some of these will fail, but they will do so in interesting and instructive ways. And still others may just make it. Specific responses include the following:

Reintegration

The whole financial services mix is being reintegrated. On one hand the first curve is consolidating horizontally, to wit all of the mergers in the traditional banking sector: the consolidation of Western banks—Wells Fargo with Crocker and now First Interstate, Bank of America with Security Pacific—and among Eastern banks—the Carolina banks, and the large deal with Chase and Chemical combining under the Chase label (even though Chemical is the dominant partner) to be a powerhouse in New York City. This isn't the end of these consolidations; they're likely to continue as a response of the first curve. The second set of changes involves the putting together of new pieces of the banking system and financial services system in different combinations.

Got Milk? Got Mutual Funds?

Wells Fargo has committed itself to a strategy where it becomes a virtual bank, but it is also trying to increase its physical presence by providing more and more points of contact with the customers, while closing as many branches as possible. The bank's strategy is to enter into an agreement on an exclusive basis to be the financial partner with all of the grocery stores in California, the exception being Lucky, which entered into an exclusive relationship with Bank of America. Wells Fargo's stated intent is to provide, in selected supermarkets, a large presence, which will essentially be a sort of three-window system: one that's traditional ATM, one that's a videoconference facility for customer service, and one that's staffed during appropriate hours by what is really a sales/customer representative who will be walking the aisles trying to capitalize on the opportunity and the number of traditional Wells Fargo products, including its own money market and mutual funds. It's not inconceivable that you could go to the market to buy milk and come out with mutual funds. An extreme case, but a good example nonetheless of retailing's increasing recognition of banking, and of the likelihood that the tools of retailing—branding and promotion—will increasingly be used in the financial services sector.

Outsourcing the Customer

As the financial services industry came under earnings pressure over the last twenty years (especially during the recent periods of market deregulation), the implementation of performance and profitability measurement systems has led to a reevaluation of how products get delivered. In many areas, financial services companies realized that the costs of delivery of products exceeded the revenue potential, if measured on a stand-alone basis. In order to take advantage of economies of scale, outsourcing of transaction processing has become the rule of the day for many financial products (credit card processing, merchant servicing, ATM management). In many cases, new companies arose to fill the outsourcing needs. However, the problem that has developed is that the financial institution not only outsourced the computer services and transaction processing, but ended up outsourcing customer management as well. The result is that the outsourcing companies now basically own the customer relationships and stand ready to eclipse the financial services companies that they were created to support.

Building New Brands

Credit card companies like Visa and MasterCard have been more successful than the banks in building the brand image of the card. Because consumers trust Visa so much, they are almost indifferent to the bank that issues the card, an attitude that has opened the door for affinity cards: if you got miles or gas or discounts or—better yet—money, you would use an affinity card.

Open your wallet and pull out your cards. What bank issued them? My United Airlines First Card Visa card was issued by the FCC (First Chicago Corporation) National Bank, an affiliate of First National Bank of Chicago, but it took me a while to figure that out. The rise of affinity cards has anesthetized consumers, so that we trust the brand on the card, not the bank behind it. Joseph Nocera describes the first drop of Bank of America's credit cards in Fresno in September of 1958 as a disaster for the bank in terms of bad loans, fraud and abuse, and bad press, but it sowed the seeds of the credit card industry. We've learned to trust a new medium of transaction before, and most likely we can do it again.

Created to facilitate the development and acceptance of a world-wide card-based payments instrument, Visa has created a brand far stronger than any of its card issuers or owners. As a member-based organization with thousands of presumed masters (its owners), it is an organization that has developed a mind of its own. With the growth of the affinity card marketplace—affinity cards are credit cards issued by automakers, airlines, phone companies, and others with tie-ins to their products or services—consumers have repeatedly demonstrated greater brand loyalty to Visa and the affinity partner than they have to the underlying issuer of the credit card. In fact, in many cases, the only relationship that affinity card holders perceive is the one with Visa—not with the bank. So here's the question: Since consumers seem to think they have a relationship with Visa, and since they have demonstrated greater loyalty to the Visa brand than to the brand of the underlying bank card issuer, will Visa some-day seek to take over the customer relationship directly (i.e., become principal to the transaction) in lieu of its bank owners?

First Data Resources (FDR) is ideally situated to become a new American Express or Visa. FDR entered the credit card servicing business as the processor for financial institutions and now owns the merchant services side of the business, including Citicorp's portfolio. Formed in 1969 as the processing operation for Mid-American Bankcard Association, the company incorporated as an independent company in 1971, hoping to expand beyond the association's mar-kets. Because FDR has financial access to the customer, it is in a po-sition to distance the banks from their clients.

The evolution of the ATM interchange networks, such as Star, Plus, and Cirrus, has permitted the commoditization of the ATM environment. The existence of such networks permits any bank to utilize the once-proprietary ATM infrastructures developed by Citibank and Bank of America. Furthermore, the pricing of these networks essentially provides any authorized user with services at the average operating cost of all members. In other words, there is a transfer of operating expense from the users to the providers of ATM services, but there is no value ascribed to number, location, or functionality of ATMs. These networks permit banks like Bank of California to offer extensive ATM networks without making any investment in an ATM network themselves (other than network connection fees). The networks also permit companies like Electronic Data Systems (EDS) to leverage their experience as ATM outsourcers for banks into providing proprietary ATM services sold directly to consumers (nonbank branded ATM machines at airports, 7-Elevens, etc.).

The creation of these interchange networks also sets the stage for new entrants into the electronic currency and payment business, such as cybercash and online resources (i.e. easy and existing electronic access to every checking account in the country). At the same time, interchange regulations are in flux as banks, in a first-curve response, scramble to get a return on their network investments.

Selling Core Competencies

So you've made a big investment in product development, operating capacity, systems resources. You've got lots of capital, customers, market share. You're in a regulated industry with lots of perceived barriers to entry. You're one of the great business barons of your community. The mayor calls, everyone calls. You don't have to lift a finger to do any marketing and rarely do you have to leave your desk to generate new business. Customers come to you. You're king of the first curve. You're a banker of the 1960s.

So what do you do? Offer correspondent banking services. In other words, sell your core competencies to others so they can build their businesses. And that is exactly what happened in the 1970s and 1980s. Investment banks sold correspondent services to individual brokers and dealers. Banks sold clearing services to other banks and special-purpose corporations. But at the same time, smart people were beginning to ask some basic questions. Why can't brokerage fees be negotiable? If I can send my mutual fund a letter to redeem shares, why can't I use a check? What's so special about FDIC insurance? Do I really need a bank? Smart lawyers were helping to find

new answers to these questions and create nonbank banks, nonde-
posit deposits, nonloan loans.

Managing Risk

Prior to 1978, U.S. interest rates were regulated. Demand accounts
paid no interest and the standard bank consumer asset was a thirty-
year fixed-rate mortgage loan. Banks perceived little or no interest rate
risk. All of that changed in the late '70s with the deregulation of interest rates and the creation of money market deposits to compete with
money market mutual funds. In one fell swoop, the large mortgage
players, such as Bank of America (the largest mortgage bank then and
now), developed large long-term interest rate risk mismatches. In
other words, long-term fixed-rate loans were being funded by deposits
with interest rates of between three- and six-month terms.

In order to control interest rate risk, the big mortgage players developed new types of financial instruments, most of which were securitized and sold to third-party investors. With the encouragement
of the big investment banks and mortgage lenders, the U.S. government also entered the picture by creating quasigovernmental agencies to assist in the pooling, securitizing, and credit enhancement of
mortgage loans (Fannie Mae, Freddie Mac). The bottom line was
that mortgage lenders were able to continue to write long-term
mortgages, but immediately have a way to sell them in order to manage interest rate risk and earnings volatility. Problem solved!

The side effect of creating the securitized mortgage marketplace
was the ability to break up the value chain of mortgage lending into
three distinct pieces: origination, funding, and servicing. No longer
did the originator of the loan (the entity that has the customer) need
to own the asset. This led to the creation of new businesses which
would create loans, sell the asset immediately to the secondary market (perhaps through one of the quasigovernmental mortgage companies), and sell the servicing rights to a transaction processor.

Banking on Relationships

Bankers have always believed they were in a relationship business.
And customers, in turn, have always wanted a relationship with their
banker. But, when you look at the way banks sold products to customers, very rarely did relationship mean anything. Banks, in general,
have always sold their services on a transaction-by-transaction basis

with each deal priced on its own merit. And the customer buying on a product-by-product basis, in most cases, is given very little incentive to do business with the same financial institution. Banks sold commodity products to consumers who weren't that loyal. This is not how you deal with the new consumer. This disconnection in the banker's mind between relationship and transaction management has led to the banker's needing to be all things to any customer the banker elects to do business with. And, in needing to be all things, the bank tends to spread itself thin, offer too many products at mediocre quality, have too many stereo salespeople who call themselves bankers, and, in general, provide little value to the consumer. Furthermore, because the customer is sold on a transaction-by-transaction basis and deals with different bank employees all the time, the customer perceives little advantage to placing most or all of his or her eggs in one financial institution's basket.

When you look at the shift in where financial transactions are purchased, you don't see the development of a new full-service financial institution that does it all right. In other words, the shift was not from Bank of America to Wells or Citibank. Or even from Merrill Lynch to Shearson. Rather, over the last thirty years, we've seen the development of new competitors who offer a targeted product set with great service, enhanced value, and a passionate focus on the new consumer. And, in most of these cases, the new competitor is able to take advantage of new regulation (or a more aggressive regulatory interpretation), technology, the evolution of the educated and more financially savvy consumer, and a stagnant bank marketing and product development culture that is, to give them the benefit of the doubt, hamstrung by regulators.

Signs of the Massive Second Curve

SIGNS OF THE APPROACHING SECOND CURVE are already here. Take a look: here are a few.

The Rockefellers Meet the Internet

The middle class now has the banking once enjoyed by the Rockefellers: access to the stock market through mutual funds and discount brokerages, to cash or credit anywhere in the world through global ATM networks and credit cards, and to sophisticated money management advice via financial helplines and the personal financial publishing industry. All this is going to be coupled to the power of the new technology.

The emergence of a new electronic infrastructure is a key driver of the second curve in most industries. The pieces have been built consistently over the last twenty years. First is the basic global infrastructure for communication of financial information that has enabled stock markets and banks to operate and move cash on a global basis in real time. Second is the increasing sophistication of retail banking's ability to reach consumers through ATM networks and the increased integration of those networks on a global basis. Third is the development of the EDI and EFT systems that allow for electronic document interchange and electronic fund transfer as a tool for consistent payment and new forms of financial integration.

Newest and perhaps most exciting is the platform for electronic commerce that is being created for the Internet. Until very recently, no one in their right mind would do financial transactions over the Internet (just as in the early days of credit cards and ATMs); some would still argue that it's unwise. But a number of protocols and encryption systems have been developed to allow for the secure transmission of credit card numbers over the Net, and several banks, including Wells Fargo, one of the leaders, have committed to an electronic infrastructure where the Internet will be a basis for secure transactions. But the Internet is only one of many dimensions of this coming electronic infrastructure. Another key area is the rise of smart cards, which can be updated and replenished with cash remotely by phone.

Mondex, developed by National Westminster Bank, is a tool that will enable users to carry electronic cash. The other forms of "new money" are digital cash, virtual cash on the Internet, where account holders agree that a virtual amount of money is available to them over the Internet and that amount is held through organizations like Cybercash.

The New Insurance Agent

Agenting technology, such as that being developed by General Magic, will also have a dramatic effect on how we purchase commodities such as financial services. Soon you'll be able to keep your

risk profiles online and have your intelligent agent constantly searching worldwide for investment, borrowing, and insurance opportunities that match your appetite for risk. Think of this as program
trading for the rest of us.

Payment Services

A major core competency of large commercial banks is their check
clearing operation. More corporations bank at Bank of America because more consumers bank at Bank of America. Therefore, within
Bank of America's serving area a business is more likely to get same-
day availability of funds if they utilize B of A's check clearing operation than if they use any other service.

With the growth in electronic payment instruments, this paper
"on-us" advantage of large commercial banks will go away. What are
the business opportunities to replace these services? Is there such a
thing as an electronic "on-us" advantage? Enter the world of electronic bill payment and electronic bill presentment.

Consumer-to-Consumer Lending Made Possible

Consumer credit rating and insurance services permit direct consumer-
to-consumer lending. With the creation of more communications
mechanisms and services (BBS, e-mail, online services, Internet) and
the proliferation of computers and communications services into the
home, you can imagine the development of an automated matching
service to support direct consumer-to-consumer lending. Such a service
would be dependent on the existence of a reliable consumer credit rating service that would evaluate the credit worthiness of each participant and a credit insurance product that would serve as the loan loss
reserve pool.

Authentication Services

The digital signature process for network transaction leverages a
bank's investment in ATM card issuance and acceptance technology.
In effect, the card/PIN number is analogous to a public/private key.
Since financial services companies will require digital signature technology to permit remote transactions over networks and since consumers most likely will want one digital signature to use for all
network transactions, unless the banks become the issue/escrow

agent of keys, they will find themselves being forced to purchase at a premium services they provide to themselves today.

Smart Card Real Estate Management

Financial services players are all looking at the chip card. Dubbed "smart cards," these cards hold monetary value that can be deducted as purchases are made until the card has no value. Some cards are disposable, others rechargeable. Other smart cards may simply hold information. Airlines like them for electronic ticketing. Universities like them as universal ID cards usable in the library and cafeteria. The medical community is looking at the card for health records and the banks see it as a way to curb credit card and ATM fraud as well as an electronic purse. But what do consumers want? Most likely not to have to carry twenty smart cards in their wallets. Enter the business of smart card real estate management.

Interstate Versus Intergalactic Banking

Reform of the 1927 McFadden Act in the U.S., which set forth a restrictive framework for bank branch expansion, is already here. The rush of bank consolidation in 1995 alone was a whirl! A done Chase/Chemical deal, the Wells Fargo/First Interstate merger, a possible BankAmerica/NationsBank merger: every major financial institution is looking at ways to create the nationwide franchise. But at what cost? Systems and employee cultural integration nightmares. Acquisition of lots of real estate called branches. And account conversions that lead customers to rethink their whole relationship with banks just as often as they sign on with you. There's got to be a better way.

Virtual Banks

Everybody's talking about building a virtual bank. We'll put the accounts online and you'll be able to pay bills, buy investments, borrow money, all from the convenience of your living room. At least, that's what the traditional financial services companies think is a virtual bank. But consumers know better and have built their own virtual banks over the last twenty years. They've purchased day-to-day transaction services from a local commercial bank, savings and loan, or credit union. They've opened investment accounts with discount and full-service brokers and mutual fund companies. They've got credit cards from their schools, unions, supermarkets, and online services companies, not to mention from airlines, phone companies, and auto manufacturers. They save through their employer, borrow through their real estate agent, and have six or seven financial "relationships." In the meantime, each of the financial services companies claims these fickle consumers as their valued customer.

Bill Gates calls banks dinosaurs and every banker thinks that Microsoft wants to be a bank. Banks, as we know them today, are dinosaurs, and Microsoft does want to be a bank, but not what we think of as a bank today. Rather, the Microsofts of the world are riding the second banking curve, agenting transactions and relationship management. Consumer experience in building virtual banks coupled with the advancement in database tools and communications technologies is opening the door to a whole new industry of brokerage banking. A broker bank provides the infrastructure for the consumer to purchase financial products and services from the most cost-effective source, regardless of where the consumer and where the provider of the product or service are located. These new entities are not banks, just the important first screen on the way to a myriad of financial products.

The Schwab One Account is a good example of this. With one phone call, you can purchase securities, deposits, and mutual funds from almost any service provider worldwide. You can borrow against your assets, pay for purchases with a debit and credit card, and write checks—and you'll soon be able to pay bills as well. All of your transactions come nicely reported on one bank and investment statement each month.

Directory and online services will also play an early role in the further disintermediation of relationships. You can already log on to CompuServe, America Online, Prodigy, and the Internet to find out which bank is paying the most on CDs that day, which credit offer has the incentives right for you, and who's offering the best mortgage rate in your local community. And, within a few months, you'll be able to click on that rate or product feature to move to the vendor's home page to initiate the transaction. Directory services companies like InsWeb and Morningstar, and the major online services themselves, will provide these services.

Around 60 percent of the most affluent one fifth of the U.S. population own PCs; of those, over a fifth use their PC for financial management. Intuit's Quicken program claims around 70 percent of the

personal finance management market, with more than 7 million customers. Other contenders include Microsoft's Money, which is available to users of Windows 95 and Windows NT. Most of the banks
that offer Intuit offer Microsoft as well, although competitive pressures may separate them as platforms. And third is MECA Software
Inc., a Connecticut company (briefly owned by H&R Block, and now
jointly owned by Bank of America, NationsBank, Fleet Financial
Group, First Bank Systems, and the Royal Bank of Canada) that's
approached the situation a little differently. MECA Software offers
banks substantial control over personal financial management and
acts as a front end for banks that want to reinforce their relationships
with their customers through a personal finance management product, but don't want that product competing for customer favor.
MECA Software provides a front end that can be customized so that
it looks as though it were made exclusively for a particular bank.

Within a few years, Intuit's Quicken will be the electronic equivalent of the Schwab One account. Already you can have a Quicken
credit card which can be automatically downloaded to the software,
and you can pay virtually anyone through Intuit's electronic bill payment services. (Such services have already made an impact on the
check printing business. In December 1995, Deluxe Corporation,
the largest check printer in the U.S., announced that it would be restructuring its business in anticipation that the traditional 1 percent
per year growth in check volume will be leveling off by 1998, and de-
creasing after the turn of the century.) Soon you'll be able to have
data from transaction accounts at selected banks, as well as mutual
funds transactions, integrated with the software. As long as you use a
Quicken-enabled vendor, the software will be your relationship manager. And, as soon as Intuit provides links for consumers to purchase
any Quicken-enabled financial product through the software, Quicken
will be the virtual bank.

Intuit grew to prominence in 1994, with Microsoft's proposed acquisition that included an offering of seventy-five times earnings for
a company in the personal financial management software business.
The prospect of having Intuit's capacities to provide personal financial management and a link to transactions embedded in Windows
95 shook everyone up, but no one more so than the banks. Wall
Street worried that Microsoft was hoping to become a bank. Microsoft decided to pull out of the Intuit deal under the threat of the Justice Department Investigations for Antitrust, and in the wake of that
announcement, Intuit stock dropped by 20 percent, although it

came back up a month later, and the company subsequently signed agreements with several other banks and financial institutions.

Intuit CEO Scott Cook, an ex-P&G-er who has strong feelings about customer service, wants to make technology accessible to those of us who aren't software engineers; he hopes to enable what he's called "an electronic wallet," where Intuit would be the conduit between banks and consumers, and through which consumers would maintain their financial records and engage in various financial transactions—the selection and management of mutual funds, for example.

Intuit is extremely responsive to the electronic user of personal financial management software. The key to the company's success isn't necessarily the elegance of their programming—though the program does work well, *and* it even accomplishes all the things it says it will—but the company's high degree of responsiveness, from both a customer service and a customer feedback perspective. The company saw an increase of 77 percent in revenue from 1994 to 1995, and although that includes revenue from two acquisitions and is therefore somewhat artificially inflated, it's still impressive. The company has branched out from their base of Quicken (formerly the center of all their revenues), and now offers products for both the small business and the home. Intuit has also embraced European and other international markets, where they feel they can find the profile of users they're looking for. That market, simply put by Scott Cook, is defined by a two-by-two matrix of affluence versus PC use. Intuit hopes to claim the quadrant of affluent households with heavy PC-based financial interests, the infomated households discussed earlier.

Quicken users and customers of financial institutions who have hooked up with Intuit's online private network can use Quicken to handle a variety of banking tasks, including balance inquiries, money transfers, and bill payment. The network, which includes technology from Teknekron Software Systems, encryption algorithms from RSA Data Security, and additional firewalls on Sun Microsystems servers, provides consumers with a secure high-speed connection to accounts at up to three financial institutions. For each institution, the customer will see that particular bank's logo in the online service menu.

Intuit and America Online Inc. (AOL) have signed a strategic agreement to jointly provide electronic banking to AOL members. Intuit will make over its online area on AOL and include links to its recently launched Internet web site known as the Quicken Financial

Network, and AOL will make Intuit software products available for sale on AOL. Both companies will sponsor joint promotions to introduce their products to each other's customer base.

New Competitors in Insurance

InsWeb, started in October 1995, is one of a selection of insurance centers on the Internet. InsWeb provides in-depth industry-wide information on agents, brokers, insurance companies, and coverage. Founder and chairman Hussein Enan's initial idea was to create software that would allow individual insurers to develop their own online services. But, realizing the difficulty that customers would have in locating all the different insurers' sites, not to mention comparing policies, he changed direction and focused on providing consumers with the information they need to make solid purchasing decisions. And once you've made your decision, you can also electronically purchase different kinds of insurance and establish contact with the agents and brokers in the company of your choice. Security measures are included, and are available to both hosts and consumers. Host organizations (those providing source material) include educational institutions that provide unbiased information for glossaries and common questions, and nonprofit organizations that publish consumer information such as agency rankings in terms of product and price, as well as insurance companies.

Companies, agents, and brokers pay to be on InsWeb on a graduated scale. Pricing for insurance providers is based upon the number of product lines and the number of states in which the lines are offered. Pricing for agents, based on the complexity of the agent's site, is lower. Insurers can also advertise their products and employment needs on InsWeb. And consumers don't have to just browse through company policies to find what they want; they can fill out application forms, allowing insurers to offer policies that match their requirements, a process that will potentially reduce policy prices.

Direct to Consumer

There are several examples of financial services players going directly to the consumer, bypassing brokers, agents, and branches. Schwab made a big purchase in the U.K., expanding its base, and Nations-Bank has hired three hundred security dealers to operate inside their bank. Virgin Direct is another example, as are First Direct and

Lloyd's, which is going to go direct to provide services. Virgin Group, the British airline and leisure group headed by Richard Branson, launched its first financial product in March 1995, with one of the cheapest personal equity plans (PEP) on the market, Branson's attempt to attract new customers to financial services by targeting the under-forty-five age group with a simple product and tie-in discounts with Virgin's travel business. Branson reportedly decided to enter the market after trying to invest his own fortune. "My impression was that it was packed with hidden charges, pushy salesmen, poor performance, and meaningless jargon. I couldn't believe it was so complicated, so I put a team together to do it better. The objective was to offer products which are the cheapest on the market and easiest to understand."

Virgin formed Virgin Direct Personal Financial Service, VDPFS, a fifty-fifty joint venture with British life insurer Norwich Union. The company used telephone sales to keep its costs down, benefiting from new rules established to make the British insurance industry more transparent in terms of costs and commissions. Within the U.K., VDPFS will sell life insurance over the telephone, with new products initially being available without advice; but the company plans to provide financial advice over the phone soon. And there are reports that Virgin plans to expand to overseas markets where the Virgin name is strong, the margins are high, and the service is poor—probably Europe and North America, with Australia less of a possibility because of the commonality with the Australian Mutual Provident Society.

Looking Ahead: Second Curves for the Future

THE MASSIVE SECOND CURVE of financial services will be driven by the slow buildup we have seen—middle-class consumers with a range of financial instruments at their disposal and no loyalty to the component issuers—coupled with the dramatic growth of technology-based second-curve actors like Intuit. The decline in the value of relationships coupled with increased consumer education and sophistication, advancements in communications technologies, further breakdown in barriers between financial market segments, and the free movement of capital cross-border will lead to new ways that commerce can be conducted with the creation of new financial products and services to support the new commerce. The change will be fast and furious, and it will shake to the core many of the biggest first-curve players of the twentieth century.

It's terrifying to first-curve financial services companies to see how dramatic the effect could be. Recently, we met with a large East Coast life insurance company. Like most life insurance companies, this one had built a huge business selling life insurance via armies of salesmen and saleswomen with big hair and strong handshakes, who knew how to prospect for new customers and close them on a high-load, high-commission plan. As we explained to company leaders, however, that world is ending. It is quite conceivable that in the very near future an intelligent agent embedded in a home PC will automatically identify the insurance plans I might need on the basis of my social and financial profile. The electronic agent would automatically go to InsWeb or even out to the home pages of all the vendors on the planet and develop a tailored side-by-side comparison of the best term rates connected to all the different insurance vendors. As this major insurer said to us, "The last thing we want is a side-by-side comparison of group term rates."

Increasingly, savvy purchasers will buy financial services through intelligent networks like the Internet rather than from an army of big-haired salespeople. They will interact with global markets, and they will be steered by new global brand names like Virgin, facilitated by Intuit, General Magic, First Data, RSA, Netscape, and First Virtual. This is the second curve.

Managing the Second Curve

WE'RE NOT IN KANSAS ANYMORE; the world we live and work in is a dramatically different place than it was twenty years ago—or even ten. We're different as consumers and we're different as businesses; you would not be hard-pressed to give your own examples of the changes described in these pages. The advances in technology, the changes in consumer habits and outlook, and the global expansion of the marketplace have had far-reaching effects, creating second curves that offer both challenges and opportunities. Whether you look at the emergence of China as an economic giant, the growth of new consumer markets in middle-class cities around the world, or the rise of new technologies and new means of doing business, second curves are here to stay.

And to wreak havoc, if you're not careful, turning boardrooms into war rooms, when top management has to consider the solid (or at least *existing*) financial returns from the first curve to meet the expectations of those ever-present shareholders, versus the feeling—

and hope—that the second curve will yield a sustainable business for the long run. It's risky business, but it can be done.

The second curve is a phenomenon that businesses have to address to survive. But it's more than that; it's a model, and a good one. Because of its simplicity, the two-curve model is a wonderful tool for planning strategically during times of great change, a simple diagnostic that can help companies think about their business and markets as they are, and as they might become; about their attitudes toward risk; and—most important—about the direction and pace of change. Using the two-curve model can help companies stretch their time horizons to five, ten, and even twenty years. Pitney Bowes has gone so far as to incorporate the two-curve language into the job descriptions for senior executives at the highest level of the company. And health care companies—including pharmaceutical, medical technology, managed care, and provider organizations such as Bristol-Myers Squibb, SmithKline Beecham, and Kaiser Permanente—have used the two-curve model to fully understand the demise of the first curve. Automakers, banks, and technology companies like Volvo, Chrysler, Chase Manhattan, and Telia have used the two-curve model to help them think about what to do when their longtime market matures.

Managing on two curves is a metaphor that can help companies think about great change—not incremental growth, the kind of change that occurs as every company moves through its life cycle, but widespread, fundamental, universal change on the order of the comet that wiped out the dinosaurs in the Mesozoic era. The two-curve model resonates with companies because it provides a tool for handling the essential strategic dilemma that arises in times of change: You know things are changing, but you don't know how or how fast. All you know is that you can't just wait for change to happen to you; you have to go out and do something about it.

Signs of the Second Curve

SOME OF WHAT YOU NEED TO KNOW about the second curve, and responding to it, depends on where you stand—the specifics of your business and industry. But there are some characteristics about the second curve that apply, and that you need to be familiar with, no matter where you are. The following trends go hand in hand with the second curve, across the board:

The Shift from Goods to Services to Knowledge

The information revolution is taking us to a knowledge-based society in which services become increasingly important vis à vis goods. Where what you know counts more than what you manufacture, and where owning the customer is more important than owning the factors of production. Even in the manufacturing sector, we're seeing more and more of the jobs being created in knowledge work as opposed to drudge work. Increasingly, value is added to goods only when it contains the knowledge content that comes out of services like R&D.

Fragmented and Consolidated Markets

Today's consumers demand response, including everything from product quality (whether it's information or service that's being sought) to when and where the sale takes place. One way that vendors try to provide that response is by appealing to and focusing on smaller, more specific groups of consumers fueling the second curve. And the effect of that focus is a fragmented market. Second curves are often attempts to open new markets for what was a particular segment of an existing market. We'll see more and more markets aimed at smaller, more specific groups of consumers. Some have called this one-to-one marketing, where pluralism and technology meet head to head to create unique transactions between buyer and seller. As a United Airlines flyer, my travel preferences are stored to enable United to better tailor their service to my needs. With many of the new online services, I could customize my own newspaper. I don't, but I could. But the shifts to highly fragmented second-curve markets like the ones emerging on the Internet are balanced by the massive consolidation on the first curve of retailing in response to the value-driven consumer. Overall retail sales per square foot in all forms of retailing are declining in constant dollar terms. This is a function of overcapacity in every mass marketing category—grocery stores, drugstores, club formats like Costco, and even large-scale department stores. Major grocery chains, drug chains, and book chains are each consolidating to fight over market share. The first curve tightens down, even as the second curve opens up.

An example is the publishing industry, where the second curve is coming to books, and the dilemmas posed by two curves are everywhere. Consolidation of the bookstore retail channel has already occurred, touched by the changes in distribution and retailing discussed earlier. Value consumers, new technology, and new logistics have greatly increased the clout of big chains. At the same time, outlets like Barnes & Noble are opening new channels (in the form of superstores). Together these shifts threaten the first curve of low-tech publishers with traditional markets.

What's a publisher to do? Ballantine, a division of Random House and publisher of this book, has embraced the second curve. Ballantine saw that the new technology offered an opportunity to do things differently by using new computer technology as a vehicle for producing, managing, and distributing books. Starting first in 1989 with automation of bookstore sales information through PROS (Professional Re-Order System), they built an electronic spine for the distribution side of their business. Through PROS and its successor BOOKNET, which was integrated with bookstore systems, they got closer to the customer and had real-time information about what was selling and what wasn't, thanks to rigorous in-store inventory and data collection, initially by Ballantine's sales force, but later through EDI links.

But the big step to the second curve came in 1993, when Ballantine moved to Lotus Notes as the platform for virtually all of their interactions. Not just the collection and distribution of sales data, but interaction among editorial, publicity, sales, marketing, and business functions. Notes is the lifeblood at Ballantine. This means they can respond faster; they can flatten their organization and shift from meeting so much in physical space to meeting in electronic space.

RandomSoft is Random House and Ballantine's foray into the software publishing business. They have a superb channel, a superb sales force, and a series of customers (like Media Play and Borders) who are bridging the gap between book sales and software sales. Ironically, the retailing of software is in need of a dose of the second curve. And Ballantine has set its sights on delivering.

As in a true second-curve situation, the vast majority of Ballantine's revenues is and will be on the first curve of books. That doesn't mean you can't incorporate second-curve thinking in the traditional book retailing business. Ballantine will continue to bring second-curve thinking to the base publishing business. The payoff: although Ballantine and Random House are privately held, insiders say they outperform the industry by a wide margin.

The Shift from Big Technology to High Technology

In many areas, the economies of scale that favored big technology are being actively challenged by newer technologies that can produce specialized (and often high-value-added) products for specific market segments that are better tailored to their needs and can be delivered more quickly and at less cost. Futurist Stan Davis has termed this "mass customization." The combination of today's information technology—which makes marketing, distribution, and inventory control much more cost-effective—and today's processing technologies—which allow efficient smaller assembly line runs—makes smaller production for market niches an option more and more often in the contemporary industrial world. The Chinese manufacturing revolution is not big technology. It has focused on incorporating the light manufacturing principles found in Hong Kong and Taiwan with computer-integrated manufacturing. Dick Wong's factory described earlier is making light electronics products; it's not doing heavy engineering. Similarly, the explosive potential of companies like Netscape and Silicon Graphics isn't based on *big* technology; it's based on *high* technology.

The End of Economies of Scale

The technology advances that allow companies to learn of customer needs quickly, turn out products and services to meet those needs, and get those products to market have ended the dominance of economies of scale that we've seen for basically the last century. And that's had a cyclical effect, allowing today's already-calling-the-shots consumer to gain even *more* control over the market. Levi's personalized jeans are a leading-edge example of new technologies being brought to bear to make a mass-market product tailored for individuals.

The End of Supply and Demand

In a society where consumers are as powerful as Superman—stronger than steel and faster than a speeding bullet—the good old model of supply and demand doesn't seem too relevant anymore. Creating some product (or service), and then setting out to convince people to buy that product or service just doesn't work anymore. In real estate terms, it's a buyer's market, big time. We're moving toward an economic order that's more in the middle, where the consumer and the producer work together to develop the product or service that best combines the needed—what consumers want and need—with the possible—what the vendor can provide. In retailing, Wal-Mart and others shape new products with their vendors, but are driven by the end consumer. In information technology, new applications emerge from the messy middle ground where users and vendors discover the future together.

Managing on Two Curves

FUNDAMENTALLY, managing on two curves means confronting the uncertainty of change and getting comfortable with it. And it means being willing and able to pursue the future—to let go of the first curve and follow the second, whatever it may be—when the time is right. Uncertainty is one of the names of this game, and while there are no guarantees, there are some "probablies," some things that will make life easier, and more profitable, and less of a roll of the dice.

LEARN TO JUMP

Speed and flexibility are crucial; you have to move like a gazelle. Throughout this book we've seen examples: Netscape's push to be the browser of choice, Ed McCracken's belief in being so fast you can start later and still win, Black Cat's getting sea urchins to you fresh. And those leaps of faith? Whether they be to serve the new consumer better or to start a whole new second-curve business, they're not into the abyss; they've got to be focused. The second curve may be the unknown, but you still have to have some idea of where you'll land before you jump. An uncertain future doesn't mean no vision. Companies who jump to the second curve have some view of what the second curve might become. And when you do jump, do so with your eyes open and your mind clear, working from a strategy that's well-developed and clear and as thorough as it can be. When Nestlé jumps to an emerging market, they clearly follow the hierarchy of needs in the market.

SERVE THE NEW CONSUMER OR FAIL

Responsiveness to consumers—providing them with whatever they want, whenever they want it, wherever they want it (anything, anytime, anyplace)—is paramount. And because in a two-curve world consumers are calling the shots, expect battles over the control of those consumers. In a bid to capture a share of mind (and share of market) of the new consumer, many software companies are giving test products away free.

BUILD A DIVERSE MANAGEMENT TEAM

Cultural talents can help you make the jump successfully. Remember: diversity enables success. A culturally diverse leadership will have more skills in jumping to the second curve.

OUT WITH THE OLD, IN WITH THE NEW

Forget the old; bigger isn't always better, and old faithfuls like the economies of scale, supply and demand, and monopoly channels are things of the past. Value-added services are no longer just in the mind of the vendor—it's that omnipotent consumer again. The new world is about transforming the value chain and coming up with new products—and new channels to market them—and it's an environment where smaller second-curve players can find a niche and come to dominate.

FOCUS ON THE PACE OF CHANGE

The language of change is all around us. But people both over- and underestimate the pace of change. Don't live in the future before it happens, but be prepared to deal with the ever-accelerating forces driving change—a stance that requires investment in, and attention to, the measurement and monitoring of change. Not just forecasting, but scenario planning, creation and tracking of leading indicators, and systematic top-level review of the long run. In corporations today there's an increased awareness of the need to think systematically about the future—not in the hope of prediction or of creating elaborate, inflexible five-year plans, but as an ongoing discipline of strategic management. At the core of this strategic long-term thinking is a focus on discerning the true pace of change. Managing on two curves demands it.

BUILD A SECOND-CURVE CAPACITY

The second curve is radically different from the first curve. It requires new competencies, new people, new customers, and whole new business systems. To a large, fat, successful corporation it seems too much like hard work to really make the transformation to the second curve. But you have to do it or die.

Strategies for a Two-Curve World

SO HOW DOES THE SECOND CURVE—and what others have done—affect your business? Companies can choose to stay on the first curve (at least for a while), to jump to the second curve, or to play both curves. But regardless of direction, the decision must be informed by intelligence (in both meanings of the word) and hard strategic choices.

Analyzing Your Business in Terms of Second Curves

LOOKING AT YOUR BUSINESS in terms of second curves involves two general steps: learning how to spot the real thing and gauging the pace of change.

The first step is figuring out whether or not what you *think* is a second curve really is one—or whether it's a phantom, just something going bump in the corporate night. It's tricky business; even those experienced in the world of the second curve never quite know whether the second curve is real or not. Is that blip on the screen a true emerging technology, something like a PC in 1977, or groupware in 1985? Or is it an *almost*, a kind of gadget-technology that will always be a big deal "ten years from now"—a videophone or personal helicopter. Could even be just a fad that flames out. Does anybody remember CB radio or videotext? How about Betamax and eight-track tapes? Wing-walker's rule number one applies big time here: Never leave your position on one wing (or curve) until the next one is a sure thing.

The question becomes particularly tricky where emerging technologies are concerned. When sales take off, it's very difficult to know whether they represent a real trend or just an illusion. When it comes to new technology, there are two million Americans who will buy anything, and two million Americans who will use anything, no matter how user-ugly. So selling four million units isn't quite as impressive as it sounds. It could be that you just saturated the idiots and the folks of high tolerance.

Sorting out the new technologies that will take off from those that will fail, even if they fail in interesting ways, is incredibly difficult—and critical. And sorting out real growth potential from hype is difficult even in nontechnology areas. Is the second-curve candidate a Starbucks Coffee, or a Bartles & Jaymes wine cooler? Is it a Southwest Airlines or a People Express Airline? Is it Toys "R" Us with its 22 percent market share or Child World, a chain that once had 130 stores with $180 million, but went bankrupt a few years ago? A lot of businesses like to innovate, even when it doesn't do them any good. They're good at selling ideas, which leads to enormous hype. Most of the markets from the 1980s that were supposed to reach a billion dollars by 1990—technology niches and new product ideas—turned out to be worthless junk.

As emphasized earlier: *There is a tendency to overestimate the impact of phenomena in the short run, and to underestimate it in the long run.* This tendency is particularly acute in today's culture, with its obsession with self-improvement, novelty, and the march of linear progress ever onward and upward. We are a forward-oriented culture, tireless, enamored of the frontier, living on the leading—if not bleeding— edge. Further, it's the export of this stance to the rest of the world that is one of the key drivers of the second curve worldwide. And with this bias for movement comes the tendency to mistake activity for action, to see short-term forays as the start of long journeys. We buy a ticket on the next plane out, even if we're not sure where it's going. No wonder it's hard to know a real second curve when you see one.

Staying on the First Curve

PLAYING THE SECOND CURVE isn't always the best choice; sometimes it simply makes more sense to stay with the first curve—

as long as you've examined that second curve thoroughly. Even if you're a committed first-curve player, you need to know something about the second curve, if only to know what to expect from your competitors.

The scenario for a company for which staying with the first curve might be the right decision would go something like this: The company recognizes that massive structural change is on the way—its industry will soon change dramatically—and that this change will create a second curve. But there's a strong market share on the first curve, and the company's core competencies suggest that it can get more out of the current market than it can by jumping to the new one. So you don't jump—you stay with the first curve. You still have a number of choices, none of which are mutually exclusive:

OWN THE FIRST CURVE

You're in a first-curve business, but maybe it's going to take ten or twenty years to die—video stores, facsimile machines, or nuclear submarines, for example. Or maybe the curve isn't ever going to grow; think of basic metals. It's clear that the first curve will disappear in the long run or show very little growth, but you can own this curve in an absolutely or relatively declining market. The commodity steel business, the oil business, and the global defense industry (or should it be global *offense* industry, since we can't all be defenders?) are currently experiencing huge consolidations. Some fancy fighters and frigates are still going to be built, just not as many as there used to be. As a consequence, Lockheed, Grumman, and Martin Marietta have dramatically consolidated. Similarly, Rio Tinto-Zinc and Toronto-based Inco Ltd., the world's leading miner of nickel, have come to own the commodity metals business by cutting jobs and investing heavily in techniques to boost productivity.

SLIDE DOWN THE DEMAND CURVE INTO OBLIVION

You milk the market. You don't make any investment on the first curve that doesn't have a short-term payoff. You wring the profit out of the first curve, and either sell the company at the top, or simply take the money and run. Many corporations behave like this—although they rarely admit it. Defense contractor General Dynamics pulled off the mother of all sacrifice flies by simply winding down, selling all its assets to players who wanted to fight it out on the first curve, and sending the proceeds to shareholders in a nice big check.

EXPORT THE FIRST CURVE

GE has been at the top of the Fortune 500 for the last thirty years and will likely stay there for the next thirty years. Its genius is that it moves old businesses like jet engines and railcars to some other place on the planet, and focuses on providing value to sophisticated new business consumers. Volvo is another company that uses this strategy effectively. Sören Gyll, Volvo's CEO, has substantially reversed the diversification strategy of Per Gyllenhammar, his predecessor. Gyll has divested Volvo of pharmaceuticals and consumer products to focus on the core transportation business, where the Volvo brand is strongest. In the United States and some other parts of the world, Volvo is thought of as a small luxury car company. In reality, it has a 1 percent global market share in cars (closer to 10 percent in the segment it serves), but it has a 10 percent global market share in heavy trucks, and is well on the way to becoming perhaps the world's biggest bus company. It is already the second biggest truck company in the world, behind Daimler-Benz. Big trucks and buses are first-curve businesses in the developed world, but there is huge and growing demand in second-curve markets in developing countries. Part of Volvo's declared future strategy is to provide the transportation infrastructure for the rapidly developing regions of the world.

A second form of export shared by GE and Volvo is exporting technology from one industry to another. Turbine technology can be used for generating electricity just as well as it can be used for making jet engines. Similarly, Générale des Eaux, the massive French water utility, is buying utilities in other places and expanding its hold on a flat first curve by adding value in water treatment and waste management technologies.

KILL THE SECOND CURVE

Some of these stories are the stuff of myth. The auto manufacturers reputedly killed the various carburetion people that came up with the 70 miles-per-gallon engine, and a railroad company bought and replaced the emerging public transit system (consisting of electric trolley cars) of Los Angeles early this century. A less extreme example is the debate that went on in the United Kingdom and is still going on in Germany about retail hours. This debate is fundamentally motivated by first-curve players (including organized labor) whose costs and competition will be increased by longer hours. Hence their desire to preserve the status quo. Indeed, much of domestic European industrial policy is aimed at propping up the first curve at the expense of the second. By conferring preferred status on domestic first-curve mainframe computer businesses like Groupe Bull or Siemens-Nixdorf, the Europeans have stifled the emergence of smaller, more entrepreneurial second-curve technology companies. Where are the Oracles, Sybases, or Silicon Graphics of Europe? Similarly, tight control of landing slots at European airports has prevented the emergence of effective competition from new European-based domestic and international airlines. Europe has no Southwest Airlines. It took the entrepreneurial second-curve genius of renegade Brits like Freddy Laker in the 1970s or Richard Branson in the 1990s to break through this first-curve thinking with charter airlines.

IF AT FIRST YOU DON'T SUCCEED, RENAME IT

In many businesses, people just put second-curve labels on first-curve companies: We are not a Blue Cross plan anymore, we are a managed health care company. We are not a drug company, we are in the disease state management business. We don't make commodity PCs, we sell solutions. Yes, we are good at renaming; it's the "new improved" mentality. Swatch did this with watches. To some extent, the accounting firms that now tout themselves as consultancies are doing the same thing.

Jumping to the Second Curve

BUT SAY YOU HAVE SOME LUCK, or smarts, or both, and that the second curve is looking pretty real, and you're thinking about making the jump. The next question is when, just as it is with any big decision: you decide *what* you're going to do, then you decide *when* to do it. Only in this case, the "when" is crucial. Do you jump now and walk away from your best customers? Jumping to the second curve too soon could mean walking away from a still viable source of revenue or—worse yet—going head-to-head with yourself or your best customers. Baxter built a new business in health care delivery in the 1980s focused on alternate site (nonhospital). But the business—Caremark—was in direct competition with Baxter's big hospital clients who were diversifying into similar businesses. The result: Caremark was spun off as an independent business. And Baxter is about to do a second-curve spin-off again. They will create a new cost-containment business separate from their growth-oriented biotechnology and new product business.

If you jump too early, you can lose a lot of money; ask Chase or Citibank about the home banking trials of the 1970s and 1980s, when they poured tens of millions into premature experiments. Ask Apple about the Newton that was supposed to usher in the golden age of personal digital assistants and the new economic base for Apple.

But if you hang on, will it be too late? If you stay on the old curve too long, you may never get a chance to move to the second curve and get into the game, and (once again) you can lose a lot of money. Ask Western Union. They owned telegraphy—they still do—they just missed out on radio, television, and the computer.

The first part of figuring out when to jump is gauging the pace of change on the second curve, the same way you'd be pretty interested in the speed of a moving train if you were going to try to hop on. If the curve is moving too fast, staying on is going to be tough. Is this a three-year growth phenomenon like the diffusion of color TV, Starbucks Coffee, or Cindy Crawford? Or is it a three-decade phenomenon like cable TV, managed health care, or mail order?

Stein's Law is helpful in thinking about the problem of forecasting the pace of change on the two curves in general, and in getting some perspective on the second curve in particular. Herb Stein is a distinguished scholar at the American Enterprise Institute who developed an interesting observation about the demise of communism that he has applied to broader societal phenomena and formalized as Stein's Law: *If something is unsustainable in the long run, it will end.*

And there's a corollary: *If something is going to be a big deal in the future, it's got to start sometime.* And if it has to start sometime, it will tip its hand, show up on the radar screen somewhere, even if only as a tiny, unidentified blip. So you need to ask the following question: If the second curve is real, how do you measure it? It has to be out there somewhere.

In the case of Pitney Bowes, it was helpful to identify a series of important indicators of second-curve mail users. One of these was the infomated household. Tracking and exploring the mail use and behavior of these infomated households helped to identify opportunities for new businesses for Pitney Bowes on the second curve, as well as potential substitution threats to the traditional mail stream on the first curve.

For many of the leading pharmaceutical companies like Bristol-Myers Squibb and SmithKline Beecham, as well as for health care consultants like Price Waterhouse, it was helpful to develop indicators of managed health care that could be tracked to measure progress on the second curve. One such indicator of advanced managed health care is the presence of medical groups capable of organizing and managing all of the care for their patients for a single fee per capita, per month. Tracking the number, size, and distribution of these groups helped to develop a better perspective on the direction and pace of change.

Conventional wisdom may tell us that it's smarter to be lucky than it's lucky to be smart, but luck won't do it all here. Since by definition there's a dearth of good metrics for the second curve, you'll usually have to come up with at least some of these calculations on your own. You may have to invent the metrics as you go along and develop an infrastructure for tracking them. One such measure for tracking cities most likely to attract "knowledge workers" was a "three-star-restaurant-to-bowling-alley ratio" that proved a useful leading indicator of the yuppie enclaves of the future. It's this kind of creativity the second curve demands of those companies and their leaders who want to make it in a two-curve world.

Entrepreneurs and venture capitalists breathe, eat, and sleep the second curve. But for a well-established company, the second curve is an alien notion, and certainly not an easy jump. Here are five basic strategies to make playing that second curve possible.

EAT THE CORPORATE LUNCH

Second-curve minnows can take on huge corporations and huge markets by going after them one nibble at a time, eventually taking over and becoming giants themselves; Microsoft, Apple, Oracle, and Genentech all began this way. And Federal Express parlayed a wacky business plan to deliver high-priced letters through Memphis overnight into a multibillion-dollar global business with a reputation for speed, efficiency, and value. Enabled by a piece of legislation that allowed it to compete in a tiny sliver of the mail stream, FedEx built a dominant position in overnight document delivery. Everyone says it's a great miracle that FedEx moves all this stuff around so fast and so cheaply—yet FedEx moves half a billion mail pieces a year at an average cost of several dollars per piece. The U.S. Postal Service, on the other hand, moves 171 billion pieces at several cents a piece—sure it's slower, but not by much. Federal Express focused on one great lucrative niche and ate the corporate lunch.

You find another good example in health care. HMOs like U.S. Healthcare, United HealthCare, FHP, and PacifiCare were able to pick away at the business held by traditional health insurers and Blue Cross plans. As a result, many of the old first-curve players are trying to move to the second curve.

Internationally, Sony and Samsung took on established American giants in consumer electronics and ate their corporate lunch. They focused on features, quality, and value. Conventional televisions, VCRs, and stereo equipment are primarily Asian products now.

In publishing and media, Rupert Murdoch is a second-curve player who has stuck it to the first-curve players of Fleet Street and the big three U.S. TV networks. Murdoch parlayed bad taste and good marketing into a multibillion-dollar global enterprise.

TURN A SMALL BASE INTO BIG BUCKS

The leading venture capitalist Kleiner Perkins Caufield & Byers is delirious if something goes from a $2 million investment to a $50 million return in five years. If they can do that a hundred times over the course of a venture fund, they get quite excited about it. But if you want to talk to the average Fortune 500 CEO about a $50 million business in five years, you can't even get on the calendar.

All of which leads to a huge competitive advantage for second-curve players. First-curve players only go after big numbers—at least one decimal point on the balance sheet. But second-curve players—the successful ones—are these passionately hyperfocused humanoids who are personally going to go from Worth Nothing to Worth A Lot. Xerox's Palo Alto Research Center (PARC) has developed more important innovations in information technology in the last thirty years than any other R&D organization except Bell Labs. But while PARC was a second-curve player, until recently Xerox itself could never capitalize on its innovations because it wasn't managing on two curves. Instead, PARC alums spawned Silicon Valley giants like Apple. Xerox's new venture capital orientation may reverse this.

DEVELOP A BRASS NECK

Anyone brought up in Glasgow knows the expression, "He has a brass neck," meaning that so-and-so has so much self-confidence he is willing to stick his neck in places he shouldn't and risk having his head chopped off. The Yiddish term is *chutzpah*. Imagine the young Bill Gates—practically a teenager—going in to convince IBM that he could provide the operating system for its new line of personal computers. A lot of us would think at least twice, but second-curve entrepreneurs perform these feats every day. Michael Dell of Dell Computer has a brass neck. He started a multibillion-dollar discount PC business from his college dorm. Marty Wygod of Medco built the mail-order drug business into a marketing powerhouse that tempted the world's largest and richest drug company to pay an astonishing $6 billion for the illusion of control over the distribution channel. Richard Branson of Virgin delights in shocking the establishment by walking in and competing in new fields on the strength of the Virgin brand name. An individual with a brass neck often has the Midas touch as well, though it's likely that the brass neck came first.

LOOK FOR EXPONENTIAL MARKETING

Exponential marketing is a socially acceptable form of pyramid selling. Some of the potential businesses that will emerge from the Internet are likely to be exponential, meaning that they'll go from nothing to millions of customers and transactions (albeit very small ones) almost overnight. More traditionally, many growth businesses work like the old Clairol Shampoo commercial: "You tell two friends, and they tell two friends, and so on." Amway grew to be a gigantic business this way. Exponential franchise businesses are built all the time—you turn an idea into one store, then into a whole lot of stores—if not overnight, then in fairly short order. The power and perils of franchising combined with the connectivity of the Internet could lead to some very interesting franchises in cyberspace.

But franchising isn't the only form of exponential marketing. New fashion-oriented businesses have used massive word of mouth (and millions in advertising the world over) as a form of exponential marketing to create new products that consumers "have to have," things like Vuarnet sunglasses and Nike athletic shoes (a global gold mine in sneakers). The success of the Republican party and the Christian right over the last fifteen years is in no small part due to exponential marketing through direct mail and cable TV.

TAKE UP PARADIGM SURFING

Some people handle the second curve like the Big Kahuna, that wave they've been waiting for all their lives. They know, from a sort of sixth sense, when the second curve's coming and when it'll take off. Couple that kind of intuition with a keen sense of when the first curve has peaked, then act on it by putting your money where your mouth is, and you're in the business of paradigm surfing: sell at the top, move on to the next wave.

Paradigm surfers make a lot of money for themselves and their investors. And while these second-curve surfers may have better-than-average antennae about change, it's not only their forecasting ability that makes them successful; it's their surfing ability. It's one thing to *see* the wave coming, and quite another to get up on the board with the surf roaring over your head. You can often identify paradigm surfers by their necks: solid brass. Take a look.

Jim Clark of Netscape fame and fortune is a paradigm surfer. So is Bob Patricelli, who left a big corporate job running CIGNA Health-Care to found Value Health. He understood that the paradigm was going to shift from monolithic health care providers to players that manage the subcomponents of health care, such as pharmaceutical benefits managers. And Craig McCaw is a paradigm surfer. He founded McCaw Cellular, sold to AT&T at the top, shopped for PCS (personal communications systems) licenses in the name of bidding up the price, and then decided not to do that, leaving the price high for the next player and investing himself in yet another pioneer company in information services.

Playing Both Curves

WE'VE TALKED ABOUT SITUATIONS in which a company might choose to play one curve or the other, and there are certainly times when that's the best choice. But for most large companies, the reality is that choosing one curve or the other isn't really an option; it's a luxury they can't afford. The forces of change driving the second curve aren't going away. Those changes—and certainly others that we can't even define yet—will continue to generate two curves, and to make it to the twenty-first century, most companies will have to learn to manage on both curves.

Easier said than done: most large companies don't know where to start. They know how to continuously make a profit, to innovate, and to be competitive in the short run, but that's not the same as managing on two curves. Corporations will have to go beyond reengineering, time-based competition, and core competencies, and focus instead on long-term growth. To perpetuate themselves as market leaders, companies will have to build second-curve organizations, while continuing to get as much as possible from their first-curve businesses. Those that don't won't survive.

The strategies that follow are *just a little different* from those last two lists. Those were suggestions, possibilities—things to consider. These are *musts*, five key steps that large corporations have to take to manage successfully on two curves.

REDEFINE THE VALUE CHAIN

Most second curves are created by a redefinition of the value chain. Somebody sees a way to reconfigure the existing game or create a new game with a different set of rules. The explosive growth comes when customers see the value in the new chain and tell their friends. Large corporations hunting for second-curve opportunities should look first at the value chain, but they shouldn't do it alone. Engage some crazy people from inside and outside the organization to challenge your assumptions, change your perspective, and build new models of value. Reengineering core business processes won't be enough.

CREATE SECOND-CURVE PORTFOLIOS

A large company can make the small numbers of the second curve worthwhile by acting as its own venture capitalist and maintaining a portfolio of second-curve opportunities within the first-curve company. This means taking risks, knowing how to build a portfolio of new ventures, and tolerating—even encouraging—failure.

PRUNE THE SECOND CURVE

A corollary to creating second-curve portfolios. Companies should continually reevaluate their second-curve opportunities to determine which are succeeding and which are not. You have to be brutally honest. Remember our corollary to Stein's Law earlier: *If something's going to be a big deal, it's got to start sometime.* But if nobody, but nobody, buys it—pay attention.

SHIFT CURVES ON THE BASIS OF CULTURE AND COMPETENCIES

Most large organizations are threatened by change, but to compete on two curves, you have to learn to master change. But it has to be change that has a basis, some kind of logic to it, not change for the sake of change. The key to managing on two curves is developing second-curve strategies that harness existing culture and competencies. It doesn't mean that the existing culture and competencies are the only ones for the second curve, but there must be some linkage. If the second curve is too alien, it will have to be separated from the first, usually as a spin-off.

Pitney Bowes is building its second curve on the basis of its customers, its competencies in encryption, and its ability to manage the logistics of putting paper-based messages in motion. With these competencies, Pitney Bowes can participate with new partners in filling some of the key niches that will emerge in electronic commerce. Their second curve will be very different from their first, but it will draw on the company's strengths in the first. But to pull it off, the company will have to invest in understanding, teaching, learning, and managing the pace and direction of change. That means fundamentally altering the internal political economy of the organization. Most large organizations have evolved to an equilibrium where power and money have been brokered to a point where everyone tolerates the behavior of everyone else. Pitney Bowes and other companies managing on two curves must reshape the culture to master change.

ORGANIZE FOR TWO-CURVE SUCCESS

To successfully manage on two curves, large corporations have to address four common organizational pitfalls: scale, incentives, organization, and people.

Scale. Companies must learn to honor small numbers. Most big organizations are pathological about rewarding largeness as an end, rather than a means. Compensation is based more on the *size* of the empire than on its true contribution to the current and future health of the organization. Honoring and supporting small but rapidly growing businesses within a large first-curve corporation is a first step toward two-curve success.

Incentives. Corporations have to create two-curve incentives. Most organizations reward current or short-term performance. But the second curve is about *future equity*, not current income. Organizations have to find ways to design second-curve incentives inside first-curve organizations—for example, big bonuses for keeping and building market share on the first curve, mega options on the second curve. This may involve creating fictional stock in emerging second-curve businesses—why should the growth and success of CompuServe be rewarded in parent H&R Block stock, which is viewed by Wall Street as a play for the first-curve investor, albeit a rewarding one?

Organization. The classic corporate hierarchy is not a good place to grow the second curve. As we saw in chapter 2, you are more likely to see the second curve come out of chaords, or fishnets, or shared-risk alliances. And whatever you do, keep the reengineering merchants away from your second-curve jewels.

People. You can't build a second curve without them. Do a second-curve audit of your human resources. Who is building the second curve, who understands it, who is a champion? Do you have the classic skunkworks working? Hongkong Telecom's Interactive Media System (IMS) was built as a separate second-curve unit. Seen as a little bit crazy and a little bit out of control—not only by Hongkong Telecom, but by the folks at Cable & Wireless in London—they went and built a second-curve capacity. Volvo built a brand-new prototype car in record time with a tiny team who went into exile in Norway. Applied Materials is searching for second-curve people inside the organization and empowering them to build the company for the next decade of growth.

And Away We Go:
Some Final Thoughts on Leadership

FOR THE EXECUTIVE in the big corporation stuck on the first curve, this book may be a bit depressing. I hope not. It should help you see the second curve more clearly and give you some way to respond.

It can be done. Nokia, a Finnish manufacturer, was a giant (by Finnish standards) in the forest products and rubber industries, making matches and rubber boots. They recognized that they were not exactly in huge growth businesses, and in 1992 they began to specialize by concentrating on high technology equipment. The move has paid off: net sales in 1994 were $6.4 billion, and today they are one of the world's leading companies in the production of cellular phones and high-end computer monitors, with a bottom line and growth prospects that have Wall Street excited. The company runs its North American sales from a tiny San Francisco office, and they have concentrated on sales to businesses with a small marketing group that delivers good quality at low prices.

The second curve cries out for leadership. Yet no CEO in their right mind should touch it. The payoff from investing in the second curve will come on someone else's watch. But that's what leadership is about: you combine vision and courage with a sense of responsibility for the legacy of the first curve. It doesn't mean you have perfect foresight (although we believe that improved foresight can be learned or acquired), but it does mean that, as a leader, you step up to the obligation of dealing with the second curve.

You don't have to jump recklessly to the second curve. You don't have to freeze on the first. My generic advice for CEOs who want to hedge is to give $60 million to the three craziest people in their organization and ask them to send back equity from the twenty-first century.

But you do have an obligation to your shareholders, your colleagues, and yourself to think about growth for the long run and the second curve. Is it happening to your organization? If so, then do something about it. If you step up to that challenge, then this book will have achieved its purpose.

Selected Bibliography

Davidow, William H., and Michael S. Malone. *The Virtual Corporation*. New York: HarperBusiness, 1992.

Davis, Stanley M. *Future Perfect: A Startling Vision of the Future We Should Be Managing Now*. Redding, MA: Addison-Wesley, 1987.

Hawken, Paul. *The Ecology of Commerce*. New York: HarperBusiness, 1993.

Johansen, Robert, and Rob Swigart. *Upsizing the Individual in the Downsized Organization*. Reading, MA: Addison-Wesley, 1994.

Morrison, Ian, and Gregory Schmid. *Future Tense: Preparing for the Business Realities in the Next Ten Years*. New York: Morrow, 1994.

Nocera, Joseph. *A Piece of the Action: How the Middle Class Joined the Money Class*. New York: Simon & Schuster, 1994.

O'Hara-Devereaux, Mary, and Robert Johansen. *Globalwork: Bridging Distance, Culture, and Time*. San Francisco: Jossey-Bass, 1994.

Overholt, William H. *The Rise of China: How Economic Reform Is Creating a New Superpower*. New York: Norton, 1993.

Rothschild, Michael. *Bionomics: Economy as Ecosystem*. New York: Henry Holt, 1992.

Sapenian, AnnaLee. *Regional Advantage: Culture and Competition in Silicon Valley and Route 128*. Cambridge, MA: Harvard University Press, 1994.

Wolffe, Richard. "Virgin Launches Financial Product." *Financial Times* (London). 4 March 1995, p. 7.

Index

About the Author

IAN MORRISON is the president of the Institute for the Future (IFTF) and advises major corporations on planning and forecasting, including Chase Manhattan, Bristol-Myers Squibb, IBM, Daimler-Benz, Cable & Wireless, plc., and John Hancock, among dozens of others.